Modernism after Postcolonialism

HSM **Hopkins Studies in Modernism**
Douglas Mao, *Series Editor*

Modernism after Postcolonialism

Toward a Nonterritorial Comparative Literature

Mara de Gennaro

Johns Hopkins University Press
Baltimore

Printed in the United States of America on acid-free paper
9 8 7 6 5 4 3 2 1

Johns Hopkins University Press
2715 North Charles Street
Baltimore, Maryland 21218-4363
www.press.jhu.edu

Library of Congress Cataloging-in-Publication Data

Names: De Gennaro, Mara, 1972– author.
Title: Modernism after postcolonialism : toward a nonterritorial comparative literature / Mara de Gennaro.
Description: Baltimore : Johns Hopkins University Press, 2020. | Series: Hopkins studies in modernism | Includes bibliographical references and index.
Identifiers: LCCN 2020011212 | ISBN 9781421439464 (hardcover) | ISBN 9781421439471 (paperback) | ISBN 9781421439488 (ebook)
Subjects: LCSH: Modernism (Literature)—History and criticism. | Modernism (Literature)—English-speaking countries. | Modernism (Literature)—French-speaking countries. | Comparative literature—English and French. | Comparative literature—French and English. | Postcolonialism in literature. | Postcolonialism.
Classification: LCC PN56.M54 D43 2020 | DDC 809/.9112—dc23
LC record available at https://lccn.loc.gov/2020011212

A catalog record for this book is available from the British Library.

Special discounts are available for bulk purchases of this book. For more information, please contact Special Sales at specialsales@press.jhu.edu.

Johns Hopkins University Press uses environmentally friendly book materials, including recycled text paper that is composed of at least 30 percent post-consumer waste, whenever possible.

The poets declare that never again will anyone on this planet have to set foot on a foreign land—every land will be native to all—nor will anyone remain in the margins of citizenship—every citizenship conferring on all its graces—and that citizenship, caring for the world's diversity, cannot decide what cultural luggage and tools it might wish to choose.

—Patrick Chamoiseau, *Migrant Brothers*

Contents

Acknowledgments

I owe a great debt to the friends and colleagues who have considered my work valuable and who helped me to refine and develop it in ways I could not have done alone. My deep thanks go to the extraordinary scholars who became my close readers purely out of friendship and professional passion. Vince Sherry, Joan Scott, and Gary Wilder have been indispensable interlocutors and advocates whom I cannot thank enough for their meticulous readings of my drafts and for the many ways they inspired me, supported me, and patiently but persistently coaxed me to bring the project to a conclusion. That I first met Vince when we were fellow participants in a peer seminar of the T. S. Eliot Society, and that I first met Joan, and came to know Gary, when we were fellow participants in an ongoing weekly seminar of the Committee on Globalization and Social Change (CGSC) at the CUNY Graduate Center, impressed on me how beneficial faculty forums can be when they are voluntary and egalitarian in spirit. The happy surprise of finding myself a visiting fellow and continuing participant in the discussions of the CGSC reinforced my faith in the collaborative nature of even the most seemingly solitary intellectual work. Between 2016 and 2019 I presented three chapters in progress to the CGSC faculty and fellows, who generously read and commented on my drafts while also exposing me to a wealth of interdisciplinary scholarship on globalization that I would not otherwise have encountered. I am thankful to everyone in the group who responded to my work and offered support, but particularly to David Joselit, Julie Skurski, Uday Mehta, Herman Bennett, Susan Buck-Morss, Grace Davie, Duncan Faherty, Mischa Suter, Colette Daiute, Karen Strassler, Libby Garland, Amy Chazkel, Nikos Evangelos, Francisco Fortuño Bernier, Michael Gillespie, and Red Washburn. My research also benefited from the two years that I was affiliated with Columbia University's Institute for Comparative Literature and

Society, first as a postdoctoral fellow and more recently as a visiting scholar. I am especially grateful to Hamid Dabashi, who crucially encouraged me and advocated for my work at ICLS.

It is no doubt often the case that the mentoring a young scholar is offered while she is writing her dissertation most visibly bears fruit in the work that follows her early scholarship. Certainly in my case, innumerable wise and trenchant insights that I appreciated but was not yet ready to address in my early-career research on comparative primitivisms have remained with me and helped to light my way as I pursued this study. I hope my mentors and early guiding influences, especially Ursula Heise, David Damrosch, Brent Edwards, and Andreas Huyssen, will see how foundational their teaching and writing have continued to be for me. As the book's argument reflects, this is true above all of Gayatri Chakravorty Spivak, and I thank her for her transformation, over many years, of what comparative literature means to me.

From our first correspondence, Doug Mao has been a model of graciousness and professional generosity. I thank him for encouraging me to see the potential of my project early on and for his discerning advice as I was revising it. My readers at Johns Hopkins University Press were rigorous, generous, and swift in producing their responses, for which I am deeply grateful. I am delighted that the book was selected to be part of the Hopkins Studies in Modernism series, and I thank everyone at JHUP for bringing my book to press with such admirable efficiency and professionalism. I owe particular thanks to Catherine Goldstead and Kim Johnson, along with copyeditor Jeremy Horsefield.

I have received invaluable comments on the manuscript or parts of the manuscript over many years at conferences and other professional associations such as journals. I am especially grateful for the constructive suggestions, challenges, and encouragement offered by Bruce Robbins, Achille Mbembe, Paul Breslin, Ato Quayson, Anjali Prabhu, Peter Boxall, James English, Susan Andrade, Gayle Rogers, Jed Esty, Laura Doyle, Rita Barnard, Lawrence Rainey, Mark Wollaeger, Rosemary Jolly, Martin Munro, Alex Gil, Elizabeth Ault, Sejal Sutaria, Martin Harries, Urmila Seshagiri, Liesl Olson, Christina Britzolakis, Janice Ho, Benjamin Kohlmann, and my anonymous readers at *Textual Practice* and *Comparative Literature Studies*. I am also grateful to scholars who generously shared their own work in progress with me at my request: Susan Stanford Friedman, Jahan Ramazani, Joey Slaughter, and Eric Hayot.

Let me close by honoring the friends, colleagues, and family members who inspired and sustained me as I labored on this book. I am grateful for the judicious advice and warm reassurances I received at pivotal professional junctures by Susan Krakenberg, Bill Cloonan, Jeffrey Huskins, Nicole Rizzuto, Andrew Rubin, Ranji Khanna, Surya Parekh, James Peterson, Alf Siewers, Paula Closson Buck, Greg Clingham, Chris Camuto, Heather Hennigan, Lauren Feldman, Karen Hornick, and Marnie Brady. My closest friends have animated and deepened my thinking in singular ways by sharing with me their creativity and commitment to social justice, their intense scrutiny of ideas in everyday conversations, and above all their good humor and compassion. I have delighted in the company of Elisabeth Guerrero, Roosevelt Montás, and Darren Gobert, and I thank them for our wide-ranging, always rejuvenating conversations. I thank Matt Smith for his abiding friendship, which has been such a reliable source of pleasure and insight for me, and for urging me to share my book manuscript with Doug Mao. My deepest thanks go to my most faithfully optimistic friends, who steadfastly attended to my progress on the book as well as to my daily well-being and who always made me feel that the book would, one day, come to light: Ellen MacKay, Shirin Khanmohamadi, and Laura Lomas. I am thankful to have had the adventure of writing this book with all of these friends at my side and on my side, no matter how far-flung our homes and institutions.

I am immensely thankful to my loving and devoted parents, Jean Mellor and Thomas de Gennaro, who passed on to me their high respect for reading, learning, the beauty of language, and the value of questioning conventions of thought. Beyond this, my mother has been a constant source of affection and affirmation through all the years I wrote this book, while the memory of my father's perfectionism and earnest commitment to his goals and ideals has invigorated me to keep striving.

As for Alex Dunlop, I cannot imagine what the writing of this book would have been like, or what the book itself would now be, without his dedicated support and companionship. Dedicating the book to him seems not nearly enough in exchange, but it's a start. For his humane intelligence, his equanimity, his playfulness, and his generosity, this book is for him, with love and thanks.

An earlier version of chapter 1 appeared in *Textual Practice* as "States of Absence: Stein, Coetzee, and the Politics of Despair," copyright 2014; the revised essay is reprinted here courtesy of Taylor & Francis. An earlier version of chapter 2 appeared in *Comparative Literature Studies* as "A Return to *The Waste Land* after Césaire's *Cahier*," copyright 2015; the revised essay is reprinted here courtesy of The Pennsylvania State University Press.

Modernism after Postcolonialism

Introduction

Anxious Mastery and the Forms It Takes

> The comfort of a world of known limits derives precisely from the known measure of things.
>
> —Ranajit Guha

> There are more pathways and horizons in trembling and fragility than in full command.
>
> —Édouard Glissant and Patrick Chamoiseau

We know that anxiety can propel the building of walls—anxiety that manifests itself as a fear of intruders and the disruptions they might bring, the clarity of their menace standing in for more nebulous forces of change. In 2010, Wendy Brown attributed "the striking popular desire for walling today" in otherwise disparate national contexts to a shared "identification with and anxiety about" waning state sovereignty, misrecognized as a terror of "The Alien."[1] For anxious citizens who see globalization as weakening their nation's sovereign independence and in turn their own, "walls generate what Heidegger termed a 'reassuring world picture'" (26). And yet the anxiety persists, is even reinforced, within the bounds of these reassuring world pictures. Stories of rightful belonging and righteous authority produce what Édouard Glissant has observed to be "the anxious satisfaction" of those who "consent to be reduced: to sectarianism, to stereotyped discourse, to the ardor of guarding definitive truths, to the appetite for power," all in "pursuit of a happiness limited to fragile prerogatives."[2]

In ascribing to anti-immigrant advocates of national wall building a latent anxiety about diminished state power, Brown echoes postcolonial accounts of anxious imperialists shaken by a world too vast and manifold for empire to master. When, more than twenty years ago, Ranajit Guha asked, "Can we afford to leave anxiety out of the story of the empire?" he had in mind the colonizer's anxiety about the discrepancy between "'a world whose limits were known'" to him and "a colonial environment where the 'unimaginable' scale of things was beyond his comprehension."[3] Confronted with the strangeness of a world "beyond limit, hence beyond knowing," Guha's colonizers, like Brown's border proponents, redouble their identification with state power and attempt to scale back what exceeds it through a self-imposed entrapment. What Glissant calls a "consent to be reduced" appears in these readings of anxious worldliness as consent to circumscribe one's thought and sociality for the still-anxious satisfaction of securing the order one knows.

We find this consent at the pivotal moment of George Orwell's autobiographical essay "Shooting an Elephant" when Orwell, as a colonial policeman in Burma, must decide whether to shoot an elephant to satisfy the expectations of the native onlookers, even though the animal's rampage has ended and it is no longer a threat.[4] Although Orwell understands his predicament as one of fearing the crowd's ridicule, Guha's discussion of this essay emphasizes Orwell's oblique expression of anxiety at the crucial moment of decision. Contrary to Orwell's own explanations, Guha attributes this anxiety to the colonial policeman's sudden, uncanny realization that he might not do what his position of mastery demands, that he might instead act in a way that would put him outside empire's conceptual confines (488). Orwell glimpses "the possibility of not being at home in empire" but quickly retreats from it; by shooting the elephant, "he overcame the anxiety of freedom by coming down firmly on the side of unfreedom" (493, 492). A policeman's *raison d'être* is to maintain order, after all, and even if the elephant is no longer disruptive, a break with imperial norms of command would be.

Imperial anxiety is here understood as a response to the perception of an unforeseen and still uncomprehended freedom of thought and action. The elusiveness of this freedom to an imperial mindset—even an ambivalent, in some ways liberal imperial mindset such as Orwell's policeman has—is conveyed by the indefinite, negational terms in which Orwell describes his anxious response to it: "I was not afraid in the ordinary sense" (153) (Guha 488). In reading Orwell's essay as the story of a colonizer's anxious avoidance of an unnamed and barely perceived freedom, Guha draws on Kierkegaard's distinction between fear and anxiety, where fear is defined as having a nameable cause and anxiety's cause is indefinite.[5] The stakes of interpreting Orwell's dilemma in light of this distinction are, for Guha, historiographic. Too often histories of empire have reiterated a statist discourse of law and order, he contends, mistaking the "indefinite and pervasive anxiety" of Europeans living in the colonies—an anxiety whose avowal is potentially disruptive of imperialism itself—for imperially manageable and soluble fears (485). Similarly, Brown demonstrates that contemporary ethno-nationalist discourse converts unruly anxiety into vanquishable fear by substituting the sharply defined and containable threat of alien invaders and lax border control for broad-based systemic transformations of national identities, international relations, and state power. Though she does not cite Kierkegaard's definition, her argument also depends on a distinction between a misleadingly transparent, well-articulated fear and an unspoken, perhaps unspeakable anxiety, difficult to decipher because its causes are complex but also because they are disavowed.

These critical readings of anxious negotiations with a world of shifting parameters emphasize the xenophobic, confining, and self-defeating cultural politics of such negotiations. They reveal affectively fraught discursive patterns in which individuals are made to take notice of unexpected, immeasurable horizons beyond the worldviews of their home regimes, only to look away and maintain their prior views through psychological and social repression. On the other hand, when Guha interprets "Shooting an Elephant" as indirectly revealing a freedom beyond empire that Orwell's liberalism fails to admit, he implies that literary form can evoke alternative possibilities for thought and action even in texts that ostensibly deny their viability. Though the focus of Guha's reading is not literary form per se, but historians' symptomatic inattention to the anxiety expressed by colonialist settlers and enforcers of empire, he construes form as a politically significant expression of this anxiety. In identifying Orwell's shift into uncharacteristically elliptical language to recount a moment of uncertainty, a moment when he might have freed himself from his prescribed imperial role, Guha demonstrates that the political promise of a text may lie not simply in the conclusions its narrator draws but in their interplay with textual modes of summoning forth what such conclusions sidestep or preclude. Such a text acquires its power by exceeding the ostensible control of the narrator.

Difficult Poetics and the Politics of Uncertainty

Orwell's surrender of narratorial transparency and authoritativeness at the moment he might renounce his identification with the authority of empire connects two kinds of mastery—rule over others and knowledge of oneself in relation to others—and hints that a liberation from the imperative to rule entails a liberation from the imperative to know definitively. It follows that there is a value, at once political and ethical, to "difficult" literary language, difficult in the sense of enacting, whether subtly or conspicuously, conceptual dilemmas that an expanded awareness of the world as distinct from one's habituated worldview poses to perceptions of coherence. This is the value of what Gayatri Spivak describes in *Death of a Discipline* as "difficult, even mysterious texts" that "stage the question of collectivity" without providing easy answers, "curious texts, where collectivities become undecidable."[6] Proposing a comparatist practice of reading that will "let literature teach us that there are no certainties, that the process is open, and that it may be altogether salutary that it is so," Spivak, like Guha, looks to literary figuration— twentieth-century literary figuration in particular—to find "an indefinite structure of possibilities" (26, 23).[7] As when Orwell figures an unrecognized possibility of freedom through an elliptical language of negation, this "indefinite structure of possibilities" defamiliarizes and potentially deauthorizes what had seemed secure positions in a known world, "making our home *unheimlich* or uncanny" (74). The value of these "difficult, even mysterious texts" is a value that already in *A Room of One's Own* Virginia Woolf assigned to "the difficulty of modern poetry." This difficulty consists in averting the "rapture" (which we might translate as a lack of worldly awareness) inspired by beloved Victorian poems to which "one responds easily, familiarly, without troubling to check the feeling, or to compare it with any that one has now."[8] Woolf's view is that her contemporaries, unlike the previous generation of poets, "express a feeling that is actually being made and torn out of us at the moment. One does not recognize it in the first place; often for some reason one fears it; one watches it with keenness and compares it jealously and suspiciously with the old feeling that one knew. Hence the difficulty of modern poetry" (14).

These reflections on a distinctly modern quality of poetic abstruseness, at once foreign, self-implicating, and self-violating, anticipate Orwell's formal association of disorienting language with anxiety or unaccountable fear.[9] Woolf goes further and explicitly theorizes this quality as both expressing and further generating a self-consciously uncertain comparative practice of reading the familiar and the unfamiliar together, hence its emotional and intellectual difficulty. By offering these reflections immediately after reminiscing about a strangely disturbing Manx cat she saw trespassing on the cultivated quadrangles of the men's college at Oxbridge, Woolf implies that this difficult language of uncertain comparisons is a means of thinking differently by admitting the alien into ingrained and institutionalized spheres of knowledge—admitting, too, that the alien may already be there, not yet recognized as part of those spheres. Glimpsing the tailless cat during a lavish luncheon at the college, Woolf's narrator is made a witness to the intrusion of difference into what had been a scene of harmony and unquestioned privilege around her (11–13).[10] If the male scholars who surround her at the luncheon seem for the moment to share their prewar predecessors' serene faith in the continuity and worth of cultural traditions from which they still benefit—a faith that there is "no need to be anybody but oneself"—the narrator's "sight of that abrupt and truncated animal" reminds her with a jolt that now "everything was different" (11). Being oneself as one has always been—which Woolf here frames in collective, cultural terms—is precisely what is no longer enough, no longer even possible.

Weaving together these comparisons of Victorian rapture and modern difficulty, of an apparently staid community and its unexpected alteration, Woolf makes comparatism itself the distinguishing practice of the literature she espouses—and not just any comparatism, but an anxiously self-reflexive and inconclusive comparatism that emerges out of the unanticipated convergences of durable structures of privilege with forces that upset their smooth operation. It is noteworthy that what we have come to know as the conceptual difficulty of early twentieth-century European and transatlantic modernist poetics, so often understood in isolated formal terms, is made here, in this most canonical of literary works, a political matter.[11] "Difficulty" for Woolf is not the difficulty of comprehending allusions and cryptic but sure ordering principles likely to elude all but the most classically educated of readers, though this notion of difficulty, conservative and hierarchical, has come to be associated more than any other with modernist literature between the wars. The difficulty that Woolf finds in the comparatist poetry of her time is one of comprehending social and textual relationships that are unresolved and perhaps irresolvable. The inconclusive and thus potentially nonnormative comparative forms she attributes to the literature of her age, and that she herself produces, evoke an expanded and rightly unsettled sense of the world, a world that in its fullness defies mastery. With this new sense of the world comes an awareness of strange figures of difference that may infiltrate, however circumspectly, ostensibly bounded communities and their self-affirming discourses, entering into images of untroubled, innocuous wholeness and changing their meaning.

To recognize the inchoate ethico-political promise of what Marjorie Perloff long ago called a "poetics of indeterminacy," we must reconsider persistent associations of poetic difficulty with cultural elitism, taking our lead from postcolonial revaluations of textual uncertainty as a potentially democratizing political force.[12] Such revaluations have figured indispensably in Anglophone diasporic theories of subalternity and the decolonization of disciplines such as history and comparative literature, on the one hand, and in Francophone diasporic poetics and theories of negritude and creolist relation, on the other. We might consider, for example, the work of Dipesh Chakrabarty, a historian of British colonialism in South Asia who is widely known across humanistic disciplines for his book *Provincializing Europe* and for his earlier participation in the Subaltern Studies Collective that also included Guha and Spivak. He has argued that the writing of history should entail "an acknowledgment of the opacity of the world," an explicit formal avowal that pasts cannot be altogether illuminated because "they are a play of the visible and the invisible; they partially resist discursivity in the same way that pain resists language." A theory of the past "always somewhat gropes and . . . takes a leap in the dark," and historical narratives should mark this rather than erase it.[13]

Chakrabarty's appeals for an openly self-critical historiography have traveled well beyond the field of history to interdisciplinary efforts to decenter European notions of modernity and the human subject, a decentering he influentially conceived to be a process of "provincializing Europe." Yet critical responses to his vision of a Europe no longer occupying modernity's center stage rarely engage with the formal and affective terms in which he frames that vision. When he urges historians to bring their "fear and anxiety" to the writing of the past in *Habitations of Modernity*, as when he proposes a historiographic "politics of despair" in *Provincializing Europe* (which he concedes he has not pursued in that book), he makes anxious uncertainty in the face of a never fully knowable or translatable world the catalyst for writing that attests to its own partiality, even complicity: "I ask for a history that deliberately makes visible, within the very structure of its narrative forms, its own repressive strategies and practices." Historians should write "translucent" narratives "so that the world may once again be imagined as radically heterogeneous."[14]

In numerous works, including more recent essays on what the crisis of climate change reveals to be "the limits of historical understanding," Chakrabarty's elaboration of this idea resonates closely, if in different linguistic, disciplinary, and imperial contexts, with Glissant's philosophical reflections on striving, always inconclusively, to understand the world's totality of relations without remaining bound by the constraints of either identitarianism or a universalizing humanism.[15] With his paradoxical image of *relation* as "open totality, moving in itself," a totality from which the principle of unity has been subtracted, Glissant urges us to reenvision the world's dynamic relations as constituting a kind of borderless force field, an unlimited expanse of diverse elements unforeseeably interacting among themselves, without any unifying impetus or end. To envision relations in this way entails replacing the "imagined transparency" of unity with "the opacity of the diverse," whose "poetic force" makes us "sensitive to the limits of every method" (Glissant, *Poetics* 192; trans. mod.; *Poétique* 206).

It is in the context of his revaluation of poetic opacity as a means of countering practices of domination that Glissant turns to a concept that recurs in his theoretical work and in his collaborations with novelist and theorist of *créolité* Patrick Chamoiseau: "the beauty of the world" (*la beauté du monde*). In *Poetics of Relation*, Glissant attributes to the world a beauty both indomitable and continually under threat. The threat comes from sometimes manifestly, but other times more subtly and insidiously, "tyrannical" modes of representing others that reduce the complexities of difference to a self-interested knowledge sufficient to propel and naturalize acts of domination. In contrast, he proposes "the thought of wandering" (*la pensée de l'errance*) and, more recently in *Philosophie de la relation* and in political manifestos written with Chamoiseau, "the thought of trembling" (*la pensée du tremblement*) as attempts to conceive of the world without the "totalitarian" impulse to fashion generalizations that "sum up the world with conspicuous transparency, claiming for it a presupposed direction and purpose" (Glissant, *Poetics* 20; trans. mod.; *Poétique* 32–33).[16] In an increasingly technologized era when internationally disseminated information seemed to offer deceptively easy access to others around the globe, Glissant turned to esteemed aesthetic categories of poetry and beauty—but, more precisely, to anti-realist and anti-scientistic connotations of these categories developed in literary and visual artists' revisionist appropriations of them earlier in the century—to cast doubt on the value and scope of isolated and readily assimilated knowledge. As I discuss more fully in this book's conclusion, what Glissant and Chamoiseau suggest, indefinitely and incipiently, to be the alternative to illusory assumptions of mastery and certainty is a "beauty of the world" that circumvents and transcends efforts to wall off relations of difference within that world.[17]

Theories such as Chakrabarty's and Glissant's share a methodological commitment to resist imperial legacies by dispensing with positivist modes of representation used in the past to justify European cultural triumphalism, and instead devising new forms of writing that signal the incapacity of any discourse or system of knowledge to comprehend the world in its totality. Such a commitment engages in varying degrees of explicitness with Jacques Derrida's delineations of responsibility in light of discourse's necessarily limited access to singularities that elude and belie its self-validating measures. When Glissant and more recently Chamoiseau ascribe a liberatory political value to recognizing beauty as an ongoing searching out of relations that are "unforeseeable" and "beyond measure" (*démesuré*), they echo Derrida's association of the "always possible" with what cannot be mastered: "the irruption of the new . . . should be anticipated *as* the unforeseeable, the *unanticipatable*, the non-masterable, non-identifiable, in short, as that of which one does not yet have a memory."[18] Derrida couples this imperative with what appears contrary to it, the imperative to remain suspicious of claims to absolute newness or otherness that would suppress all memory of prior, potentially applicable (and comparable) identifications (18–19). With this qualification, Derrida signals another important aspect of all the self-questioning theories of modernity and postcoloniality on which this book builds: their refusal to interpret as mutually exclusive a commitment to acknowledge singularities and a commitment to compare them, provided that such comparisons concede their own provisionality and, in so doing, foster more awareness of the unspoken in the spoken, the hidden in the seen. While Chakrabarty in particular has heightened our awareness of incommensurabilities that cannot be reconciled in comparative frameworks, he also makes the comparison of the known and the unknown essential to his vision of a writing that defies imperial legacies of domination. We find this in his own citation of Derrida in *Provincializing Europe*, where he writes that "subaltern pasts" are "supplementary in a Derridean sense" to "the historian's pasts": "they enable history, the discipline, to be what it is and yet at the same time help to show what its limits are" (Chakrabarty, *Provincializing* 112).

A Modernist Language for the Unsayable: Comparing Forms of Anxious Mastery

Notwithstanding their shared methodological and theoretical commitments, Chakrabarty and Glissant exemplify Anglophone and Francophone currents of transnationalist thought rarely put into direct dialogue with each other in interdisciplinary postcolonial scholarship, not only because of their authors' disparate origins, languages, and disciplinary affiliations but also because their immediate objects of analysis seem unrelated or only tangentially related. Even more rarely are they considered in relation (as opposed to merely in contrast) to earlier transatlantic literary experiments whose difficult—which is to say, indirect and inconclusive—forms of comparison instigated a crucial but now often discounted process of conceiving, with a necessary vagueness, the "impossible unions" to which T. S. Eliot refers in the *Four Quartets*, and which, as I discuss in chapter 2, C. L. R. James made the basis for his own comparison of Eliot and Aimé Césaire. When read without being translated into unified, transparent narratives and arguments, these difficult poetics open possibilities for readers to recognize and even revalue the uncertain horizons that have displaced serene worldviews.

A guiding contention of this book is that postcolonial historiographic, philosophical, and literary-critical theories that promote self-questioning and inconclusively comparative forms of representation participate in a still-ongoing transnationalist literary project dating back to the early twentieth century, in which otherwise disparate writers have sought a special language through which to convey an otherwise incommunicable "experience of the impossible" (Spivak, *Death of a Discipline* 101). The dream that has kept recurring since as early as Gertrude Stein's *Three Lives* (1909) is of a newly self-critical representational language entangled with what it disputes, whose critical power is not to unveil the unfamiliar as if it could be made transparent but to give form to interpretive and representational difficulties posed by encounters with difference within and across cultures. To evoke such encounters and the totalities of which they are part without denying them their singular and untranslatable aspects, this language points to its own limitations, its own silences and absences; it conveys its inability to make sense of some experiences and perspectives, but it also conveys enough about what is missing to induce readers to want to know more. In diverse formations of what Chakrabarty describes as translucence, they offer us the possibility of imagining what is unspeakable within their own frames; they turn apparent absence into an elusive impression of presence. In summoning the unspeakable these languages may or may not reflect their authors' manifest intentions or aspirations, but they share the effect of intimating that "a world of known limits" always coexists precariously with the possibility that, as Françoise Vergès declares both critically and hopefully, "the future is elsewhere."[19] Striving to recognize and imperfectly represent this precarious coexistence is not to discount the exigencies of the local; it is to refuse to sanctify the local (and the already known and communicable more broadly) as the exclusive or even preeminent site of particularity, now and in the future. As Brent Edwards emphasizes in his analysis of "a particular set of 'elsewheres'" envisaged by black transnationalist writers between the wars, what Glissant calls the "point of entanglement" from which a forcibly transplanted population begins to transform into a new collectivity "may in fact be 'elsewhere' rather than in . . . the native homeland."[20] Throughout the book, I will return to these notions of "elsewhere" and their implications for a politics of poetic resistance and transformation.

I refer to this special language and its formal operations as a poetics, following Glissant's use of the term to describe dynamics of language that defamiliarize and thwart operations of dominance. Glissant also applies the term more broadly to intercultural dynamics of languages and discursive systems in unpredictably generative relations. With his metaphorical conception of a "poetics of relation," he imagines social and cultural relations as amounting to a poetry of sorts, specifically one reminiscent of densely intertextual and elliptical literary languages that came to define a preponderant current of transatlantic modernism. Glissant's interrelated uses of the word "poetics" to denote a counterdiscursive function of language have numerous antecedents in both French and Anglo-American thought since the late nineteenth century, notably, as I consider further in chapter 2, Stéphane Mallarmé's and later Jean-Paul Sartre's differentiations of a richly oblique, polysemous "poetry" from a purposeful utilitarian "prose."[21] Even more explicitly, Georges Bataille distinguished a systematizing, definitional "discursive language" from "poetic language" that disrupts dichotomies of self and other, subject and object, presumed by a systematizing discourse.[22] Bataille's interest in poetic imagery as a means of rousing an unmediated sense of physicality repressed in idealist and scientific discourses is an example of his impulse to transcend the bounds of custom and language, but even more directly pertinent here is his general formulation of the "poetic" as a use of language that can, in the moment, violate ingrained expectations and conceptions of relation. Though the language Bataille designates as poetic (including his own aspirationally "heterological" prose) may not altogether achieve the detachment he seeks from conventional referential functions of discourse, it strives to embody the tensions, incongruities, and perversities that disrupt coherent, mutually exclusive definitions of identity and otherness.

What follows in this book is a theory of transnationalist literary modernism as a poetics of anxious mastery, a comparative practice of writing peculiar to a time when the global North is becoming increasingly uneasy with itself and aware that the legitimacy of its authority is in question. My own comparative readings identify modes of narration and figuration that constitute this poetics and that, when taken together, emerge as a subversive engagement with imperialist modes of comparing the known to the alien. Reading their uncertain forms of comparison as difficult negotiations with a never fully comprehensible or communicable otherness unsettles longstanding assumptions about aesthetic modernism and, more particularly, transatlantic modernist literature—its signal contribution, its cultural politics, and its relation to postcolonial theory's contestations of imperial positivism and territorialism.

In passages quoted above, Glissant, Guha, and Brown all point to the lurking anxiety, the mastery under threat, that underlies adversarial and racializing cultural rhetoric. Through such rhetoric, the expression of anxious mastery takes forms that reaffirm a dominant community's "known measure of things," walling off troubling relations that would derange its "reassuring world pictures." But we have also seen that anxious mastery may be expressed as well through forms that qualify or refuse the satisfaction of reducing disconcerting relations and their transformative possibilities to a state of familiar divides. These forms harness the power of tensions, contradictions, and points of opacity that come of perceiving otherness; they admit and, in varying degrees, affirm anxieties of encountering an expanding world, and through them we can learn that negotiations with others and the newness they bring need not culminate in an ethos of walling off.[23]

My subject, then, is the denser, more ambiguous, and characteristically more difficult expressions of anxious mastery, which display rather than repress or purport to resolve the intercultural "muddles" that E. M. Forster puts at the center of his portrait of colonialist disorientation and discrimination in *A Passage to India* (a focus of chap. 3). Such muddles constrain the vision of poet-seers who aspire to represent a collectivity of others in Eliot's *The Waste Land* and Césaire's *Cahier d'un retour au pays natal* (*Notebook of a Return to the Native Land*) (see chap. 2); they animate and frustrate attempts at reasoning through racialized sexual impasses in Stein's "Melanctha" and J. M. Coetzee's *Disgrace* (see chap. 1); they propel the painful negotiations with powerful distant or indifferent audiences in polemics on imperial state violence by Woolf and Césaire and in Edwidge Danticat's testimonial depictions of genocide and economically exacerbated earthquake devastation in Haiti (see chap. 4). Of particular interest in these images of perplexed communions with otherness are figures and patterns of uncertain, inconclusive comparison, which destabilize polarizing definitions of race, gender, and culture that have historically served the interests of modern expansionist states, as well as dominant groups within socially stratified states and communities. I take these unsettling forms of comparison to be a remarkable and yet critically neglected innovation of twentieth-century transatlantic literary conjunctions of interculturalism and formal avant-gardism, as well as an essential contribution to what has since developed into a more broadly and explicitly democratic transnationalist poetics.

Variously but repeatedly in modernist poetics of anxious mastery, these innovative forms of comparison compete with speakers' habitually contrastive and hierarchizing assertions and hint at unrecognized and not yet existing relations obscured by preconceived boundaries around selves and others. The unrealized freedom from the imperial relation that Guha sees obliquely figured in "Shooting an Elephant," for example, may be read as a form of uncertain comparison that interrupts and effectively competes with, or stands as an alternative to, the many explicit comparisons through which Orwell conveys his sense of an insuperable divide between himself and the people under his command. While some of these comparisons are more sympathetic to the Burmese than others, all are definitively polarizing and leave little room to imagine cultural relations otherwise: "Theoretically—and secretly, of course—I was all for the Burmese, and all against their oppressors, the British" (Orwell 148); "All I knew was that I was stuck between my hatred of the empire I served and my rage against the evil-spirited little beasts who tried to make my job impossible" (149).

I propose in this book that indefinite, self-questioning forms of modernist comparison deserve our attention for the ways they rival and dispute hierarchizing territorialist comparisons that normalize self-enclosure and exclusion and that reinforce the demonization and conquest of those excluded. The chapters that follow are organized around literary forms of comparison that illuminate what a narrator cannot say because it is unsayable in the world the speaker knows and perhaps wishes, at least ambivalently, to preserve. Recent theoretical arguments informed by a poetics of anxious mastery, such as those by Glissant, Chakrabarty, and Spivak quoted above, have made the discrepancy between the forms they must use and the forms they need—which is also to say, the discrepancy between what their interpretive language can and cannot (yet) articulate—a primary means of evoking what escapes the language of cultural imperialism. In tracing the politics of an argument to the politics of its form, they help us to recognize what Guha's analysis of Orwell's anxious language also suggests, namely, that the form of a text can qualify, even contradict, that text's manifest content and ostensible cultural politics.

Reading the Politics of Modernism: Toward a Nonterritorial Comparatism

In arguing this, I am responding in part to an abiding preconception about prewar and interwar transatlantic modernist literature, especially Anglo-American "high modernism": its formal innovations are undeniably impressive and valuable, the idea goes, but it is permanently marred by the elitist and sometimes outright racist cultural politics that its motifs and authors' own pronouncements betray. This idea remains entrenched despite new transnationalist approaches that have put the work of these authors—perhaps some authors (Woolf, Joyce) more than others (Eliot, Stein)—in reconfigured and more capacious artistic and historical fields of relation, affording new comparative frameworks that have begun to shift our sense of their work's possible political implications. There have been numerous interventions in comparative reading practices that have probed the politics of poetic form and that, in the process, have recast the meanings and values of transatlantic modernism or particular texts associated with it, such as Susan Stanford Friedman's "paratactic comparativism," which takes inspiration from the juxtapositions of collage, and Laura Doyle's "regional transnational approach," which interprets expressive forms as arising not out of distinct national cultures so much as out of broader regional configurations of "nations in relation, and in clustered relation."[24] This book builds on critical interventions such as these in order to reassess the politics of transnational modernist poetics, including early twentieth-century transatlantic poetics whose formal ingenuity is still routinely divided off from its putative political commitments.[25] Readings that treat poetic form as discrete from political content and ascribe a stable, coherent cultural politics to texts posing manifold challenges to self-certain, noncontradictory discourse reduce the diversity of implications to be found there, not least by foreclosing the challenges these texts direct against their own repressive responses to apprehensions of (and about) difference. Such responses may be overt or subtle, deliberate or inadvertent, exclusionary or assimilationist. Their convergence with the challenges that push against their authority is not ancillary to the signifiable effects of these texts but distinctively generative of them.

My readings bring into dialogue a heterogeneous selection of transatlantic, diasporic, and transnationalist writing from the early twentieth century to the present in what we might describe, echoing the indeterminate negational language of Orwell and numerous others central to this study, as a nonterritorial comparatism. By "nonterritorial" I do not mean "extraterritorial," a precise designation in international law for conditions in which a state's legal jurisdiction extends beyond its own territorial borders. Extraterritoriality has lately emerged as a compelling area of research in global literary studies,[26] its exceptional zones of authority reminiscent of the "no-man's land between public law and political fact, and between the juridical order and life" that Giorgio Agamben called the state of exception.[27] "Nonterritorial" is deliberately inchoate; it identifies what it resists being, but it will not specify and delimit what the contrary is or should be, as if there were a binary choice. An adjective, not a noun, a shifting modifier, not a determinate thing, "nonterritorial" clearly opposes "territorial" in both its associated senses of "proprietary" and "bound by or restricted to a particular territory," but its prefix "non" leaves open how to imagine what the not-territorial could be at different times, in different contexts. Nonterritorial comparatist reading does not seek to resolve textual difficulties into a reassuring state of coherence; rather, it seeks to recognize these difficulties as at once informed by their authors' immediate contexts and affiliations and, potentially, transformed by their conjunctures with other textual forms in variable but also overlapping fields of cultural knowledge. Reading for what is repressed, resistant, or excessive within texts summons forth ideals of collectivity less readily conceivable, and perhaps inconceivable, without the benefit of prior or concurrent encounters with related but differently imagined ideals elsewhere, sometimes far afield from those to which they are being compared. This is not at all to dispute the importance of connecting these relations and ideals to the specific local conditions in which they arose, but it is to insist that, in a long century of imperial incursions and withdrawals, international wars, global marketing and communications, and mass migrations, local conditions of both textual production and textual interpretation are not merely cultural but intercultural and increasingly creolized.

In their theory of a creolization particular to the Indian Ocean and their native Réunion, a former French colony and now an overseas department of France, Françoise Vergès and Carpanin Marimoutou argue that to be native to their island "means not simply to be born there" (and indeed Vergès was born in Paris, though to a prominent Réunionese family) "but to care about it, to care about . . . reappropriating its territory and revaluing its distinct practices and means of expression."[28] They understand this process of retaking and revaluing their territory as one of according recognition to a long-subjugated region's multilingualism and multiculturalism, a linguistic and cultural diversity they regard as both historically inevitable and now indispensable to its inhabitants' participation in an intercultural world (9). If this is a claim to a territory, it is one profoundly aware of that territory as creolized and interdependent. A nonterritorial comparatism in no way rejects what Césaire advocated as "a deepening and coexistence of all particulars," but rather rejects what obstructs their deepening and coexistence; as Césaire explains, "there are two ways to lose our way: walled segregation in the particular or dilution in the 'universal.'"[29] Both of these reductive tendencies rest on proprietary claims that deny the variety and reciprocity of exchanges across cultures and social formations more broadly (including disciplinary fields and schools of thought).

The texts I examine all in some way mark the limits of cultural and other territorial measures of meaning to render otherness communicable; I have suggested that these texts all enact a struggle to impart communicable form to differences and totalities of relation without occluding their uncomprehended and untranslatable aspects. Even as these texts make us acknowledge that comparisons are necessarily approximations and thus unable to represent the singular, they do not avoid comparing seemingly incommensurate figures and perspectives. Nor should we who interpret these texts avoid comparing them because their origins, stated goals, and histories of reception are wide-ranging and often discrepant. On the contrary, a premise of this book's necessarily incomplete attempts to deterritorialize texts and our practices of reading them is that the texts I consider are united in a particular, indeed a special way: beyond the disparate forms they take, they show, both within and among themselves, that what cannot be figured, defined, or represented directly may be evoked through comparisons—specifically, comparisons marked by uncertainty, inconsonance, and unease.

This mode of literary reading is allied in important respects with Françoise Lionnet's "transcolonial" readings that identify nonhierarchical patterns of intertextual relation across colonial contexts, with a focus on the "minor transnationalism" revealed not only through South-South literary comparisons but also through North-South comparisons that alert us to chronically overlooked implications of well-traveled texts we thought we knew. Like Vergès and Marimoutou, the Mauritian-born Lionnet traces her vision of comparatism to her formative experience of creolization arising out of the diverse colonialisms that converged in the Indian Ocean's Mascarene Islands.[30] Like them, she is committed to bringing her knowledge of the region's long-neglected particularities into transnational comparatist debates: in her critique of Anglophone postcolonial readings of Baudelaire, for example, she notes a systematic neglect of the poet's geopolitical references to Mauritius and Réunion and argues that the close attention in postcolonial studies to history and the colonial archive, so influential for interpreting aesthetic modernism, has not sufficiently extended to the "*geographical real* that constitutes the landscape and canvas on which colonial temporalities have unfolded."[31] Her own attention to this "geographical real" does not discourage, but indeed engenders, wide-ranging transcolonial and translinguistic comparative readings.

Lionnet credits literature in general—"literature of all eras"—with inspiring the potentially transformative process of world questioning that this study ascribes principally to an ongoing modernist practice of writing (however often its practitioners equate that practice with the poetic or singularly literary as such), whose new comparative forms, in my view, make new comparative modes of reading both possible and politically desirable (*Écritures féminines* 10).[32] Moreover, as my discussion of transnationalist conceptions and uses of anxious and uncertain representational modes attests, I see more political value, and more affinities with black Francophone theory, than Lionnet and coauthor Shu-mei Shih see in early Anglophone postcolonial theory, whose emphasis on "the constraints of representation," Shih and Lionnet argue, "has tended to generate a self-perpetuating and politically unproductive anxiety."[33] Shih and Lionnet distinguish this early work by Spivak, Homi Bhabha, and Partha Chatterjee from more recent work by Spivak and Chakrabarty that they take to "show us a way out of the impasse of anxiety" (20). My sense is that the constraints and difficulties of representation continue to figure strongly in this more recent postcolonial theory, if in different forms, and that a goal of such theory is expressly not to relieve our anxiety. Despite these points of difference, my work shares Lionnet's long-standing preoccupation with literature that "leads us beyond our singularities while paradoxically remaining anchored in the real of those who produce it," and with ways of reading that make the extensive, uneven effects of racialized and sexualized imperial domination the persistent reference point from which to "underline what these texts have in common despite their apparent distance" (*Écritures féminines* 10, 16).

One of this book's interventions is to question and contend with anticomparatist implications of some prominent recent formulations of incommensurability and untranslatability, by building on theories of transnationalism that compare widely but also uneasily and self-critically, foregrounding the risks of reduction and appropriation that cross-cultural comparisons pose. Although notions of uncertainty, obliqueness, difficulty, and opacity figure centrally in my interpretation of transnational modernist poetics of anxious mastery, I depart from theories of linguistic and cultural untranslatability where they seem to me to exaggerate the gulfs between cultures and communities whose ethnic and economic differences, often considerable, coexist with overlaps and intermixings they owe to shared imperial, diasporic, and interimperial contacts and experiences. After all, "large social formations and political fields . . . are also concrete places," as Gary Wilder argues, and if we take one of these broader-based social formations or political fields "as our unit of analysis, the case for insisting on cultural singularity or epistemological incommensurability weakens."[34] Wilder makes this argument to advance his larger critique of the "territorial assumptions underlying strong currents in both European historiography and postcolonial criticism, assumptions that often lead scholars to relate texts to the ethnicity, territory, or formal political unit to which their authors appear to belong or refer" (8–9). He identifies these assumptions not only in "Europe's territorial colonialism" but also in an enduring postwar territorial nationalism that equates African and Caribbean emancipation with national independence, as well as in some postcolonial assertions of "multiple, alternative, or countermodernities," as if the "modernity" claimed by Europe were not already a heterogeneous formation of European and non-European cultural inheritances and innovations (95, 4–6, 11). Another reason not to substitute the idea of alternative modernities for "a singular, if wildly uneven, modernity," Rita Barnard argues in her theorization of "post-apartheid modernism," Is that many Africans "have come to regard modernity, not as a matter of difference, but of lack," and she is "reluctant to foreground diversity when inequality is such a vast concern."[35]

While one would expect to attend closely to relationships between works that share a language and a regional or national history, there is much to gain from considering more subtle affinities among literary techniques and theoretical quandaries that suggest borrowings and infiltrations across languages, nations, and empires. To take such affinities seriously is to acknowledge the already intensely creolized character of twentieth-century literary practices and cultural relations. If, in the past two decades, "postcolonial theory's center of gravity seems to have shifted toward an emphasis on the incommensurable singularity and cultural alterity of non-European forms of life," as Jini Kim Watson and Gary Wilder observe,[36] the thinkers cited in this introduction and others who figure in the coming pages show that there has also developed a durable and, I believe, increasingly important current of deterritorialist interpretive practices that retain postcolonialism's defining commitment to recognizing and learning from subaltern and nondominant anti-imperial perspectives, while seeking to expand its scope through new intercultural and transcultural comparative frameworks that bring to view what escapes habituated ways of circumscribing fields of relation and interpenetration. Without discounting the disagreements among some critics I associate with these practices, especially as to the status of universalism and humanism,[37] I take this current as voluminous enough to include transnationalist approaches conceived in "geographical," "regional," or "locational" terms, like those of Lionnet, Doyle, and Friedman, respectively, as well as diversely transregional approaches, some framed as cosmopolitan (Bruce Robbins), others as planetary (Spivak, Achille Mbembe), still others as both (Paul Gilroy). These disparate and sometimes conflicting approaches have in common that they foreground empire and its legacies of inequality in the relations they ask us to acknowledge, and that their preferred way of doing so is through deterritorializing forms of transnational and transdisciplinary comparison.

More than a decade ago, Gilroy countered the "negative view of cross-cultural understanding and transnational solidarity" in "what passes for radical and critical thought"; though he did not specify which critics he had in mind, he assailed this thought for advancing "the notion that the very aspiration toward translocal solidarity, community, and interconnection is tainted."[38] Of course, the "proclamation of difference" by subjugated groups and communities is, as Mbembe sympathetically acknowledges, "an inverted expression of the desire for recognition and inclusion," and we are far indeed from having secured what he aspirationally calls "a world that is coming," a world of universal recognition and inclusion where such proclamations are unnecessary (*Critique of Black Reason* 183).[39] Maintaining a critical wariness toward our own transnationalist efforts to translate alterity across cultures, regions, and languages may help to stem the tide of imperious globalist rhetoric, which not infrequently appears more inclusive and attuned to subaltern and global South particularities than it is. But we should also stay alert to ways that a scholarly practice of walling off differences, however well intentioned, can unwittingly mirror identitarian social and political divisions that curtail dialogues across territories (by which I mean, again, not only spaces but also any formations subject to proprietary claims), along with the unanticipated discoveries and transformations that such dialogues make possible.

Francophone transnationalist thought, for example, is still considered too rarely in relation to Anglo-Atlantic modernist literature, despite close engagements with Glissant's thought on *relation* and poetics in prominent Anglophone postcolonial theories of comparatism.[40] When we assume the experience of rupture to be the defining catalyst of interwar Atlantic modernism, or, as in Friedman's temporally expansive globalist iteration, of multiple, otherwise diverse modernisms, we orient our readings toward relations of radical difference: novelty, opposition, breakage, shock, revolution. Such relations were indeed foregrounded in the explanatory discourse of interwar modernists and avant-gardists themselves, just as anticolonial and early postcolonial discourse on liberation, decolonization, and independence often orients us to see ruptures and obdurate differences—indigeneities reclaimed, colonial subservience overcome. But the Anglo-Atlantic writers central to this study, though boldly innovative, all distinguished themselves from prior artists and thinkers through negotiation and appropriation at least as much as opposition. To reorient our readings away from a preoccupation with rupture and the progress or regress that may ensue from it and toward relations of creative negotiation and appropriation, we can draw insight from the literary and theoretical dialogues emerging out of former French colonies that became overseas departments of France rather than independent island nations. Anjali Prabhu and Adlai Murdoch have traced back to the "underlying geopolitical ambiguity" of these Caribbean and Indian Ocean territories the recognition of "hybridity as a form of politics" in the work of Glissant and Vergès.[41] Unlike Anthony Appiah's "comfortable cosmopolitanism" and other theories of transnationalism that downplay structural inequalities, Prabhu and Murdoch argue, Creole transnationalist interventions attend closely to both "collective identity and the contradictions within the totality of that collectivity" (408, 409).

I have already suggested the theoretical value of postcolonial Francophone discourses on *créolisation* for comparative readings of Anglophone literature, literary and cultural theory, and historiography; in my discussion of Anglophone fictions of miscegenation in chapter 1, I draw on the aesthetic and political evolution of the related concept of *métissage* as well. *Créolité* or creoleness, still principally identified with the Martinican *créoliste* manifesto from 1989, the *Éloge de la Créolité*,[42] has since developed in overlapping theoretical and aesthetic practices, including those of the *Éloge*'s authors themselves, that remain insufficiently recognized outside Francophone and Caribbean studies. This still-evolving concept has more to offer transnational literary and cultural studies than one might assume from its familiar reception in world literature studies, where it is often recapitulated as a clear-cut response to two main questions, namely, whether Antillean literature should be written in Creole instead of colonial European languages, and whether Caribbean identities should be defined principally in terms of their hybrid mixtures of African, European, and Asian heritages, or in terms that accentuate their African heritage.

Chamoiseau, for one, has presented us with a much farther reaching vision of *créolité* in his many writings since the *Éloge*, as in his novel *Texaco*, discussed in chapter 3, in which an exuberantly collective Creole, at once the spoken language of the people and the disorderly, demotic "poetry" of their communal life, encroaches painfully but persistently on neocolonial and international corporate terrains. Here and in his political writings, some coauthored with Glissant, on the recent surge of migrants, refugees, and state walls that I consider in my conclusion, *créolité* figures as a global force that continually disrupts not only antidemocratic expansionisms but also identity politics, even ostensibly progressive articulations of identity that Chamoiseau has said he used to advocate. He and Vergès both describe themselves as having once propounded polarizing identitarian visions of cultural difference and colonial emancipation, but as having subsequently realized the greater political value of writing on relation and filiation.[43] We can take from this shift in their conceptions of resistance that their reflections, not only on processes of creolization but also on their own and potentially everyone's constitutive creoleness, have led them to question predominantly oppositional and definitive forms of comparison and to favor ones more receptive to the possibility of debts, complicities, intersections, and confluences connecting world pictures and their politics. This turn from contrastive and hierarchizing forms of comparison to more unsettling and self-implicating ones has transformed Chamoiseau's literary theory as well. Chamoiseau's new mode of comparatism is openly inspired by that of Glissant, whose readings of modernist poetics, most extensively those of William Faulkner and St.-John Perse, methodically distinguish between the signifiable effects of those poetics and their authors' own consciously held, publicly avowed opinions on racial difference. Even more importantly, Glissant shows how an oblique poetics of "doubled" and "deferred" meanings, one that "describes and *at the same time* seeks to say what cannot be said through description," can contradict the definitive adversarial logic of such opinions.[44] Chamoiseau's recent literary theory departs from his earlier propensity to divide himself off politically from Perse and Césaire and instead searches out implications of their poetics that come to light when read in nonhierarchical comparison with each other and with the poetics of Glissant and French poet René Char. Chamoiseau's method of reading, like Glissant's, explores what texts can say interactively that they cannot say independently or by authorial fiat.[45] This, too, is a kind of *créolité*, echoing Spivak's appeal for "creolity rather than kinship as a model for comparatist practice," with creolity a figure for intertextual reading that "assumes imperfection, even as it assures the survival of a rough future."[46]

Each of this book's four main chapters is a comparative reading of early and late twentieth-century literary and theoretical texts that are themselves structured around comparisons. The comparisons I draw do not grow out of any text's direct reference to another, or out of any evidence that one text influenced another. What they share is a common backdrop of imperialist expansionism and its discursive negotiations with relations of difference and the prospect of their influence. I have argued that such negotiations characteristically repress the anxieties of encountering an ungraspable world through positivist comparisons that affirm dominant hierarchies of relation. Against this backdrop, more searching and subversive, if often ambivalent, literary and theoretical negotiations with worldliness have found expression through new comparative forms that constitute what I have been calling a poetics of anxious mastery. What has provoked each chapter's particular conjuncture of texts is not only a common theme, such as racial intermixing (chap. 1) or massacres wrought by authoritarian regimes (chap. 4), but also their display of overlapping forms of representation, figuration, and critique, which, often regardless of authorial intentions, signify differently and unpredictably when read intertextually. For this reason, nonterritorial comparative readings are able to unsettle both regional and disciplinary determinations of critical categories such as "modernism" and "postcolonialism," "Francophone" and "Anglophone," "aesthetic form" and "political engagement." A reconsideration of the politics of literary forms as they pertain to imperial fields of perception and interaction would ideally enhance our experience of reading these seemingly unrelated and discrepant texts, but it would also defuse some of the less productive tensions in a discipline where global modernist and postcolonial interpretive approaches still coexist quite uneasily. Attending to ways that Euro-Atlantic texts are transformed when revisited in light of the critical imaginative training imparted by African-Atlantic and comparative diasporic literature and critical theory pushes against the persistent assumption that transatlantic modernist literature must signify narrowly as the work of mandarins at odds with postcolonial commitments to social justice. In less agonistic interpretations such as Guha's reading of Orwell, James's reading of Eliot, and Glissant's reading of Faulkner, authors' professed cultural politics are not presumed to exhaust, or even necessarily to describe accurately, the effects of their poetics, effects that can change to a significant degree depending on the critical values and methods we bring to reading them. If a text's meanings are never stable, this instability is intensified in writing where individuated perspectives and unified arguments are pervasively qualified and multiplied.

When Ann Laura Stoler poses the question, "How much do the conditions of empire produce stupefied serene states as well as racial anxieties, or something that uneasily combines both ways of not knowing and obliquely knowing at the same time?" she does so to assert that "historical ethnography is obliged to address" the difficult questions that novels by Coetzee and others raise but leave unanswered about the relationship of imperial "structures of feeling to fields of force."[47] I take her point that ethnographic scholarship can explicate genealogies of imperial actions, sensibilities, and attachments in ways that narrative fictions of empire—at least, modernist fictions such as Coetzee's, whose poetics work to disrupt rather than construct discursive certainties, especially where the writing of history is concerned—do not. But I would emphasize that literary forms may be inconclusive, ambivalent, and polysemous and still guide us to answer a question such as hers in some ways rather than others; the open-endedness that interests me in this book is not the sort that amounts to an ethico-political agnosticism.

Chapters 1 and 2 examine narrative and lyric forms of comparison that qualify the authority of speakers who attempt to represent others, and whose accounts indirectly suggest perspectives and relations unimagined or inadequately understood by those speakers. These chapters make the conjuncture of postcolonial Francophone and Anglophone concepts—*métissage*, subalternity, and the politics of despair in chapter 1, transgressive assemblies and the displacement of sovereigns and heroic romance with the imagining of bonds in chapter 2—a means of tracing new relations between Stein and Coetzee, Eliot and Césaire. These conjunctures reveal how modernist literary forms can not only generate pessimism and critique regarding trusted worldviews and states of collectivity in the present but also allow us, in different ways, to glimpse the possibility of the nondominant insinuating itself, like Woolf's Manx cat, into those worldviews and states, which in turn cease to appear whole in themselves but rather as relative parts of larger wholes we must continually strive and fail to imagine. The focus shifts in chapters 3 and 4 to hybrid narrative and essay forms that show speakers' accounts of themselves and others to be the result of dynamic intercultural and intracommunal negotiations with difference. These negotiations may be inadvertent, arising out of unexpected encounters and bewildering shocks that result in an individual's transformative learning; such negotiations are the focus of chapter 3. Or they may be willfully and strategically pursued by narrators who recognize the imperatives of collaboration and persuasion, as in the polemical and testimonial texts I discuss in chapter 4, which employ analogies as a negotiating tactic to rouse transnational audiences to begin to imagine and identify with distant and nondominant experiences of injustice.

What is crucial throughout the four chapters is that speakers, including narrators, are never in full narratorial command individually; they require others, both manifest and marginalized, to supplement, modulate, undercut, and transform the fragmentary stories they tell for more broadly encompassing but still inconclusive stories of collectivity and creolizing relations to emerge. The forms and techniques used to tell these stories of unspoken and misrecognized relations arise from, and powerfully evoke, an expanding and newly uneasy worldly awareness. Read together, these texts suggest a turn, often subtle and more conflicted in earlier modernist texts, while more overt and decisive in later diasporic and postcolonial texts, away from hierarchizing cultural comparisons and toward a comparative practice marked by a questioning of one's home ground that admits, rather than represses, the anxiety of a waning sense of mastery.

1 Troubling Classifications

Unspeakable Figures of *Métissage* in "Melanctha" and *Disgrace*

> The fear of, and desire for, *métissage* is inscribed in the history of human societies.
>
> —Françoise Vergès

We might begin with endings. "The Good Anna," the first of three stories that make up Gertrude Stein's *Three Lives* (1909), concludes with a minor character's brief letter to another character recounting the protagonist's death.[1] The account of the death is jarringly simple and prosaic, rife with omissions by a narrator who seems sadly inadequate to the task of representing the momentous end of a woman's life. Almost fifty years later Chinua Achebe would conclude *Things Fall Apart* (1958) with an abrupt shift into a perfunctory account of a protagonist's death,[2] but where Achebe's novel closes with the narrative anomaly of an uninformed colonial district commissioner taking over what had been a richly textured story of precolonial Igbos and recasting it as a minor addition to an ethnocentric anthropological report, Stein's story ends with a structural device recurrent in "The Good Anna": the revelation of significant plot developments not by the narrator directly but by a character's mediating voice. At one level these endings seem incommensurable: Achebe sharply contrasts a prototypical colonialist bias to the balanced historical realist narration that came before, while Stein contrasts the limited information communicable by a sincere working-class immigrant to the variegated knowledge by accretion that readers have developed gradually out of the story's sinuous repetitions, elaborations, evasions, and deferrals. Stein's emphasis on the partiality and tenuousness of all narratorial views would not have served Achebe's pedagogical goal of reconstructing a forgotten African history for young Nigerian readers, a goal for which the narratorial persona of a farsighted, trustworthy chronicler was advantageous.[3] In this way, the two narratives seem so clearly positioned on opposite sides of the familiar border between an immersive literary realism and an estranging modernism—notwithstanding Stein's own shifting status in the modernist literary canon over the course of the twentieth century[4]—that there has been little incentive to explore how particular formal attributes of the earlier work might accrue or shift meaning by their transfiguration in the latter.

Yet Stein's mediating narrators throughout *Three Lives*, whether clearly delineated or subtle and easily overlooked, suggest a conception of knowledge that we can now better recognize thanks to the cumulative effects of transdisciplinary postcolonial efforts, including and since *Things Fall Apart*, to excavate and imagine presences that escape, or operate subversively within, ostensibly transparent and innocently informative languages of representation. Theories of difference, subalternity, hybridity, and relation have cast suspicion on readily communicated claims to knowledge as "rough translations," to borrow Dipesh Chakrabarty's phrase, that efface complexities they cannot assimilate.[5] These theories have envisioned knowledge as potentially transformed by comparatist practices that make heterogeneity imaginable even in uses of language that obscure it. Achebe is less suspicious than either Stein or numerous, more deconstructive postcolonial thinkers have been of narratorial authority as such; in *Things Fall Apart*, he reserves his skepticism for the patently misleading narration of a colonial official whose ignorance Achebe implies to be avoidable, if typical. However, this difference should not distract us from an affinity between *Things Fall Apart* and "The Good Anna," at once formal and political: both conclude with a commonsensical description that we know is inadequate because the comparative structure of the larger text has made us see otherwise.

Françoise Lionnet has argued for a literary criticism that takes an "unwavering interest in what literature can *do*, in the real work it accomplishes in the world, in what it achieves through questioning, in the overtures it promotes and the democratic processes it favors *without having to say so explicitly*."[6] The political promise of these endings, and of narrative forms of indirection and implicit comparison more broadly, lies in their capacity to train readers to look beyond explicit textual assertions of knowledge to the position and function of those assertions in larger patterns of meaning. What would appear as conclusive information if read in isolation signifies in fraught relation with what is read elsewhere. Such forms of indirect comparison are essentially ironic and can be risky, especially when they pervade a narrative poetics as they do Stein's, often more circumspectly and ambiguously than my opening examples suggest. The risk is that their modulations and contestations of the explicit will go unnoticed, especially when the subject is highly controversial; the irony fails to translate, and the authority of the explicit is magnified and misread as the stance of the text and its author. Not, in my view, coincidentally, two of the twentieth century's most contentious portrayals of interracial sex, racial identification, and racialized sexual domination and desire unfold through extended and repeated uses of narrative indirection and implicit comparison: the novella-length middle story of *Three Lives*, "Melanctha: Each One as She May," and J. M. Coetzee's novel *Disgrace* (1999).[7] To see how both narratives make failed relations of intimacy and community indissociable from failures of definitive, objectifying language, a language saturated with colonialist logics of social and cultural classification, we must weigh what characters, including narrators, are able to think and say against what the texts imply to be missing or misrecognized in characters' reflections and communications.

As Stein's reputation as a major innovator of modernist literary form solidified in the late twentieth century, critical scrutiny of her thought intensified. The revaluation of Stein for her prescient attention to performative processes of language and sexuality has coincided with a tendency to interpret the racial politics of "Melanctha" as "undeniably troubling," in Matthew Hart's words.[8] Even scholars sympathetic to Stein rarely dispute that her early fiction's insistent racialization of characters is contrary to enlightened egalitarian discourse on race and ethnic difference.[9] The awkwardness of this position, as Hart and a long line of critics before him have readily conceded, comes from the story's favorable reception by some (though certainly not all) enlightened and egalitarian African American writers in the past. It is often noted that Nella Larsen wrote Stein a fan letter after reading "Melanctha" for having "caught the spirit of this race of mine," and that James Weldon Johnson also wrote Stein a letter in which he praised her as the first "white writer to write a story of love between a Negro man and woman and deal with them as normal members of the human family."[10] The story's most frequently cited admirer is Richard Wright, who describes his "shock of recognition" at discovering "Miss Stein's struggling words" that "made the speech of the people around me vivid": "As I read it my ears were opened for the first time to the magic of the spoken word. I began to hear the speech of my grandmother, who spoke a deep, pure Negro dialect and with whom I had lived for many years."[11] For Wright, reflecting on Stein in

1945, the critical consensus to be overcome was a socialist one that deemed "her tortured verbalisms" and bohemian lifestyle decadent and counterrevolutionary. Wright recounts reading "Melanctha" aloud to "a group of semiliterate Negro stockyard workers," whose sense of identification and engagement with the story impressed him as so strong that, he concludes, "my fondness for Steinian prose never distressed me after that" (*Selected Writings of Gertrude Stein* 338).

In assessing whether these black American writers were "correct" to take inspiration from Stein's characterization of black Americans or to hear in her stylized vernacular a distinctly and admirably black American English, we let debates over authenticity divert us from the sense of solidarity that a literary language can inspire, not by its literal realism but by its imaginative translation of what a hegemonic language is perceived to foreclose at a particular point in time. That Larsen, Johnson, and Wright found in Stein's story a provocation to solidarity at a time when there was no dearth of literary attempts at representing black characters and their speech should make us look to what was singular and counterhegemonic about Stein's forms of translation.

My phrasing here draws on Lionnet's theorization of *métissage* as a literary aesthetics and practice of critical reading, which she aligns with Édouard Glissant's use of the term, in *Le Discours antillais*, to designate the composite relations characteristic of the Antilles but also of cultures more broadly, including cultures mythologized as racially pure and exclusive.[12] Arguing that "we have to articulate new visions of ourselves, new concepts that allow us to think *otherwise*," Lionnet joins with Glissant in drawing from the subversive connotations of the French colonial concept of *métissage*, or racial intermixing. Bringing to literary criticism Glissant's metaphorical image of cultural relation as a "poetics," Lionnet translates the colonial concept of *métissage* into a textual practice that disrupts the clarity of dichotomous thinking through its "undecidability and indeterminacy, where solidarity becomes the fundamental principle of political action against hegemonic languages."[13] In other words, a poetics of *métissage* both formally embodies and guides readers toward imagining a diversely constituted solidarity, in place of the isolation of sameness from otherness normalized through languages of imperialism and white supremacism. Such a poetics is one that builds with, rather than buries, anxieties about indeterminacy and its disruption of norms.

In her history of *métissage* as a recurrent and contested concept in discourses of emancipation and assimilation emerging out of France's Atlantic and Indian Ocean colonies, Françoise Vergès emphasizes that "*métissage* was developed *in the colonial world* as a response to European racism and the discourse of mono-ethnicism, of blood and nation."[14] As "both a fact—biological mixing—and a value—the colonized's condemnation of pure blood ideology," *métissage* was "a source of anxiety and a site of rhetorical subversion in the empire" (9). Of course, the colonial conception of *métissage* as the mixing of racially differentiated bodies and their "blood" proceeded from nineteenth-century definitions of race, but it countered the ideal of blood purity, the fear of degeneration, and the notion that there existed a natural order of races that should be preserved.[15] The prospect of racial intermixing and its indeterminate social effects posed a continual threat to the conservation of ethno-territorial power that blood politics were designed to ensure, hence the paradoxically anti-racist and anticolonial implications of a concept that explicitly makes use of raciological and colonialist dichotomies. *Métissage* puts dichotomies to work toward their own dismantling.

When we trace *métissage* to its root *tissage* (weaving), as Glissant and Lionnet do, we see that the English term "miscegenation" is a misleading translation of *métissage* because it lacks the French term's politically and aesthetically productive connotations of a transverse texture, in which component elements remain differentiated, indeed must cross the grain of others to assemble and cohere as they do, instead of blending into a homogeneous unity.[16] *Métissage* is, at its root and in its historical association with physical crossings of race, sex, and power, a term that accentuates, more than comparable terms such as hybridity, creolization, and *creolité*, the operations of contrast. In crosscut weaves, differences interacting without reconciling are indispensable to the workings of larger patterns.

From this perspective, it is apparent why *métissage* as a disordering of colonialist categories of race would resonate as a postcolonial metaphor for literary and critical practices that destabilize and delegitimize divisive conceptions of identity and knowledge.[17] These formulations of *métissage* contribute to a discursive context that has been neglected in discussions of Stein's writing of the conjunction between racialized cultural discourse and sexual exploration.[18] After studying psychology and, one summer, embryology as a Harvard undergraduate, then medicine at Johns Hopkins before dropping out in her fourth year and moving to Europe, Stein settled in Paris in 1903. Two years later, she began work on her story of a mixed-race African American woman, "pale yellow" and "half made with real white blood," who is determined to mix, so to speak, socially and sexually in pursuit of "world wisdom" (Stein, *Three Lives* 60, 75). The period of the story's composition (from 1905 to 1906) and publication (as part of *Three Lives* in 1909) coincided with the writing and publication of Sir Francis Galton's memoir, in which he rejoiced that his theory of eugenics, long underestimated in his view, had at last found "an appreciative audience."[19] Galton had coined "eugenics," which he defined as "the conditions under which men of a high type are produced," in 1883, thereby giving a name to the theory of heritable intellect and "racial improvement" he had been developing since the 1860s.[20] His now-notorious belief in the "Utopias" that might result from well-funded programs of "selective breeding" was premised on the idea that men of white European "stock" were innately superior to everyone else, and that they should protect and enhance their "hereditary talent and character" by taking measures to limit the sexual reproduction of "sub-races," as well as disabled, mentally ill, or otherwise "unfit" individuals.[21] The appreciative audience that had formed by 1908 would continue to grow, notably in the United States among proponents of anti-miscegenation laws, as well as researchers in the medical and biological sciences, until eugenics fell out of public favor because of its association with Nazi practices of "racial hygiene" in the 1930s and 1940s.[22] It was in this discursive context, in which institutionally authorized, even decorated advocates of "pure blood" ideology routinely singled out black Africans and their descendants in the Americas for particular denigration, that *métissage* became a source of both anxiety and hope in the French colonies. Whether conceived more radically, as an openly multiethnic resistance to both colonialist universalism and blood politics, or more conservatively, as an assimilationist erasure of difference in keeping with French ethnocentric ideals, *métissage* signified a rejection of racially bounded sexual possibility.

Unquestionably, "Melanctha" would not exist outside the discursive context of a racialized Africa that abides in the blood of black Americans. To read "Melanctha" as if its characters' expressions of unexamined racism and blood politics are affirmed by the text, though, requires isolating these expressions from their collaborative function in a story of sharp contrasts that throw each other into doubt, while together conveying a vision distinct from any one speaker's explicit view. It is particularly tempting, but I think mistaken, to equate the narrator's focalization at any given time with the vision produced by the text's totality of crisscrossing and mutually qualifying perspectives. "Melanctha" is not a realist depiction of its titular protagonist but an enactment of the circumscribed ways of thinking and speaking through which she is imagined in an interracial small-town community in the southern United States, where upwardly mobile black residents estimate their worth in terms of how successfully they comply with white middle-class norms of respectability. The story of this community's divisive ways of categorizing each other gradually reveals itself as a quiet tragedy in which any enduring intimate relationships Melanctha might have had are precluded by a rampant local discourse propelled by communal anxieties about sexual and racial indeterminacy. These anxieties are expressed, in both direct dialogue and the narrator's "free indirect" approximation of characters' perspectives (a technique Mieke Bal calls "ambiguous focalization"), through an amalgam of blood ideology, at once racist and classist, and an ethos of bourgeois assimilationism.[23]

Vergès has linked a heightened anxiety about "mixed blood in the age of eugenics and nationalism" to "a reconfiguration of otherness that was taking place in France to situate a coherent national bourgeois identity" (95). Neither white nor the Other, the French colonial *métis* had a socially troubling "position as an 'in-between,' a 'not-quite' white," whose potential to pass as white awakened anxieties that could be dispelled by the *métis*'s performance of a nonthreatening or, ironically speaking, "good *métissage*," that is, an acceptance of social and political assimilation and an identification with the nonwhite community within the French imperial nation (95). With the figure of Melanctha, Stein imagines an alternative to the "good" *métis* or *métisse*: a racially and sexually undecided woman who refuses to choose sides and settle in to black (aspiring) middle-class married life as her accommodationist black and mixed-race neighbors do. Instead, Stein makes "wandering" in pursuit of "world wisdom" and with no preconceived destination her protagonist's chosen condition, not unlike Glissant's sense of "wandering" in *Poetics of Relation*. With this recurring, vaguely defined, polysemous metaphor, Stein evokes a hybrid process of physical and verbal exploration that leads Melanctha to cross continually into new territory and unpredictable social encounters in a town aptly called Bridgepoint. Although Melanctha, like everyone in the story, has her own biases (she credits upper-class interlocutors with having more to teach her than people of her own class), her wandering represents a rejection of the determinate identity and communal membership that assimilation would entail.

Her wandering also represents a rejection of conclusive narration, characterization, and claims to knowledge. Frustrating the anxious, compulsively reiterated efforts of her lover, the assimilated mixed-race doctor Jeff Campbell, to "know which is a real Melanctha Herbert," Melanctha "all her life did not know how to tell a story wholly" (Stein, *Three Lives* 97, 70). In a clear allusion to the story also named "Melanctha," whose language simulates processes of speaking and thinking through serial repetitions and a disconcerting preference for compound sentences and present progressive verbs, Melanctha is faulted by other characters for her preoccupation with the present, and for lacking a coherent sense of temporal progression. Her memories and sense of her own story are said to wander, while others continually seek to define her in strict terms that are variously motivated and self-interested, but also discursively constrained and formulaic. Characters who think they know how to tell Melanctha's story wholly are those whose ideal of story making is implicitly contrasted with the wandering narration that includes their voices but undercuts their positive assertions. In this way, "Melanctha" appropriates and revalues colonial psychology's generalizing diagnosis of Creoles as having a pathologically "weak sense of self"—a diagnosis that ties the standard of blood purity to a standard of selfhood as "whole," Vergès argues—and translates the notion of Creoles' tenuous individuation into an affirmative image of self-searching through convergences with others.[24] Stein's writing of *métissage*, as both a theme and a poetics, makes the *métis*—the site of contradiction, the intermixed—a form of possibility, an unanticipated convocation.

The goal, then, is to explore how narrative forms and figures of *métissage* translate absence—the absence of intimacy and understanding, the absence of difference that can be articulated and heard—into the presence of possibility. I want to suggest how our reading of the poetics and politics of race in "Melanctha" changes not only in light of Francophone postcolonial conceptualizations of *métissage* as a literary aesthetics and critical praxis of comparative reading but also in relation to formal and thematic reverberations of *métissage* in Coetzee's *Disgrace*. My readings of "Melanctha" and *Disgrace* are meant to suggest a productive convergence between theories of *métissage* and some Anglophone postcolonial theories of subalternity and transnational comparison, which together prepare us to recognize in textual irresolution an incentive to doubt the sufficiency of either division or untroubled assimilation as a solution to interpretive dilemmas posed by difference.

At the start and close of a century when the world's increasingly uncertain parameters and unforeseen relations were met with an array of anxiously absolutist claims about ethnic difference, Stein and Coetzee both drew from a potent imperial language of racial and sexual classification and juxtaposed it, along with the specious knowledge it normalized, to poetic evocations of alternative ways of knowing and communicating. Set in stratified but also transitional social spheres, their stories of *métissage* recall traumatic histories of racist domination by unearthing those histories' remnants in the present, including a mostly disavowed anxiety among the dominant and those who seek to identify with the dominant, about black self-determination and potency unleashed in a fragile and shifting order of knowledge. These remnants leave scant space, in the grim present of both fictional worlds, for indeterminate figures to present themselves directly. At the same time, these narratives represent the *métis*—as personified figure and as literary form—to summon the possibility of liberation from impasses that racialization and social division keep engendering. Together, their distinct but intersecting poetics cross not only black with white but also speech with silence, to call us to imagine beyond what any one speaker can say directly, beyond what any one narrator can direct us to know. In this lies the optimism of their manifest despair.

Crossing into the Future in *Disgrace*

"What is striking about the discourse of racism before 1945 is its nakedness, its shamelessness," Coetzee writes in *White Writing*, in an essay first published in 1980.[25] While the exposure of Nazi war crimes at Nuremberg did not put an end to racism, it did entail a thoroughgoing repression in the international public sphere of language that had worked to normalize pure blood ideology since the mid-nineteenth century: "The Nuremberg war crimes trials, and what they revealed to the world about the implementation of National Socialist race theories, put a stop to a certain way of talking about other human beings: as low-grade people, degenerate types, *Untermenschen*, the unfit, slave races, and so forth. These terms, with their claim to stand for biological and anthropological realities, disappeared from public discourse, taking in their train a number of phrases involving *blood* (*blood-consciousness, pure blood, tainted blood,* etc.), as well as certain terms from the fringes of the science of heredity (*taint, flaw, degeneration*)" (141). I have suggested, and will return to the point, that Stein's poetics of unresolved perspectives puts this language of blood on display as part of a broader interimperial racial discourse made ironic by the contradictory patterns of its articulation in "Melanctha." By the time Coetzee wrote *Disgrace*, biologically framed threats of hereditary regression had given way to culturally, religiously, and economically framed threats in mainstream racisms and ethnocentrisms.[26] By "mainstream" I mean those racisms and ethnocentrisms capable of being received on national and international stages as a kind of common sense (which is not to say an uncontested common sense, any more than eugenics was ever uncontested). A poetics that works to denaturalize more occluded languages and logics of ethnic domination, as Coetzee's does, necessarily looks different from Stein's, and of course Stein's looks different to us now than it did to readers before the language of blood had been altogether discredited. And yet, Coetzee, too, insinuates subversive figures of alterity into a rarely questioned, ostensibly high-minded common sense—in his case, a common sense about civilized humanity and its attainments of art, language, and reason—through a poetics of *métissage*: a poetics of implicit, unresolved contrasts whose difficult interaction evokes what cannot be understood or described by any one of the novel's characters. More precisely, these ironic contrasts evoke what cannot be understood or described by the narrator, who, unlike Stein's more fluid and ambiguously focalizing narrator, characteristically enters into only one character's view, that of the protagonist, David Lurie. Coetzee impugns Lurie's erudite ratiocinations with an obliqueness that exposes the novel to some recurring interpretations that, whether critically or sympathetically, overestimate the value of Lurie's conclusions and underestimate the significance of how they signify in ironic contrast to a more expansive vision. The novel's undeclared comparisons privilege the reader to see and enter this vision.

Acclaimed for its aesthetic and moral vision but also faulted for reinforcing racial prejudices, *Disgrace* takes place in the perilous terrain of a newly postapartheid South Africa, where a white woman is raped in her home by black intruders and then, learning that she is pregnant, decides to bear her rapist's child, as well as cede her property to the rapist's protector, who is also a black man, so that she can remain in the house where she was attacked without fear of further violence. The book's mixed critical reception echoes the dramatic divergence of responses to Stein's depiction of black American speech and social relations. Critics of "Melanctha" debate the implications of Stein's overtly primitivist poetics, in which some speakers, including the narrator, reproduce racist views; critics of *Disgrace* debate the implications of Coetzee's provocative plot, which reproduces a stock colonialist narrative of white grievance over the violation of a gentle white woman by brutal black men. In both cases, the narratives translate highly recognizable racisms of their time into uncanny variants, at once familiar and dubious, whose meaning is not self-evident in the narratives' larger worlds of conflicting and situated interests.

Peter McDonald has argued that the racism perceived by many of Coetzee's detractors can be traced back to their "restrictive territorialization" of *Disgrace* as a "South African novel" and, in turn, a "'South African novel' of a deeply racialized kind"—classifications that predetermine and reduce the scope of the novel's significance.[27] For McDonald, this territorializing critical proclivity is perhaps most damaging in its more nuanced articulations, such as Jeff Radebe's address to the South African Human Rights Commission on behalf of the ANC, which ambivalently characterized *Disgrace* as a valuable commentary on "white people's perception of the post-apartheid black man" but also, perhaps, a less than neutral one, and Jakes Gerwel's objection that the novel's "image of our nation" is one that excludes "the possibility of civilized reconciliation" (324–25).[28] Asking "what effects *Disgrace* would begin to produce if read without" the narrow regionalism and defensive nationalism that give rise to such readings, McDonald argues that "it is as much about the ethics of reading" as it is about "millennial anxieties in South Africa and elsewhere" (327, 330).

My own reading does not distinguish as sharply as McDonald's between *Disgrace* as an index of historically particular millennial or, we might say more broadly, late imperial anxieties and *Disgrace* as a "testament to the essential instability of the 'literary'" (330), mainly because, as I note in the introduction, I take the latter phrase to describe literary language as modernists reacting against nineteenth-century positivisms repeatedly define it, rather than a description of all literary expression. Coetzee's aporetic narratives about topical controversies such as sexual harassment and interracial rape stir up our impulses to take sides while undermining our faith in the frames of reference that would allow us to do so. The ethics of reading that these confrontational and equivocal stories prompt us to confront are inextricable from the anxious sense of precarious mastery that they both portray and elicit. I share McDonald's sense, however, that territorial critical approaches guided principally by their investment in the struggles of a particular place or group are ill-suited to Coetzee's explicitly noncommittal, subtly ironic poetics of narratorial deficiency. This poetics is difficult to interpret despite its standard syntax and veneer of realism because it leaves so much unspoken and unresolved in relation to the unreliable explanations and troubling resolutions that characters are able to articulate. As readers we must contend with the text's refusals to master its subject and achieve closure, a trial of reading that, one hopes, will impel us to try to imagine what assertions of mastery and closure elsewhere forestall. For Derek Attridge, Coetzee's difficult narrative poetics and the ethics of reading that it imparts share in the larger ethical intervention of modernism: "Modernism's foregrounding of language and other discursive and generic codes through its formal strategies is not merely a self-reflexive diversion but a recognition (whatever its writers may have thought they were doing) that literature's distinctive power and potential ethical force reside in a testing and unsettling of deeply held assumptions of transparency, instrumentality, and direct referentiality, in part because this taking to the limits opens a space for the apprehension of the otherness which those assumptions had silently excluded."[29] This ideal of poetic difficulty, with its crossing of direct referentiality to allow for the apprehension of otherness, emerges in *Disgrace* out of the totality of its transverse but interwoven perspectives, both articulated and silent. It is against this higher ideal of the text, while also functioning within it, that the abstract principles of the novel's protagonist David Lurie regularly appear in stark relief.

Disgrace maintains a tightly controlled focus on the perspective of Lurie, whose story unfolds in a seemingly open-ended present tense that precludes the consolation and catharsis of endings and accentuates Lurie's strandedness in the present, contrary to our expectation that a protagonist will develop and improve over time.[30] Lurie is a white university teacher dismissed from his job after a mixed-race student he seduced accuses him of sexual harassment. The novel opens with this sequence of events and prepares us to see Lurie as an unreliable authority figure, a sententious teacher and father who fails at the task of teaching, not once but repeatedly, because he is blind to the power inequities his culturally constrained reasoning reflects and perpetuates. Coetzee's ample use of free indirect discourse keeps Lurie's mental life at the center of the book, while the understated third-person mode of narration leads us through unsatisfying conversations and half-articulated conclusions that amount to "zones of untranslatability," in Emily Apter's phrase.[31] These untranslatable zones of the narrative not only attenuate the authority of the introspective man of letters who imagines that his erudition will yield enlightenment, for himself and others; they also undermine the credibility of discursive communication itself as a primary means to insight about cultural and sexual difference.

In *Disgrace*, Lurie's labors of reflection and argumentation fail him; the awkward efforts to communicate by this eloquent and multilingual professor of communications regularly yield only more confusion and, not infrequently, hostility. Coetzee implies the impasse to be one where the possibility of self-transformation through convergence with others is systematically blocked by received ideas infused with colonial paternalism; Lurie cannot interact with students, women, or black South Africans without falling into diagnosing and moralizing about them. After her rape, Lurie's daughter Lucy repeatedly distances herself from Lurie when he attempts to make sense of her motives: "You keep misreading me. Guilt and salvation are abstractions. I don't act in terms of abstractions" (Coetzee, *Disgrace* 112). Given his difficulty in seeing beyond inherited abstractions, it is significant that the openness to otherness he conspicuously lacks in his earnest but disconnected conversations finally emerges to some extent in his work at the animal clinic, where he assumes responsibility for disposing of the corpses of euthanized dogs. This development in Lurie's character seems to grow out of an unspoken sense of identification with the dogs, which, like him in the wake of his student Melanie's sexual harassment suit, live in a fallen state, out of favor, marginalized, disgraced. Despite his condescension toward animals through most of the book, the one potentially reciprocal bond he begins to form is with a young lame dog, whose interaction with Lurie hints at what might have operated outside the sense-making limitations that Lurie has continually run up against and inadvertently reinforced throughout the novel (214–15).[32] He resists naming the dog, but whatever name he might have conferred is effectively replaced by the dog's identifying disability, "a withered left hindquarter which it drags behind it" (215).

Marianne DeKoven has argued that *Disgrace* is "a coherent narrative of personal salvation" in which Lurie progresses ethically from a sense of indifference and disdain toward nonhuman animals and middle-aged women to a sense of humane identification with them.[33] Certainly Lurie undergoes a radical shift over the course of the novel, from an intellectually and sexually confident urban pedant to a variously peripheral manual laborer of sorts, whose social miscalculations, natural aging process, and dwindling authority have humbled and bewildered him. Coetzee portrays this shift through Lurie's evolving interactions with animals and their caretaker, Bev Shaw, and through his increasing compassion toward them. His laudable commitment to disposing of unwanted dogs' corpses and his use of the word "love" to explain what underlies that commitment, though, do not constitute a drastic transformation of Lurie's propensity to relate to others in abstract terms that exclude more than he realizes (Coetzee, *Disgrace* 219). The "love" he describes is as much an abstraction as the "honour" and "dignity" he advises Lucy to maintain when she decides to stay on her farm after the rape and accede to the terms of her neighbor Petrus's self-serving offer of protection. Lurie's "love" for animals is a generalizing one, and in the end it does not extend to the particular dog to which he has begun to form an attachment. Despite the singularity of his relation to this dog—the only figure in the book with whom Lurie communicates through music, rather than words—he does not, in the end, take him in, which is also to say that Lurie never identifies with the dog to the extent that he ceases to classify him as an other.[34] On this point, Coetzee conspicuously contrasts Lurie's feeling for the dog to the dog's feeling for him: "Arbitrarily, unconditionally, he has been adopted; the dog would die for him, he knows" (215). The dog's commitment to Lurie, based in a recognition of him as special, is unreciprocated. Soon after letting go of his ambitions to write a chamber opera, into which he had briefly considered incorporating the dog's voice, Lurie decides, in the book's final sentence (and his own), to let go of the dog as well: "Yes, I am giving him up" (220).

The idea that *Disgrace* is essentially the story of Lurie's moral awakening and redemption is unlikely to persuade those who read the novel's conclusion with a wrenching sense of disappointment, loss, and frustrated desire. I would attribute this sense to the radical discrepancy between what the narrative has shown the dog's singular relational value to be and what Lurie perceives as that dog's expendability and equivalence to other homeless animals, ones with whom he has not interacted. No doubt most critics would concur, as I do to a point, with Elizabeth Anker's assessment that "an aura of profound indeterminacy surrounds the conclusion of the novel, engendering its overwhelmingly haunting force"; the prevailing view that *Disgrace* is "a characteristically undecidable, ethically ambiguous post-modern novel" is what DeKoven seeks to refute by recasting *Disgrace* as a "salvific narrative" ("Going to the Dogs" 847).[35] The novel's conclusion, like much of what comes before, denies us determinacy and closure in multiple ways, but I would again emphasize that this denial is not an abdication of politically consequential ethical engagement. As McDonald and Attridge suggest with respect to the ethics of reading Coetzee, it is precisely by unsettling and refusing to redeem or replace ideals of moral clarity and blind justice that the text presses on readers the responsibility to apprehend new possibilities of relation in their wake.

It is fair to say that in otherwise disparate critical responses to *Disgrace*, including, surprisingly enough, those that emphasize the novel's indeterminacy and Lurie's fallibility, a striking point of agreement has been that Lurie's cryptic decision to let the dog be euthanized conveys his mature relinquishing of what he privately values for a greater communal good, and in this sense marks the moral progress that this once selfish and anthropocentric man has made over the course of the book. Such accounts typically do not attempt to explain why, in the practical terms of the plot, it is necessary or even desirable for the particular dog to die; they seem to trust in Lurie's sense of his own righteousness.[36] Rita Barnard's compelling analysis is an exception, both in acknowledging that Lurie's motivations for killing the dog are obscure and in offering a possible justification for his choice. Writing that Lurie's decision "is an act redolent of betrayal but also, one obscurely senses, of a profound love and responsibility," Barnard proposes that "in refusing to single out the special dog, Lurie is accepting, perhaps helplessly, perhaps resolutely, the claims of an infinite number of other creatures with whom he has no special connection."[37] It seems to me that Barnard's qualifications—"one obscurely senses," "perhaps helplessly"—signal her own ambivalence about this reading. The dog is never represented as competing with other dogs for his survival. It is only because he is not valued by individuals like Lurie—only because his particularity is subsumed under the category of unwanted dogs—that he must die like all the others. Lurie could not take them all in, but a community of individuals like Lurie, each doing their part, could. Let us suppose that this lame mongrel dog were a human being, one who had been consigned to a devalued class of human beings deemed unworthy of life. Let us suppose that Lurie formed a bond with this person only to continue to classify him as interchangeable with others "of his kind" and not his responsibility to save. Would this be met with unanimous critical approval as evidence of Lurie's growth and redemption, even salvation? Would the abandoned friend's presumed expendability and interchangeability not be condemned as quintessentially dehumanizing?

If Coetzee were a humanist, this counterfactual would be irrelevant. But Coetzee is not a humanist: his work has repeatedly returned to the vast and mostly unquestioned system of apartheid that human beings have created to segregate themselves from animals; he has repeatedly shone a light on the cruelties that ensue from this system, not only toward animals but also toward human beings whose likeness to animals has been declared in order to justify their subjugation and elimination. McDonald defends *Disgrace* against accusations of racism by pointing out its "oblique references to the Indian caste system, and, more chillingly, to the Nazis' final solution—the word *Lösung* recurs twice," but neither he nor other critics who identify these references connect them to the "dehumanization," shall we say (for want of a better term), of a physically impaired but otherwise healthy dog that Coetzee's narrator, focalizing Lurie's point of view, twice identifies as young (McDonald 329; Coetzee, *Disgrace* 215, 219). *Lösung* does not simply recur twice; it recurs as Lurie's designation for his weekly mercy killings of unwanted animals, which he sees (the free indirect narration suggests) in corporal terms, with a fixation on categories of disabled bodies: "He and Bev Shaw are engaged in one of their sessions of *Lösung*. One by one he brings in the cats, then the dogs: the old, the blind, the halt, the crippled, the maimed, but also the young, the sound—all those whose term has come" (142, 218).

One of the most dramatic, yet critically neglected, implicit comparisons in the novel is the contrast between Lurie's choice not to keep the unwanted mongrel dog and Lucy's decision to keep her unwanted, mixed-race child of rape. Both the dog and the child are *métis* figures of possibility, figures of collaborative crossing that represent new, indeterminate configurations in place of old segregations. Lucy consents to admit this possibility, to her home and herself, however painful it must be for her; Lurie decides against admitting this possibility. His rejection of the figure and its potential to traverse and reconfigure his own future may be read as a final test in which Lurie, once again, subordinates the singular experience of intimacy with another, and the responsibility this entails, to a general principle of what one ought to do in such circumstances. The novel's final sentence means, in effect, that he will go on, divided off from others, as he has always done. He remains true to his own self-assessment near the start of his story: that he is not someone to wake up with the next morning, and that his temperament is not going to change (Coetzee, *Disgrace* 2).

The impenetrability of Lurie's vision to what might alter it, as well as his inability to take others in and be transformed in the process, has consequences for his art as well. His equation of tragedy with nineteenth-century European ideas and aesthetics of tragedy dooms his intricate but derivative and ultimately abortive attempt at composing an opera, which, unlike Coetzee's novel, is divorced from the traumas and possibilities unfolding around him and his daughter in South Africa. In short, as desolate and marginal as his life has become, Lurie never moves beyond highly abstract ideas of responsibility, paternalistic feelings for animals, and recycled romantic visions of art to begin to imagine what he cannot readily translate. It is worth reflecting on how remote Lurie's art is in this respect from Coetzee's own. Whereas Stein figures her poetics of wandering as continuous with that of her protagonist Melanctha, Coetzee weaves Lurie's abstract pathos (or bathos) into his own decidedly unromantic narrative art, effecting a formal contrast between the partiality of Lurie's received ideas and *Disgrace*'s unrelenting engagement with an urgent political present, the present of a region but also of farther-flung transnational, interimperial, and trans-species patterns of relation.[38] For example, Lurie's contemplation of whether he should "bring a dog into the piece, allow it to loose its own lament to the heavens," suggests the capacity of the nameless dog's as-yet-unheard voice to transform not only Lurie's opera but, with sly metafictionality, Coetzee's novel as well. While Lurie fails, in the end, to "hear" the dog, that is, to recognize the dog's value to his story, Coetzee does not make this mistake. Coetzee further renders Lurie's artistic vision ironic by implicitly contrasting Lurie's depiction of women to his own. In his opera, Lurie imagines Lord Byron's abandoned lover Teresa "howling to the moon for the rest of her natural life," while his "unlovely, unloved" daughter Allegra pleads inconsolably to her father, "Why have you left me? . . . Why have you forgotten me?" (Coetzee, *Disgrace* 186). Without quite knowing why, Lurie eventually realizes that "despite occasional good moments, the truth is that *Byron in Italy* is going nowhere" (214). Fascinated by women but unable to conceive of them as evolving agents, central to their own stories and not dependent on the affection and magnanimity of men, Lurie imitates in art what Lucy observes in their relationship: "You behave as if everything I do is part of the story of your life. You are the main character, I am a minor character who doesn't make an appearance until halfway through. Well, contrary to what you think, people are not divided into major and minor. I am not minor. I have a life of my own, just as important to me as yours is to you, and in my life I am the one who makes the decisions" (198).

The novel's culminating comparison between Lurie and Lucy, the contrast between Lurie's rejection of the *métis* and Lucy's acceptance of it, is the last in a series of formal positionings of Lucy as her father's foil. I mean not simply that she contradicts what he says in direct dialogue, which she does often, but that, like Melanctha, Lucy resists being categorized through general principles, especially those that naturalize heterosexist, racist, and humanist patterns of domination. In the aftermath of her attack, Lucy counters Lurie's appeal that she "be sensible" and start over somewhere else because staying is not "a good idea": she replies that "it's not an idea, good or bad. I'm not going back for the sake of an idea. I'm just going back" (Coetzee, *Disgrace* 105). Her choices are incomprehensible to Lurie because they fail to conform to what he expects a white settler woman to do in her situation. Through her choices, unexplained and in some ways mysterious even to her, Coetzee refuses to validate commonsense assumptions about proper retaliation in the wake of violent assault. Lucy chooses to reject what Salman Rushdie has called communalism—the "us versus them" thinking that overtakes Lurie when he confronts Petrus and Lucy's attacker Pollux after the rape—and chooses instead to bear Pollux's child and bring it up as a member of Petrus's family.[39] This seems to Lurie the most abject of capitulations. But unlike the courses of action he considers sensible, Lucy's course lays a foundation for a new way of being in the world, a new mode of relation that breaks out of acculturated patterns of thinking about domination and subjugation. To evoke a future not constrained by old patterns of revenge and escape, Coetzee invites us to learn as Lucy does, not from an authoritative man of learning but from animals. Acknowledging her humiliation, Lucy tells her father, "Perhaps that is what I must learn to accept. To start at ground level. With nothing. Not with nothing but. With nothing. No cards, no weapons, no property, no rights, no dignity." "Like a dog," Lurie laments, to which Lucy responds, "Yes, like a dog" (205). Her identification with dogs here is much more concrete than Lurie's ever is. Whereas he assumes a sympathetic but detached role as animal undertaker, Lucy learns from dogs, taking them as a model for what human beings might achieve in the absence of transcendental principles and proprietary claims.

Vergès writes that the demand to be treated with dignity, "a term often used by oppressed people around the world to express a demand for 'respect,'" is also a demand for "recognition 'as a human being,' the demand to be treated like one as opposed to being treated 'like a dog'" (255n3). We can extrapolate two important implications of Vergès's point as it pertains to the position Lucy takes to the bewilderment of her father (and, indeed, many of Coetzee's readers). In rejecting the course of action that seems to Lurie the self-evidently correct one, Lucy refuses to define herself as oppressed within a system that has historically privileged white women like herself over her attackers, and at the same time she refuses to differentiate herself as a rights-bearing human being from animals presumed to lack rights and dignity because they lack a language communicable to human beings. She refuses, in effect, to lay claim to a category of dignity that is itself grounded in a kind of discursive apartheid.

In the year that *Disgrace* was published, Coetzee's Tanner Lectures appeared in print as *The Lives of Animals*, in which fictional novelist and animal rights advocate Elizabeth Costello similarly distinguishes the "sympathy and insight" of psychologist Wolfgang Köhler in his observations of apes from the poet's more immediate and self-implicating "feel for the ape's experience."[40] Taking as exemplary of such poetry Kafka's story of an educated ape named Red Peter, Costello twice refers to Kafka as Red Peter's amanuensis, counter-romantically defining the novelist as a recorder of characters' distinctive voices rather than an ingenious creator of them. By extension, Coetzee the male writer acts as an amanuensis for Lucy and Costello, women who exasperate other characters, and no doubt more than a few readers, by refusing to provide argumentative closure, a mode of resistance at the heart of Coetzee's art (see *Lives* 26; *Elizabeth Costello* 70–71). "I was hoping not to have to enunciate principles," Elizabeth Costello says at one point, and later, "I don't know what I think. . . . I often wonder what thinking is, what understanding is. Do we really understand the universe better than animals do?" (*Lives* 37, 45). In resisting the consoling closure of her father's principles, Lucy is better able than he to accept that Petrus and his family, and even Pollux, are no more minor characters than she is, and no less "full of being," in Costello's terms.[41]

Lurie's journey from his position as a professor in Cape Town to a rootless existence on his daughter's farm, where he and his daughter are attacked, adapts the Conradian topos of the privileged foreign thinker-wanderer who must confront a fearsome black otherness. Like Conrad before him, Coetzee uses this encounter to expose the inadequacy of local discursive frameworks to yield understanding across various kinds of borders: differences of sex, age, ethnicity, education, profession, and species all constitute borders that Lurie's cogitations do not enable him to cross. A significant feature of *Disgrace* is that its mode of storytelling figures the potential of self-discovery not through the realization of that self-discovery but through its failure. By the same token, storytelling figures in the text as a potential source of communal bonds, but, again, it does so through the absence of such bonds at the stories' ends. The expected developmental character study thus fails to develop after all, precisely because the character from whose perspective the story is told—the focalizer—is dominated by the very story he tells.

Where dominant views are shown to be dictated more by received ideas than their speakers realize, postcolonial comparatist reading practices may also offer some degree of access to alternative views left unspoken. This is where Francophone discourse on *métissage* and our own critical attempt at reading for the *métis* converge and may productively collaborate with Anglophone transnational comparatisms that recognize the subaltern as a guiding figure of possibility through difference.

Communalism and What Escapes It: "Melanctha" and Its Silences

The question of how narrative can call us to imagine possibility in its absence is the point from which I want to reconsider "Melanctha." We long ago gained from Stein's early modernism a sense of the inadequacy of utilitarian language and its modes of thinking to the immense task of narrating a woman's life. In choosing immigrant and black English speakers as protagonists who share a sense of foreignness to Standard English, Stein implies the unnatural relationship of their language to the visceral experiences they try to convert into communicative discourse. This shortcut of sorts foregrounds the distance between ordinary, unselfconscious language, usually deceptively transparent and governed by learned convention, and the inchoate realities such language can mask. But "Melanctha" is capable of conveying a good deal more than this as well. We have gained from poststructuralist discourse analysis a sense of all texts as sites of tension where ostensible meaning coexists precariously with repressed, nonconforming logics that threaten its coherence. Rita Felski argues that this hermeneutics of suspicion is limited in its occlusion of affective dimensions of literary texts, but I would emphasize that it is from postcolonial theorizations of power and displacement that we can draw insight into the implicit effects of silences, marginal presences, and absences in the exposition of characters situated at the margins in one sense or another.[42] In this sense postcolonial thought has, for lack of a better word, humanized the hermeneutics of suspicion while retaining a characteristically poststructuralist suspiciousness of claims to humaneness.

I began this chapter with the first story of *Three Lives*, "The Good Anna," whose concluding narration by a mediating speaker we recognize to be misleading because we have been privileged to see otherwise. "The Good Anna" is narrated by an apparent onlooker who alternately focalizes Anna's attitudes and the attitudes of her community. It is a critical commonplace that "The Good Anna" is a modernist departure from Flaubert's realist depiction of a simple domestic in "Un Cœur simple," but Stein's mode of narration is also an affectionate citation of Flaubert's depersonalization of the romantic imagination by exposing the extent to which received ideas and values dominate characters' ostensibly idiosyncratic imaginations. Foregrounding the subjectivism of characters defined principally by ethnic, gender, and class formations whose legitimacy they duly, and often self-destructively, perpetuate, Stein renews Flaubert's image of the author as everywhere sensed but nowhere seen, like God in creation, only without Flaubert's faith in language itself as a medium that, once cleared of corrupting popular sentiments, might yield a transparent literary view into a character's "inner" life.[43] What is revolutionary about the mode of narration in *Three Lives* is that, unlike realist novels' uses of disinterested third-person narration on the one hand and free indirect discourse to convey a character's distinct perspective on the other, Stein's first foray into modernist anti-realism radically dispensed with a unified narrator and substituted for it a depersonalized discourse of local impressions and values. This poetic evocation of a depersonalized, essentially communalist discourse is marked by all the unevenness, partial repetitions, and unpredictable perspectival shifts that normally constitute a local common sense.

My reading of Stein's mode of narration in *Three Lives* has an affinity with Ulla Haselstein's in her comparative essay on "Un Cœur simple" and "The Good Anna," where she writes that Stein's new realism "shows the narrator as ostentatiously dealing in stereotypes in a futile effort at mastering the main character, while at the same time falling prey to the latter's linguistic deficiencies and limitations."[44] While Haselstein interprets the voice of Stein's narrator as more unified than I do, her insight that the narrator's knowledge is formed of stereotypes and in this sense vies with Anna for control of Anna's story seems to me to hold true for the narrators of *Three Lives* generally, with the qualification that they are, in my reading, not so much agonistic mimics of the protagonists as multivocal and self-contradictory representatives of locally ingrained discursive claims to knowledge itself. In this way, Stein's early fiction anticipates a preoccupation of Coetzee's writing that in turn enables us to see it more clearly in *Three Lives*, namely, how to tell a story that evokes its own participation in silencing another story, a story we might hear if only we could imagine ourselves outside the story more readily communicable and comprehensible to us—in short, how to imagine newness that transcends our own acculturated narratives.

More extensively than the other stories in *Three Lives*, "Melanctha" foregrounds patterns of constructing and disseminating knowledge in a confined community, patterns that appear distressingly circular and self-legitimating. No less insistent than "Melanctha" on the prevalence of received ideas about race in the American South, "The Good Anna" and "The Gentle Lena" have garnered less attention, and indeed notoriety, surely in part because "Melanctha" was rare in its day for representing an African American community as both complex and central to its own story, independent of white neighbors consigned to the narrative's margins. But "Melanctha" is also, of the three stories, by far the most oblique in portraying its protagonist's understanding of herself and her world. Recognizing the boundedness of Lurie's interpretive vision even as he seems to authorize the story we read helps us see differently the predicament of Melanctha's lover Dr. Jeff Campbell, ostensibly the most trustworthy of Stein's characters who represent Melanctha because of the earnestness with which he goes about trying to "know" her. But he is just as restricted as Lurie by his culture's dominant "ways of knowing," which objectify Melanctha on the basis of prior accounts and divide her from him in moments of closeness. His method of trying to know her by fashioning a story about her that makes sense to him, rather than by trusting in his present experience and instinctive feeling, is precisely what renders her opaque to him (Stein, *Three Lives* 110–16). It is important that neither Stein nor Coetzee represents this practice as occurring at a purely individual level; the relational impasses that Lurie and Jeff try to resolve through definitive concepts are shown to be systemic even as they assume themselves to be reasoning independently. Like Lucy, Melanctha resists the discursive exercise of generalization through her silence, as in this excerpt from Stein's many iterations of Jeff's attempts to capture her and his feelings for her in language: "Then he really knew he could know nothing . . . 'I certainly did think now I really was knowing all right, what I wanted. . . . And now I certainly do know I don't know anything that's very real about her' . . . and he buried his face deep in the green grass underneath him, and Melanctha Herbert was very silent there beside him" (110). The silence and immediacy of Melanctha, like those of Lucy, are associated with a radical departure from conventional heterosexual domestic relations, as when Jeff tells Melanctha "how I certainly never did know more than just two kinds of ways of loving, one way the way it is good to be in families and the other kind of way, like animals are all the time just with each other, and how I didn't ever like that last kind of way much for any of the colored people" (111). Jeff goes on to say that being with Melanctha and loving her as he does has moved him away from "the old way" of thinking about love, but he demands that she clarify and make certain what their love is, and she says she cannot do this. His emphasis on not wanting "the animal way," not just for himself but for any of the people he includes in his community, suggests that his longing for certainty coincides with a longing for homogeneous collectivity. The story cautions us against these longings, both through the sympathetic figure of a wandering Melanctha and through its very subtitle, "Each One as She May," which seems to affirm doing "as one may" even as Melanctha's ostracism and ensuing depression are shown to follow from it.

In her reading of David Lurie and what remains, to him, the intractably opaque experience of his daughter Lucy, Gayatri Spivak adopts Bal's definition of "focalization" to develop her own useful concept of counterfocalization, the process of revealing an alternative point of view by rendering the focalized subject's point of view as dubious or limited: "*Disgrace* is relentless in keeping the focalization confined to David Lurie. . . . When Lucy is resolutely denied focalization, the reader is provoked, for he or she does not want to share in Lurie-the-chief-focalizer's inability to 'read' Lucy as patient and agent. No reader is content with acting out the failure of reading. This is the rhetorical signal to the active reader, to counter-focalize" (*Aesthetic Education* 323-24).[45] In an argument that develops her earlier theorization in "Can the Subaltern Speak?" of the subaltern's lack of institutional means of being heard, Spivak continues, "If we, like Lurie, ignore the enigma of Lucy, the novel, being fully focalized precisely by Lurie, can be made to say every racist thing" (326). Spivak's interpretation offers a means of addressing the question whether to define "Melanctha" as glaringly racist or racially enlightened. If we read Stein's narrator as a chorus of sorts, a communal narrator not to be trusted for insight into anything other than public opinion predominant among the black residents of Bridgepoint, the seeming racism of the text and its author becomes the focal point of the text's critique: a racism both perpetuated and internally challenged by characters in the world of the story. This structure in postcolonial fiction about Africa, whether it appears briefly, as in *Things Fall Apart*, or pervasively, as in *Disgrace*, helps us see why Stein's story seems at once full of racist discourse and a challenge to the racist discourse it features; it is indeed full of racial bias and stereotyping, but its effect is to undermine these by gesturing to what is missing from the discourse.[46] Melanctha's faulty memory and inability to make a coherent story as other characters do repeatedly about her put her at an acute disadvantage, as her rebuffed affection and ongoing suicidal despair reveal. For the reader, though, she productively embodies an alternative to self-interested story making and rationalization: exploring uncoercively and uncertainly.

While among the most sympathetic readers of Stein's work, DeKoven has expressed concern that "Melanctha" uncritically reinscribes racial stereotypes, for instance, when Melanctha displays characteristics that the narrator ascribes to people of African descent more generally: DeKoven writes, "Melanctha's crucial 'wandering' . . . at least partly falls into the category of, or looks like, the 'simple promiscuous unmorality of the black people.' "[47] And yet, despite the narrator's repetition of this stereotype, it remains unfounded by the action of the story itself; Stein gives us few examples of black characters who are promiscuous. Only sexually and racially liminal characters—the "yellow mulatto" Melanctha and the "white negress" Jane, who appear to have a sexual relationship with each other, as well as diverse experiences with men—are said to "wander." Moreover, the text's correlation of sexual fidelity with insularity, social compliance, self-righteousness, and intolerance makes suspect the local consensus that Melanctha's wandering is a bad thing. Thus, when DeKoven writes that Melanctha's turn to Jem, a rootless quasi-criminal, instead of a bourgeois mate like the doctor is a "gesture not of subversion but of hopelessness" because "upward mobility might not offer much, but it is the only game in town," she seems to me to put too much faith in those who tell Melanctha's story and not enough pressure on their accounts as accounts in a sexually repressive class hierarchy undergirded by white racism (74). While causal relationships are elusive in the absence of a trustworthy narrator or a protagonist who speaks authoritatively for herself, Melanctha's isolation appears to increase with her attempts to capitulate to her moralistic friend Rose's notions of propriety. The less she wanders and the more she seeks security from Jem, the more remote her voice becomes in the fashioning of her story.

Read as another, more complex example of the stylistic evocation of locally circumscribed patterns and shortcuts of thought found in "The Good Anna," "Melanctha" ceases to exemplify a well-received and at first seemingly progressive modernist primitivism, later recognized "truly" as having always masked the residual racism of transatlantic modernist experimentalism. The racial politics of Stein's black communalist vernacular are no longer "undeniably troubling" if we understand that vernacular to stand metonymically for any culturally particular discourse, which, like an ancient Greek chorus, is as capable of biased, cliché-ridden, and impressionable judgments as it is of wise speculations and partial truths.[48] Indeed, the strange language of "Melanctha" is largely continuous with the language spoken by white German immigrants elsewhere in *Three Lives*, as well as by Stein herself in future essays and lectures. This suggests that it is not verbal blackface and the thought it conveys but speech that is at once constrained by communal thinking and attempting to break out of it that the vernacular of "Melanctha" embodies. Stein's foregrounding of the limitations of the discourse through which the story is being told generates the reader's frustrated desire for what has been excluded from that discourse, which is to say, what the discourse cannot accommodate without appropriation and domestication; this is when we counterfocalize, as Spivak's reading of *Disgrace* guides us to do. Much of the narrative force behind *Three Lives* and especially "Melanctha" derives from the tension Stein creates between the account and what escapes the account. Moreover, when we read Stein's narrator not as one unified voice but as multiple voices of the local community in question, we trade in the debate over whether or not Stein's text is racist for a debate over how a text's subversions of monologism allow us to imagine alternatives to commonsense rhetoric about race, class, and sexuality not only in Stein's context of high European imperialism and rising American power but currently as well.

When modern fiction figures voyaging as a process of self-deciphering (even failed self-deciphering) as "Melanctha" and *Disgrace* do, the margins of that voyaging become as determinative as the voyaging itself. I have emphasized the salutary indeterminacy of Melanctha's wandering among lovers, both male and female, in a city whose very name implies a point of transition.[49] But it is equally significant that she never leaves Bridgepoint, nor does she or any of her acquaintances cross paths with the German immigrant neighbors whose insular community is the focus of the framing stories of Anna and Lena, stories marginal to Melanctha's life just as the texts' own margins sharply border "Melanctha." So Melanctha is a wanderer, yes, but only within her own highly circumscribed community of African Americans in a segregated southern town with stark borders inside and out. Stein does not romanticize Melanctha's experience of being different in a community that longs, like Jeff Campbell, for its own seamless assimilation with a known and hegemonic order. Melanctha is an inadvertent and bewildered outsider within a community she seems to have no conscious desire to reject, but whose codes of conduct remain foreign to her. Her baffled estrangement and sense of hopelessness are substantively closer to the experiences of marginality described and theorized in anticolonial works by Aimé Césaire and Frantz Fanon than to the willful alienation of a Stephen Dedalus or Meursault. Long before Coetzee, Fanon's theorization of black alienation prepared us to discern Melanctha's simultaneous confinement and displacement within her own homeland: "completely dislocated, unable to be abroad with the other, the white man, who unmercifully imprisoned me, I took myself far off from my own presence, far indeed, and made myself an object."[50] Melanctha is doubly dislocated because she does not fit neatly into the aspiring black middle class represented by the assimilationist "mulatto" doctor Jeff Campbell and the conformist Rose ("I ain't no common nigger," said Rose Johnson, "for I was raised by white folks"), or the black working class represented by her father, "a brutal black man who knew nothing" (Stein, *Three Lives* 60, 72). While her wandering seems in one sense a mark of her liberated quest for knowledge, at once sexual, emotional, and intellectual, her repeated urges to kill herself, never directly explained, make clear that Melanctha's perpetual wandering in this sharply divided and delimited space is linked to unarticulated trauma even before her friends abandon her.

When Fanon opens *Black Skin, White Masks* with the insight that "to speak means to be in a position to use a certain syntax, to grasp the morphology of this or that language, but it means above all to assume a culture, to support the weight of a civilization" (17–18), he helps us to relate Melanctha's displacement and rootlessness at home to her lack of control over her own story. Stein makes us hear a local chorus of narrow perspectives not only through the racializing narrator's voice but also through the dialogue of Melanctha's self-interested friends and family, such as her embittered ex-lover Jane Harden, a pale-skinned "negress" who "had much white blood and that made her see clear," the narrator tells us, even as Jane's condemnations of Melanctha to Jeff (expressed through free indirect discourse) are manifestly not "clear" but vengeful, racist, and motivated by the jealousy of a jilted lover (*Three Lives* 73):

> What right had that Melanctha Herbert who owed everything to her, Jane Harden, what right had a girl like that to go away to other men and leave her, but Melanctha Herbert never had any sense of how to act to anybody. Melanctha had

> a good mind, Jane never denied her that, but she never used it to do anything decent with it. But what could you expect when Melanctha had such a brute of a black nigger father, and Melanctha was always abusing her father and yet she was just like him, and really she admired him so much and he never had any sense of what he owed to anybody, and Melanctha was just like him and she was proud of it too, and it made Jane so tired to hear Melanctha talk all the time as if she wasn't. (78)

This excerpt from a much longer and highly repetitive passage from Jane's representation of Melanctha gives a sense of Stein's many cues of its emotionalism and unfairness: the racist classifications of Melanctha and her father that mimic the narrator's own; the tortuous logic of comparing Melanctha to her father while condemning her for trying to differentiate herself from him; and the impression, from the long compound sentence's series of clauses joined by "and," that Jane is venting her anger haphazardly and obsessively. The repetitiveness of Jane's account also prepares for Jeff's agonized repetitions of his incomprehension and distrust of Melanctha once they are lovers, feelings he explicitly traces back to nasty characterizations of Melanctha by Jane and Melanctha's mother, and which contradict his own instinctive sense that she has "got an awful wonderful, strong kind of sweetness" (97, 98). Tellingly, the more the credulous Jeff "learns" from popular opinion about Melanctha, the more Stein associates his sense of certainty (as when the narrator observes, "Jane was beginning to make Jeff Campbell see much clearer") with his isolation and loss of humane empathy ("He felt very sick and his heart was very heavy, and Melanctha certainly did seem very ugly to him") (101).

Melanctha's own perspective is remarkably elusive in the face of her friends' and neighbors' clear-cut verdicts on her character, which appear shallow and unjustified by what Melanctha is actually shown to do or say. The pronounced disparity between Melanctha's actions and the chain reaction of condemnations is an important implicit contrast through which the story's anti-communalist vision surfaces, albeit in the ironic form of a poetics that mimics communalist representation. The coincidence of the narrator's views with those of unreliable characters like Jane points to the prevalence within Bridgepoint of a white middle-class racist discourse perpetuated in part by self-alienated black characters who accept its social hierarchies and sexual moralism as all too true. Destructive rumormongering about Melanctha's presumably sexual but more explicitly socioeconomic "wandering" evokes the absence of characters opening themselves up to social exploration—wanderings of their own—in defiance of their acculturation and pressures to assimilate within a harshly judgmental and conformist society of both upwardly mobile and insular working-class black southerners. Stein conveys Melanctha's boundedness within this world through the story's seemingly errant but deeply repetitive and constrained prose, which, as Sianne Ngai has described a passage from *The Making of Americans*, "progresses into a narrative of not-progressing."[51] Of course, Melanctha's story does progress in some concrete ways, but what remains fixed is her position as an object, never a subject, of her own representation. She converses with others, especially Jeff, but her words make no impact on how her interlocutors perceive and represent her. In the confines of her community's story, she cannot speak.[52]

The Politics of Despair and Literature's Promise

In postcolonial tragedies in which colonial reason's psychosocial effects endure long after decolonization, those who lack comprehensible language can become figures of possibility, emblematic of what might have raised the storyteller, and what might still raise the reader, out of habitual patterns of thought. A challenge to reading *Disgrace* sympathetically is that the alternative Lucy offers to her father's clear limitations as a focalizer and explicator of the sexual, ethical, and political quandaries he continually confronts and to some extent creates is only minimally articulated or even understood by Lucy herself. In the absence of an explanatory language that could make her unfamiliar future seem at least consistent with courses of action already deemed reasonable and legitimate, we are compelled to try to imagine why Lucy rejects the "reasonable" response to her gang rape: why not leave her farm behind, even South Africa altogether? Why relinquish ownership of her property to Petrus, the man who seems to have been complicit with her attackers? Why not abort the child conceived during the rape? Lucy's lack of explanations—and the novel's—is what compels us to try to make the imaginative leap that an incomplete but aspirational sense of empathy with another entails. From this process of counterfocalizing, we can surmise that Melanctha's lack of explanations, with the quasi-exception of her attempts to persuade Jeff of the wrongheadedness of his own, might also compel us to try to imagine her story outside the bounds of what Stein's narrator(s) and focalizers have told us about her.

I am aware that this reading might be perceived, as both Coetzee's fiction and Spivak's theory of the subaltern have been, as idealizing the silence of the disempowered and thereby inadvertently validating the conditions that silence them. A year before the publication of *Disgrace*, Benita Parry faulted Coetzee's earlier fiction on grounds that "withholding discursive skills from the dispossessed . . . is to reinscribe, indeed re-enact, the received disposal of narrative power, where voice is correlated with cultural supremacy and voicelessness with subjugation."[53] While Parry focuses on the racialized other's silence in Coetzee's novels, Ato Quayson has added that "there is also a coincidence between inarticulacy, racialization, and disability in the writing," a point we could extend to include the lame dog.[54] On grounds similar to Parry's, Neil Lazarus has criticized Spivak's "austere construction of the subaltern as a discursive figure that is by definition incapable of self-representation."[55] To my mind, neither Coetzee nor Spivak is either idealizing or essentializing the institutionalized silence and incomprehensibility of the disempowered. Their figures for the subaltern share a propensity to signal literature's capacity to call readers to imagine identity and sociality outside the bounds of a particular form of communication favored in scholarly and juridical forums: discursive arguments whose sense and authority are based locally and communally but that are conceived to be universally applicable. Without access to such arguments or the institutional forums in which such arguments are formulated and heard, the subaltern escapes their ideological constraints and becomes a figure of what is possible to know beyond the local and the dominant.

Reading "Melanctha" via Coetzee as a chronicle of misrecognition and mistranslation enables us to see an enduring value of at least one feature of the now generally maligned modernist discourse of primitivism: its persistent skepticism of learned (in both senses), institutionally sanctioned arguments, arguments made comprehensible through tradition and acculturation, but therefore communally circumscribed, as incomprehensible to outsiders as they are commonsensical to insiders.[56] In some modernist texts, such as *A Passage to India*, *Three Guineas*, and *Discourse on Colonialism* (all of which I discuss in subsequent chapters), these arguments are explicitly represented as false or incomplete; in *The Waste Land* and *Cahier d'un retour au pays natal,* lyric poems that make use of narrative elements but subvert them in the process, such arguments are dramatically absent. In both cases what rises up in their place is an inherently comparative, *métis* literary language that makes use of unexplained, and never conclusively explicable, juxtapositions and silences, to signify what lies outside the confines of inherited discourse. If we consider how decisively the ideal of a counterhegemonic, even counterdiscursive literary language coexists with a thematics of intercultural encounter in *Disgrace*, we can better understand not only that novel but modernist practices of comparison as well. Whether or not it was always the case, as Fredric Jameson suggests, that "Stein's perspective has a good deal more in common" with our concerns in the era of globalization "than with the psychologism that dominated the interwar and also the Cold War years,"[57] it is my contention that implications of her modernism change when we read her writing after postcolonial fiction and theory that more explicitly foreground the historical contingencies and ideological limits of attempts at intercultural understanding.

Spivak's essay on *Disgrace*, like her earlier cautionary theorizations of the subaltern for intellectuals who would claim to use their knowledge to help the subaltern while misrecognizing those they seek to help, shows us how literary texts might understatedly teach humility to the intellectual who would presume to teach others. David Lurie is, like Melanctha, a "wandering" outsider, but like the narratorial voices of *Three Lives* and especially Melanctha's well-meaning but self-defeating lover Jeff, he is also an accomplished rationalizer, fashioning himself and others through explanations he considers enlightened but that bespeak his colonial social formation. Jeff, well educated by the standards of his community and excessively trusting of science and reason, paternalistically wants to educate and reform his neighbors—especially Melanctha—in what amounts to the white middle-class man's image. These educated characters who attempt to analyze and assimilate others are unable to imagine themselves and their relations to others (by turns human beings, animals, artworks, and ongoing processes of imagination) without recourse to the interpretive frameworks of colonially imported discourses on race, sexuality, and politics. Their predicament emblematizes that of the modern humanist critic trained with Western eyes and trying to interpret intercultural relations without remaining caught within old models of supremacy and inferiority, domination and submission. Despite, or because of, their intense introspection, these thinkers' stories take them in circles; they speak, in effect, only to themselves. As they try to convert strangeness into a familiar sameness, others (most importantly Melanctha, Lucy, Petrus, and the students Lurie has failed to teach, including but not only Melanie) remain translucent presences, haunting the abstract commentary of the educated who represent them.[58]

In *Provincializing Europe*, Dipesh Chakrabarty opposes the specious transparency of social scientists' "rough translations" to a preferable "translucence" of narratives and analyses more sensitive to the politics of translation (17–18). Chakrabarty conceives transparency as politically suspect in its effacement of the never fully decipherable discursive others it cannot accommodate. Instead of the arrogance of rough translations, Chakrabarty calls for a "politics of despair" as the basis of his desired "history that will attempt the impossible: to look toward its own death by tracing that which resists and escapes the best human effort at translation across cultural and other semiotic systems, so that the world may once again be imagined as radically heterogeneous" (45–46). This notion of a politics of despair is useful for exposing the latent possibility held out by ostensibly pessimistic fictions of racialized sexual impasses such as "Melanctha" and *Disgrace*, especially because it echoes Coetzee's characterization of his own critical reading practice, shaped by the relations of silence to sound in the modernist music of Webern, as profoundly concerned with what writing "does not know about itself": "Our craft is all in reading *the other*: gaps, inverses, undersides; the veiled; the dark, the buried, the feminine; alterities" (*White Writing* 84).[59] In his appeal for a radically revisionist history, Chakrabarty illuminates literature's power to defy the knowledge protocols of past historical discourses, "to write over the given and privileged narratives of citizenship other narratives of human connections that draw sustenance from dreamed-up pasts and futures where collectivities are defined neither by the rituals of citizenship nor by the nightmare of 'tradition' that 'modernity' creates" (46). These "dreamed-up pasts and futures" should defy colonial history's predominantly communalist forms of communication.

Through Chakrabarty's theorization of a history that looks toward its own death, we can better see how the translucent, wandering language of Stein's and Coetzee's narratives works against both the simplistic labeling and laborious circumlocutions of those who presume to know and tell the story of others who elude them: Melanctha's neighbors in Bridgepoint, who speak for Melanctha; and David Lurie, who tries to speak for Lucy and for a range of others, including her attackers, Petrus, Melanie, his operatic characters, and a nameless dog. "Melanctha" and *Disgrace* counter these imposing perspectives with conspicuous absences that enable readers to imagine otherwise, as Jeff, his neighbors, and Lurie cannot. These absences are what induce Lucy, enacting a politics of despair, "to start at ground level. With nothing" (Coetzee, *Disgrace* 205). Lucy recommences with nothing from the past social order to defend; in this sense her embrace of nothing reveals a rare new perspective that is, after all, something important. Only once does her father begin to imagine starting with nothing—when he forgets himself, fleetingly, in a moment of identification with Lucy's attackers: "he does understand; he can, if he concentrates, *if he loses himself*, be there, be the men, inhabit them, fill them with the ghost of himself. The question is, does he have it in him to be the woman?" (160; my emphasis). Lurie never does lose himself while trying to be the woman, and indeed, immediately after wondering this, he writes Lucy a letter pedantically informing her of the "dangerous error" she is making, and appealing to her sense of "honour." She can only tell him that he does not see, perhaps even deliberately refuses to see (161). Characteristically, Coetzee does not explain the nature of what his protagonist does not see. Instead, he makes the absence apparent to the reader, whose responsibility it then becomes.

Timothy Bewes understands the absence of narratorial metalanguage in Coetzee's novels in the context of postcolonial writers' shame at their dependence on conceptual categories indebted to colonial thought: "If there are lessons to be learned from Coetzee's shame, they are not lessons communicated directly in the texts; for Coetzee's protagonists and author-surrogates are, without exception, spokespersons primarily for the partiality and unreliability of their own speaking positions."[60] The politics of despair implicit in the partiality and unreliability of the stories these spokesmen tell might serve as a model for a nonterritorial comparatism. The never fully legible singularity of their modes of narration mimics the never fully legible singularity of the moral and affective dilemmas of the other. In these stories the self, a formerly empowered "I," is transformatively "figured as object," in Spivak's phrase, which is to say, the idea of the self is put under scrutiny by its position in comparison to the absent or silent other, who is made a presence, not a subject, by virtue of the comparison. The solution, these texts imply, to the dilemmas of identitarian entrapment of the "I" and repression of the "non-I" is self-forgetting.

In 1936, Stein wrote a lecture for an audience of Cambridge and Oxford scholars, in which she described the creative state as one in which the writer forgets herself—her self as her audience and her little dog know her—and thereby imagines identity anew.[61] With this imaginative self-forgetting, a new "I" comes into being, not an object of others' expectations and representations, but not an "I" that exists through its opposition to and domination of the "non-I" either. Stein opens the lecture, entitled "What Are Masterpieces and Why Are There So Few of Them," by remarking that she "was almost going to talk this lecture and not write and read it" but decided against this because it is impossible to talk about masterpieces.[62] One can *write* about them presumably for the same reason one can write masterpieces themselves—an absence of concern, during those magical moments of creation, for how one's audience will respond and in turn create the identity of the writer; an obliviousness to the preoccupations of identity and its temporal constraints even as one writes about identities in time: "Think about how you create if you do create you do not remember yourself as you do create. And yet time and identity is what you tell about as you create only while you create they do not exist. That is really what it is" (500). The writer of the masterpiece and the masterpiece itself mirror each other's capacity to transcend the exigencies of the present and to offer up a vision of the real beyond the merely apparent in the here and now: "But what can a masterpiece be about mostly it is about identity and all it does and in being so it must not have any. I was just thinking about anything and in thinking about anything I saw something. In seeing that thing shall we see it without it turning into identity, the moment is not a moment and the sight is not the thing seen and yet it is" (499). The "something" Stein sees when she thinks about anything—the imagined real beyond the merely apparent—comes to her mind's eye through a creative process hidden from the view of others; their look back at her would interrupt the self-oblivion she needs to imagine outside bounds of communal remembrance and recognition.

Stein thus makes memory's constraining aspects central to her theory of identity's relation to artistic creation, in defiance of memory's usually indispensable place in modern fictional narratives built around character development. She analogizes her audience to her dog to illustrate her claim that "identity is recognition": "I am I because my little dog knows me but, creatively speaking the little dog knowing that you are you and your recognizing that he knows, that is what destroys creation. That is what makes school" (Stein, "What Are Master-pieces" 496). She returns to the analogy at the end of her lecture to emphasize the hierarchy of values that audiences introduce into a writer's perception of what, during the creation of a masterpiece, had been a level field of values, level precisely because of her own self's indistinction when beyond the scope of onlookers: "When you are writing before there is an audience anything written is as important as any other thing and you cherish anything and everything that you have written. After the audience begins, naturally they create something that is they create you, and so not everything is so important, something is more important than another thing, which was not true when you were you that is when you were not you as your little dog knows you" (501).

On one level, Stein's metaphorization of animality would seem distinctly opposed to Coetzee's. Stein's lecture envisions a dog as exemplary of the limited perspective that the artist needs to escape in order to forget herself and write freely, while *Disgrace* envisions the dog as a model for the artist who would communicate freely, that is, nondiscursively. Stein's dog is, like human beings caught in local knowledge systems, a barrier to inspired art. Coetzee's dog inspires art, but only so long as he is approached in his singularity; once reduced to another in a series of others, he emblematizes the serial generalities that David Lurie, the aspiring but failed artist and communicator, is reduced to creating. But in the context of a broader discussion of productive silences and absences in the narratives, Stein's comparison of the dog to an undifferentiated group of human perceivers takes on other dimensions. Stein's comparison dispenses with the well-worn colonial dichotomy between the discerning human being, whose defining knowledge is based in sensible language and self-reflexive consciousness, and the animal that lacks these endowments and therefore lacks a comparably meaningful knowledge. From this dichotomy and its corollary—the opposition between an eloquent and reflective (civilized) population of superior individuals and an inarticulate and instinctive (animalistic) mass of rural/lower-class/foreign/brown-skinned natives—Stein shifts attention to a dichotomy of her own: the self-conscious "I" whose ideas form in dialogue with the historically conditioned ideas of other consciousnesses, and an "I" whose awareness of historically conditioned ideas is temporarily suspended by an act of imagination, understood as the source of artistic creativity. The theory of imagination she builds around this dichotomy extends Flaubertian doubts that the mental accumulation of communally formed knowledge necessarily empowers human beings to perceive lived realities. Stein's remarks on speaking and writing on masterpieces suggest that making up stories about others entails imagining an impossible conjuncture, namely, that what could be there is already "truly" there, at a moment in time when it is not (yet) there or does not (yet) exist.

Lucy's different uses of "nothing" in *Disgrace* clarify this point. The "nothing" Lucy conceives as the ground of her creative recommencement is fundamentally different from the "nothing" the rapists had presumed her to be: "I meant nothing to them, nothing" (Coetzee, *Disgrace* 158). Comparing the hunter's relation to the hunted animal with the colonizer's relation to the native, Achille Mbembe has shown that both relationships depend on a rationale of human exclusivity, in which the "radical opposition between the *I* and the *non-I*" imputes humanity to the *I* while "privileging a definition of the *non-I* and the *other* which makes this latter a 'thing' or 'object'—at any rate, a reality external to me."[63] Lucy's explicit rejection of the human aspiration to "a higher life" associates the immediacy of animal existence with what, for Lurie, might have been a new idea of the human self, had he not misinterpreted it as a simple declaration of atheism. When Lucy tries to explain to her father, "This is the only life there is. Which we share with animals," she offers a way of seeing herself and others, human and animal, as cohabiting consciousnesses that need not objectify each other, as European colonizers and slave traders had objectified black Africans and as hunters objectify their prey, in order to exist (74). Lurie's idealization of human transcendence, she implies, motivates these very processes of objectification and domination. Lucy does not seek to avenge her rape by asserting her subjectivity at the expense of the rapists; unlike Lurie, she has no desire to reverse the power arrangement. She accepts being nothing—no object—in contrast to the self-other divide that gave rise to the attack in the first place.

As for Melanctha, she is bewildered when her friends, especially Jem and Rose, cast her off as if she were nothing. This is especially traumatic when Rose deserts her, after Melanctha has painstakingly cared for Rose's child and home in exchange for Rose's domineering company. As with Lucy, the question presents itself of whether Melanctha is essentially subjecting herself to another—as Hegel's bondsman is to the master—even as that other refuses to reciprocate the recognition necessary for subject formation.[64] Like Lucy, Melanctha is depressed but never thinks in terms of debts to be repaid or vengeance to be exacted. Most importantly, she never tells anyone's story, including her own. But as with Lucy, this is far from submitting to the other's will. Rose's final account amounts to a long-winded complaint that Melanctha has persistently refused to comply with her advice, presumably to stop "wandering": "She didn't do right ever the way I told her. Melanctha just wouldn't, and I always said it to her, if she don't be more kind of careful, the way she always had to be acting, I never did want no more she should come here in my house no more to see me" (Stein, *Three Lives* 167). Lucy's tenacity in resisting Lurie's advice and admonitions, and in setting the terms of her arranged concubinage with Petrus, helps us see around Rose's indignant representation of Melanctha (which is directly followed by the narrator's sketchy and abrupt account of Melanctha's illness and death in a clear echo of a local character's rudimentary account of Anna's death in "The Good Anna"). Lucy helps us see that Melanctha, too, is tenaciously who she is, even as she lacks the impulse to dominate others by representing and seeking to change them, however much they represent and seek to change her.

Both Lucy and Melanctha are, in effect, like nonhuman animals, not distinguished by their verbal expressiveness or even, apparently, by their possession of memories or explanations. Their silence constitutes a counterhistory to communal attempts to domesticate them according to their cultures' dominant standards. As I have argued, these communal attempts to domesticate them are characteristic not only, or even especially, of the less educated "masses" but also of purportedly freethinking intellectuals who, far from independent of popular categorical thinking about race and sexuality, succumb to its lures and inadvertently legitimate it through elevated language and intricate arguments. In "Melanctha" and *Disgrace*, the trauma of the new and different—embodied by the *métissage* to which Melanctha and Lucy are uniquely receptive—becomes the better option, both aesthetically and politically, when set against an all too formulaic present weighed down by the past.

What David Lurie has not yet learned at his story's end is how to experience intimacy without conquest, how to disrupt his own acculturated reasoning through an imaginative leap of faith into the unknown, like that of Melanctha and Lucy. He remains caught in the inherited value systems on art, politics, and sexuality that as an educator he has helped to maintain in a postcolony ravaged by the outcomes of a failed racist regime. Like that regime, he cannot imagine himself and the communities around him outside the confines of colonial European arguments about culture and sexual, artistic, and political mastery. His recapitulation of these arguments and values in his attempts to understand what is politically and humanly foreign to him shows the poverty of these arguments in the new historical contexts in which he finds himself. His status as an exile, a homeless voyager with nowhere to return to, evokes the bankruptcy of his conceptual origins; the only roots he can claim as his own do not apply and cannot be retrieved without regression or self-delusion. In *The Waste Land* and *Cahier d'un retour au pays natal*, subjects of chapter 2, a utopian, inexpressible plenitude may be glimpsed, if distantly and indefinitely, rising out of an alienated present. Here we find no image of transcendence, only the irony of overreaching, identitarian professions of dignity and tolerance that cannot assimilate contrasting figures of openness to a new, as-yet-unimagined community. Read intertextually, Coetzee's *Disgrace* prepares us to see that "Melanctha" evokes the desirability of such a community by representing its absence from the narrative language at hand. Both texts use dichotomies as means of their own dismantling; both offer in their place figures of the *métis*, formal and thematic, as what thwarts the reproduction of sameness and otherness and ushers in an unanticipatable future. The hope we can draw from the enigmas of Melanctha and Lucy emerges from their stalwart refusal of what is for what might come, their acceptance of an ongoing anxiety of freedom from demands of the pure and the proper.

2 Troubling Sovereignties

Intimations of Relation in *The Waste Land* and *Cahier d'un retour au pays natal*

> France was dying of prose. And then came the great nervous trembling in the face of adventure.
>
> —Aimé Césaire

> If the world presents itself to me as a unity as well as a diversity, that is because I myself am one as well as many.
>
> —Aldous Huxley

On the occasion of Patrick Chamoiseau's novel *Texaco* first appearing in English translation, Derek Walcott wrote a review that begins as a letter to Chamoiseau and by turns metamorphoses into critical commentary, anecdotal history, and a love poem of sorts to the languages and landscapes of Walcott's native Saint Lucia and Chamoiseau's native Martinique.[1] Walcott tells Chamoiseau that he is choosing to write the review as a letter because its form allows him "to be impulsive, elliptical, to indulge in that simultaneity which you call 'opacity'": "Its style, like yours, is adjectival rather than nominal, a style that lies in the gestures of a storyteller, and it is in the metre of Creole. It is what we both grew up with. The countryside at night with kerosene lamps and crickets" (214). When Walcott interweaves epistolary intimacy with the critical dispassion of book reviews, he puts distinct expressive modes into play simultaneously. He addresses Chamoiseau as a confidant and fellow Antillean who traces their singular *literary* languages—even as Walcott writes in English and Chamoiseau in French—to a shared formative landscape where locals came together to watch oral storytellers perform. He establishes this rapport without relinquishing the general reader, who could be local or foreign, as his other addressee, whom he educates about Chamoiseau's writing and its contexts as one would expect any reviewer to do. The essay affectionately mimics *Texaco* not so much in its specific deviations from established forms as in its ambition to conjoin forms or generic attributes in such a way that they signify in relation, rather than isolation, within a multiform text.

It is not just by writing his review as a personal letter, then, but by conjugating the review and the personal letter so as to surpass the limitations of each that Walcott illustrates what it is "to indulge in that simultaneity" he equates with *opacité*, the concept Chamoiseau and fellow *créolistes*, following Glissant, have used to describe the unceasing, never fully legible relational encounters and interpenetrations of languages and cultures, selves and others. Walcott treats this conjugation of genres and the migrant, mutable voices it unleashes as a *poiesis* that defies the fixed categories of preponderantly "nominal" writing in favor of an improvisational "adjectival" writing, a language of potentially infinite modifications—additions, qualifications, contradictions. Walcott here appears to assume a mutually reinforcing relation between the preconceptions of a "nominal style" and the foreclosed expressive potential of conventional genres left intact and insulated from each other, reiterating instead of multiplying the "modes of emplotment" expected of them.[2] In claiming for himself and Chamoiseau a preference for the adjectival, Walcott amplifies not simply what brings color and distinction but, more fundamentally, what comes into contact with another and modifies it, modifying itself in turn.

This is not what literary evocations of "simultaneity" have generally been thought to signify in the post-realist composite texts that came to define interwar Atlantic modernism and came to be defined by it. As Walcott's delineation of a literary genealogy going back to Baudelaire makes clear, Antillean creolist poetics shares Atlantic modernism's poetic inheritance from French symbolism. In contrast to contemporaries who distrusted this inheritance and who advocated aesthetics of social realism or indigenism in its stead, Glissant and Chamoiseau reclaimed poetic density as a counterdiscursive, polysemous force for imagining relational dynamics of language, sociality, and the material world. If we take opacity, which is also to say "simultaneity" in Walcott's sense, to be a density of semantic possibilities left unresolved, then it is not new to recognize the signifying power of opacity in interwar literature's multiperspectival montage forms, which Michael Levenson traces to advances in early cinema "when the point of view became as mobile as the scenes it recorded."[3] What opacity connotes in these images of unstable and incongruous points of view should be open to change with the shifting of predominant methods of reading and the ongoing creation of such forms. Nevertheless, some of the most recalcitrant poetics of simultaneity from the phase that Levenson pithily calls "Montage Modernism" are still widely read as abiding reflections of their authors' professed (or presumed) beliefs (240).

Perhaps most intractably *The Waste Land*, T. S. Eliot's famously opaque magnum opus from 1922, has been received as the expression of a fixed worldview, its language far from "adjectival," "open," or attuned to the ongoing mutations and interpenetrations that come with unexpected contact. As Peter Nicholls writes of *The Waste Land*, "The different movements of the poem, from 'The Burial of the Dead' to 'What the Thunder Said', do not establish a strong forward-moving trajectory but tend rather to create a simultaneity of effect."[4] On the one hand, Nicholls here persuasively (and refreshingly) resists the temptation of ascribing to *The Waste Land* a linearity many of us perhaps inevitably desire and try to reconstruct as we move through the indeterminate relations of its discordant voices and scenes. On the other hand, it is not at all obvious why we must conclude, as do Nicholls and Franco Moretti (whose argument Nicholls develops), that this "simultaneity of effect" gives the impression of timelessness and immutable values.[5] Although the poem's manifestly plural and discontinuous language of representation coaxes the reader to search for a lost or elusive coherence, it also implies what may be excluded from any semblance of coherence—nonconforming perspectives, fluid identities, narratorial fragility, textual instability. Approached this way, the world of *The Waste Land* is not timeless but untimely.[6]

It is true that Eliot's own critical commentary can be read as inviting conclusions such as Nicholls's and Moretti's, as when he describes what I take to be the defining formal feature of a modernist poetics of simultaneity, not in reference to *The Waste Land* but to his translation of *Anabase* by French Guadeloupian poet St.-John Perse, as "the suppression of 'links in the chain,' of explanatory and connecting matter."[7] Following a "logic of the imagination" rather than a "logic of concepts," Eliot argues, the poem's "sequence of images coincides and concentrates into one intense impression of barbaric civilization. The reader has to allow the images to fall into his memory successively without questioning the reasonableness of each at the moment; so that, at the end, a total effect is produced" (10). It is precisely this feature of *Anabase*, together with its "*declamation*, the system of stresses and pauses," that distinguishes it for Eliot as poetic: "Its sequences, its logic of imagery, are those of poetry and not of prose" (11). Eliot seems to approve of the poem's capacity to fix "barbarian civilization" in the mind, erasing the vitality and historicity of particular places and times. Really, though, it is not this putative civilization, timeless and immutable or not, that interests Eliot, but rather the form of *Anabase* and what he believes it achieves. Together the poem's accumulated images, in mutual relation but without that relation ever being denoted or delimited, make "one intense impression" on the imagining reader. Eliot contrasts this new knowledge—the "total effect" of poetic images whose connections and implications remain undecided—with another, quite separate kind of knowledge that conceptual discourse is able to produce with its hypotactic explanatory structure.

Tonally, *Anabase* is idiosyncratically, even radically, aloof, more so than *The Waste Land* and far more so than *Texaco*, and it lacks their chorus of voices, however dissonant that chorus may be. Yet it shares with these other, characteristically paratactic works a refusal of the personal—self-consistent and progressing through time and discourse—as sovereign in determinations of identity and value. It is this sense of a distinctly "poetic" opacity that keeps resurfacing and altering the significations of its antecedents as it resounds with them. Echoing Glissant and Chamoiseau in their alignment of *opacité* and *poésie*, Walcott repeatedly identifies Chamoiseau's novel as "poetry," explaining that *Texaco*, like Joyce's *Ulysses*, is "a large prose-poem that devours the structure of narrative fiction by its ruminative monologues" ("Letter to Chamoiseau" 219). We can surmise from this comparison that for Walcott the singular difference of poetry, exemplified by *Ulysses* and *Texaco*, lies in its fluid permutations, where voices predominate over an anticipated form and vernacular invention insinuates itself into a colonial language. Walcott's admiring comparison of *Texaco* to *Ulysses* reflects a view more recently expressed by French Mauritian writer J. M. G. Le Clézio that Joyce brought to the novel and to literature in general—previously "personal" forms of expression "tied to habits of reading and writing" and to modern social processes and notions of history—"a plural voice" that approaches the collective voice of myth.[8] Just as it overcomes narrative constraints (as Eliot famously claimed *Ulysses* did), Chamoiseau's "poetry" also succeeds where the "theory" of his collaboratively written manifesto, the *Éloge de la Créolité*, fails: it brings to literary language the "sinuous, incantatory emphasis on *oralité* that characterizes Creole" (224).[9] Whereas the *Éloge* celebrates Creole orality in French polemical rhetoric far removed from Creole orality, *Texaco* "is not a work clouded by theory" (230).[10] Had Walcott adopted Eliot's terms, he might have said that *Texaco* follows a logic of Creole imagination, however faintly Chamoiseau's intimate attachment to local speech and viewpoints resembles the logic of exilic imagination in *Anabase*. What endures from Eliot's essay to Walcott's is the idea, central to both, that poetry—an incantatory poetry not bound by the "chain links" of clarifying explication—should not be conflated with plot-driven or concept-driven discourses, or measured by their standards.[11]

Walcott's sentence comparing *Texaco* to *Ulysses* flows immediately out of a reference to another opaque magnum opus of modernist poetry, Aimé Césaire's *Cahier d'un retour au pays natal* (*Notebook of a Return to the Native Land*), and immediately into a second reference to it, both of them noting Césaire's influence on *Texaco* but noncommittal about the relationship or degree of likeness Walcott finds between the *Cahier*'s own pervasive use of ruminative monologues to disrupt narrative coherence and that of the other two works. He does call the *Cahier* an "incantation," and later in the essay he includes Césaire (as well as Perse) among the modern poets since Baudelaire and Rimbaud whose inventions of the French "prose poem with its incantatory metre, its protracted breath" opened the way for the "tribal incantation" of *Texaco* (Walcott, "Letter to Chamoiseau" 219, 231). As I will argue in more detail, the *Cahier*'s declamatory poetics presumes a collectively identified but still exceptional poet-speaker, whose succession of monologues and the metamorphoses of identity each engenders afford a view into the multiplicity of that speaker and his poetic voice, not a multiplicity of speakers and their voices. This distinction may underlie Walcott's more direct contrast between the *Cahier* and *Texaco* later in his essay, although there his focus has shifted to diction: "The novel speaks in the voices, the Creole, of its population and not with the centralized authority of the Cité, that is, in the vocabulary of Césaire" (228). While he does not illustrate this point about Césaire's vocabulary—Walcott's review is indeed, as he attests early on, elliptical—he circles back to it eventually with another point that extends it: Césaire's limitation was not that he wrote in French instead of Creole, as the theorists of *créolité* charged, but that he could not visualize how to go beyond "the distant tenor of imposing particulars that are racial despite the protests of a Creole universality" (229).

Like *The Waste Land*, Césaire's *Cahier* is so often associated with a certain discourse of its time that it can seem continuous with that discourse, its still-acclaimed poetics an exemplar of "nominal" rather than "adjectival" style. Walcott's objection to Césaire's poetic appropriation of racial rhetoric resembles the preponderance of criticisms still amassing on the subject of *négritude*, Césaire's dignifying Latinate abstraction for experience rooted in the white supremacist insult *nègre* and the multifaceted system of subordination this insult historically served.[12] Long defined with a discursive fixity and directness at odds with Césaire's own mercurial use of the term, negritude as both a politics and a poetics has found recent forceful defenses but continues to trouble readers who find in it an "iteration of the very autonomies it was battling" and, in particular, a blood politics that tends toward "ethnic absolutism."[13] While Walcott does not go so far as to argue, as Nick Nesbitt would several years later, that the *Cahier* "uncritically deploys the ideological tools of fascist and racial oppression" even as it seeks to defend "the downtrodden of the world,"[14] he offers the milder but related criticism that Césaire's poem undercuts its appeal for a more just and diversified sense of universality by retaining notions of racial identity imported from the metropole. Because of the centrality accorded to these notions in the *Cahier*, "the passion of argument peters out" at the point where Césaire might have moved beyond them (Walcott, "Letter to Chamoiseau" 229). It is instructive that Walcott here equates the *Cahier*'s imagery of race to an argument about race. While it is fair to probe the ways that Césaire's poetic engagement with an imported discourse on race might compromise his vision of collectivity, criticisms made on these grounds rarely consider the imaginative effects—which is also to say, the new knowledge—achieved by Césaire's specifically *poetic* engagement with this discourse, an engagement distinct from argumentation.

I will return to *Texaco* in the next chapter to consider its enactment of a creolist mode of historical narration that illuminates the historiographic implications of E. M. Forster's earlier conjuncture of racialized discourse with epiphanic testimony and multiperspectival narration in *A Passage to India*. In light of the Antillean creolist vindication of opacity both as the authentic quality of sociality and as a quality of poetry through which that sociality may be imagined, the present chapter turns back to the unsettled and unsettling poetic worlds of the *Cahier d'un retour au pays natal* and *The Waste Land*. I argue that the political promise of their difficult, inconclusively comparative forms often goes unrecognized because the very source of their difficulty—the counterdiscursive operations of their disjointed but mutually implicating images—is obscured by exegetical habits of deciphering that effectively translate the evident disorder into a conclusive message or story. Walcott's ideal of a mutable poetic language that frees the writer to "indulge" in "simultaneity" offers an alternative starting point for approaching these early twentieth-century forms of simultaneity, even though Walcott's criticism of racial rhetoric in the *Cahier* does not address the possibility that Césaire's appropriated racial language could signify multiply at once, and is in this way representative of the pronounced mutability and lexical dynamism of Césaire's poetics in general.

Walcott implies that to evoke collectivity through a multiform poetics, each of whose contributing genres has its own expressive mode, is to display a seemingly simultaneous presence of voices, conditions, and qualities of experience usually consigned to separate domains. To "indulge in that simultaneity" is to effect through poetic form an untimely, transgressive kind of assembly, whose justifying principle is one of bringing into relation what had appeared unrelated and definitively disjunct. In revisiting two of the most intractably multivocal and *at the same time* socially and ethically engaged montage poems of transatlantic modernism, this chapter seeks to show how their implicitly comparative forms bring such untimely, transgressive assemblies into being and why we should reevaluate the politics of identity and collectivity in their images of homelands made foreign by the absence of vital communal bonds. *The Waste Land* and the *Cahier* beckon with familiar images of native lands and natural landscapes, social festivities and holidays, authority figures and authoritative discourses, and render them strange by resituating them in a vast world of relational significance that can only be intimated, never made transparent in the present of the poems. In their fraught embodiment of what Milan Kundera, following Césaire, has called "multiple encounter," these poems imply that mimetic representation and coherent narrative unfolding are not adequate to convey the fullness of the world or to animate readers to imagine what might be missing from untroubled views of it.[15] Instead, they convoke discrepant voices and textual fragments together with gaps in what can be read or said, and in doing so they induce us to imagine relations obscured in the present or existing *in potentia*. This is salutary as long as the relations we come to imagine remain uncertain and in tension with the gaps we consent to continue to see as openings in the text.

Impossible Union and the Turn to Poetic Worlds

In 1963, Trinidadian historian C. L. R. James published an appendix to the revised edition of his 1938 account of the Haitian Revolution, *The Black Jacobins*, in which he characterizes interwar anti-imperialism by way of an improbable comparison of poets: the Anglo-modernist T. S. Eliot and the French Martinican anticolonialist Aimé Césaire.[16] The comparison concludes James's discussion of Césaire's *Cahier d'un retour au pays natal*, at once the lyric, dramatic, and epic journey of a Paris-educated Afro-Caribbean poet caught between imperialist and colonized worlds, whose dawning recognition of his bonds to dispossessed peoples of the African diaspora enables him to transform his initial state of alienated anger and despair into one of intense communal identification and creativity.[17] James's reading is not concerned with the generic hybridity of the poem or with what poetic form has to do with Césaire's persistently misunderstood language of racialized bonding. With this comparison, though, James models a way of thinking beyond estimations of the *Cahier* as a reparative, and in the main reactive, declaration of pro-black racism whose political value could only ever have been transitory.

James does acknowledge the poem's reparative dimension, but he rejects the notion that Césaire's invocation of a transnational black fraternity with shared African ancestry amounts to "the unconditional affirmation of African culture," as Frantz Fanon had characterized it in *The Wretched of the Earth* two years before.[18] James contends that "it would be the most vulgar racism" to find in Césaire's poem only an affirmation of African origins or black difference without recognizing how that affirmation culminates in "a poetic incarnation of Marx's famous sentence, 'The real history of humanity will begin'" ("Appendix" 401).[19] For James, negritude in the *Cahier* is a radicalized humanism that locates social bonds in the intercultural pursuit of an "integrated humanity" still unrealized: "Negritude is what one race brings to the common rendez-vous where all will strive for the new world of the poet's vision" (402, 401).

"The new world of the poet's vision" resonates not only as futural and planetary but as specific to the culture and geography of the West Indies as well. James broadly conceives negritude as a recurrent, if previously unnamed, West Indian ideal between the First and Second World Wars: the ideal of an African homeland, espoused by writers reacting against Euro-American dominance in the Caribbean by seeking a national identity of their own ("Appendix" 395–96). After the war, he argues, "the West Indian quest for a national identity" continued but shifted its focus to the Caribbean and its own population as the source of a distinct national identity (396, 411). James's materialist reading of negritude's regionally particular political stakes lays the groundwork for approaching what he, following Césaire, calls this "one race" as a diasporic social collective constituted historically rather than determined biologically, formed from overlapping lived realities of racism, economic exploitation and deprivation, territorial incursion, and stigmatized displacement. Through the *Cahier*'s fluctuating, increasingly nebulous sense of *négritude* (not to mention *nègre*), Césaire acknowledges the historical singularity of these lived realities and revalues the perspectives arising from them, while allowing the term to signify more variably and indeterminately than James himself does. Though the *Cahier*'s lexical volatility is beyond the scope of James's discussion, Césaire's homophonic wordplay in the poem's final lines prepares for the double entendre in James's "new world," evoking both the utopian future of humankind and the West Indies as a region (deemed Europe's *Mundus Novus* in the Age of Exploration). With the exhortation "*monte, Colombe / monte / monte / monte / je te suis*," the *Cahier*'s poet-speaker expresses his desire to follow the ascendant *Colombe* (dove), whose name puns on *Colomb*, the French form of Columbus.[20] In the new world of Césaire's vision, a rapacious colonial "exploration" in pursuit of new territory has been superseded by a communal flight of discovery that transcends territories. The pun at once summons the dove and the history it must rise above.

Although James's reading of the *Cahier* attends mostly to its historical context and narrative content, it culminates in a brief but emphatic reflection on this counterdiscursive or conceptually transgressive character of Césaire's poem, or what I have been calling its poetics of simultaneity. What interests James is the way the *Cahier* confronts a world marked by repressive divisions between African and Western, past and present, external and internal, and reconfigures that world through a unifying act of poetic imagination: "The *Cahier* has united elements in modern thought which seemed destined to remain asunder" ("Appendix" 401–2). It is here that James offers his novel and surprising comparison of Césaire to Eliot, citing Eliot's "Dry Salvages" from the *Four Quartets*:

> It is the Anglo-Saxon poet who has seen for the world in general what the West Indian has seen concretely for Africa.
>
> Here the impossible union
> Of spheres of existence is actual,
> Here the past and future
> Are conquered, and reconciled,

> Where action were otherwise movement
> Of that which is only moved
> And has in it no source of movement—
>
> Mr. Eliot's conclusion is "Incarnation"; Césaire's, Negritude. (402)

James does not elaborate his comparison beyond this provocation, and although there have been a few considerations of it since, notably in Edward Said's *Culture and Imperialism*, no one to my knowledge has pursued James's comparison at length.[21] This is not surprising when considered from the standpoint of late twentieth-century postcolonial criticism, in which Eliot's professed cultural conservatism and polarizing images of racial and sexual difference made him a suspect, even discredited, figure.[22] And yet James directs our attention to a feature of Eliot's writing not reducible to the poet's political convictions at any given time, or to the Anglican theological import of the *Four Quartets* from which James quotes: he directs us to a late articulation of Eliot's long-standing aspiration to evoke "impossible unions" transcending entrenched polarities, an aspiration subtly but fundamentally compatible with Césaire's own.[23]

When James suggests that negritude integrates disparate particulars previously conceived as contradictory or fundamentally incompatible (and, because incompatible, as necessitating the suppression or conversion of some particulars by others), he himself resists the polarities he has inherited by seeking an analogue to negritude outside the categories of social identity that more predictably complement that of race: class, nationality, sexuality. It is James's resistance to predictable patterns of narrative unfolding and theoretical self-positioning that Said finds valuable in the comparison and identifies with the "particular sort of nomadic, migratory, and anti-narrative energy" driving anti-imperialist liberation discourse at its best (279, 281). James instead compares Césaire's "vision of the African unseparated from the world, from Nature, a living part of all that lives" ("Appendix" 400) with Eliot's meditation in the *Four Quartets* on the "point of intersection of the timeless / With time" that marks the logically impossible union of God and man in the figure of Christ.[24] Césaire's vision of a "new world," like Eliot's, is not the stuff of "economics or politics, it is poetic, *sui generis*, true unto itself and needing no other truth" (401). James thus points to the power of both poets, writing in the years of fascism's rise and the outbreak of World War II, to transcend divisive applications of rationalism through poetry conceived as a singular kind of world maker.

David Damrosch argues in *What Is World Literature?* that too little work has been done to consider "hypercanonical" and "countercanonical" writers "beyond the boundaries of national or imperial spaces," with the result that in both teaching and scholarship we are generally left with "an either/or choice between well-grounded but restricted influence study and an ungrounded, universalizing juxtaposition of radically unconnected works in the mode advocated by Alain Badiou."[25] Damrosch wrote this in 2003, a time when global modernist studies was not yet so prominent a field as to foresee now-commonplace debates on whether it has productively extended postcolonial studies or overtaken and displaced it. In the latter view, global modernist approaches reap the rewards of prior postcolonial innovations in North-South comparative reading while de-emphasizing or outright abandoning the commitment that motivates such reading, to elucidate meanings and values of literary and cultural expression in any of the manifold ways they might relate to geopolitical structures of power, relations of inequality, and social injustice.[26] Since then, transnational, intercultural, and interimperial critical approaches have become more plentiful and have vigorously challenged once-standard criteria for making literary and cultural comparisons. Jahan Ramazani's far-ranging comparative readings of Anglophone poetry, for example, emphasize "the mutually transformative relations between the poetries of metropole and margin," the interplay of hybrid, heteroglossic forms through which "postcolonial hybridity 'confirms yet alters,' reworks yet revalues modernist bricolage."[27] Ramazani argues that postcolonial poets' openly espoused formal engagements with earlier modernist poets such as Eliot and Ezra Pound imply that it is not enough to ascribe a reactionary Orientalism to *The Waste Land* and *The Cantos*, which in his view "retain at least some capacity to question both their Western host texts and the ways in which the non-West is represented" (*Transnational Poetics* 109). Like James, Ramazani is looking beyond established dividing lines of cultural politics to recognize textual imbrications that only our own, historically distinct critical training has enabled us to see. On the other hand, major recent transnationalist readings of Eliot such as Ramazani's tend to center on more direct authorial influences and inheritances than James has in mind when he compares Eliot's incarnation to Césaire's negritude. We could still do more in James's vein of comparing texts in pursuit of their oblique, even disavowed patterns of relation, patterns that extend beyond writers' explicit preoccupations to implicit affinities born of convergent impressions of an expanding but stratified world where polarizing approaches to knowledge appear wanting, intellectually and morally.

To compare texts as James does is not to dispense with considerations of the political but to reconsider our habits of discerning a text's political implications, which may not correlate reliably with its author's stated views. The previous chapter's discussion of poetics of *métissage* traced how literary forms might signify beyond, and even against, isolated assertions within texts, as well as extratextual assertions about texts, any one of which may have acquired enough authority to obstruct alternate views into the text in question. James brings together two disparate poets' apparently exclusive concepts—incarnation and negritude—because the concepts themselves bring together apparently exclusive elements. In this way, he advances his broader diasporic Marxist critical project, which characteristically pits communitarianism against the isolationism of individualist values he finds at the core of tyranny. These communitarian values are central to *The Black Jacobins*, his revisionist history of Enlightenment from the standpoint of Toussaint Louverture and the slaves of Saint-Domingue, who together won their freedom from France and founded the republic of Haiti, and they are central to *Mariners, Renegades and Castaways*, James's lesser-known, revisionist interpretation of *Moby-Dick* from the standpoint of the crew, whose collaborative labor and democratic ethos he opposes not only to Ahab's authoritarian monomania but also, more controversially, to Ishmael's intellectual solipsism.[28] James's work thus anticipated a defining postcolonial practice of reimagining institutionalized readings of textual and historical relationships from the perspectives of disempowered collectives and with a recognition of the formative place their labor and discursive positioning have had in consolidating the power of the dominant. To be clear, I use "postcolonial" not literally as marking the successful overcoming of colonial social structures, but strategically and aspirationally, as a politically charged shorthand for the thinking through of transnational forms of inequality and injustice from the position of the nondominant.

Clearly, this practice of reading for communities on the margins (that is, seeking them out as guides to the text, as opposed to reading on their behalf, with its pitfalls of paternalism), pioneered by James and still evolving as literary and critical production from the former colonies has intensified, has generated an increasingly influential conception of canonicity indebted to the global South and its diasporas. Consequently, we can no longer hold up Achebe's *Things Fall Apart* or Walcott's *Omeros* as uncomplicatedly countercanonical texts, and notwithstanding Anglophone literature's persistent dominance in global literary studies, the same is true, in the English-speaking world, of widely circulated translations of works by Césaire and Fanon. Even as notions of canonicity have shifted, however, on questions of which new or neglected texts might be included and which long-canonical texts are compromised or even made unworthy of inclusion by their now-suspect cultural politics, there remains little attention to how the cultural politics of canonical texts might change—which is to say, how our perceptions of their range of potential meanings change—when they are read in different frames of reference than were previously available. One example would be Nicholls's interpretation, aligned with Moretti's, of Eliot's untimely simultaneity as connoting timelessness and immutability; another example would be Glissant's early critique of the *Cahier* and negritude more broadly as appealing for "a return to the dream of an origin, to the immutable oneness of Being" rather than to "the point of entanglement."[29] Even Ramazani, when he writes that *The Waste Land* and *The Cantos* "retain at least some capacity to question both their Western host texts and the ways in which the non-West is represented," is qualifying his recommendation that we take a more expansive view of their possible implications, at least with respect to what they signify about cultural politics.

On this point, we have still not engaged as much as we might with what the "contrapuntal, non-narrative turn" of James's argument from Césaire to Eliot might mean for reimagining Eliot's poetry itself, in all its own contrapuntal, nonnarrative promise (Said 281). James's reading of Eliot after learning from Césaire, like his much more extensive reading of revolutionary France and its democratic ideals after learning from the Haitian Revolution, or of the politics of sociality in *Moby-Dick* after learning from Caribbean diasporic patterns of migration and labor, exemplifies a mode of politically engaged interpretation in which we, too, might read texts and relational networks newly, from a perspective that comes with our own critical moment in which interimperial and transoceanic comparatisms are increasingly visible. Building on these earlier ideas of diasporic transnational solidarity, with their shared commitment to learning from the nondominant, we can more closely scrutinize how modernist aspirations to create new collectivities through distinctively counterdiscursive poetic languages generate, both within and across texts, dynamics of power and authority that extend well beyond, and not infrequently undermine, the explicit cultural politics of texts and their authors.

Foreign to the Language

To pursue this argument, let me now shift from "The Dry Salvages" to Eliot's earlier poem, *The Waste Land*, for several reasons. Like the *Cahier*, *The Waste Land* is widely perceived as its author's signature expression of a sensibility now dated and justifiably surpassed, a sensibility made, in my view, all too clear-cut by discourse external to the poem. Second, both the *Cahier* and *The Waste Land* enact a comparative poetics, neither obscuring through translation nor thematically resolving the mutual foreignness of the languages and discourses they interweave. And finally, in both poems cultural plurality and an attendant psychic confusion are figured through formal unpredictability and inconclusiveness, the enigmatic results of which have historically inspired attempts to demystify the poems by translating the multiple significations of cultural difference within them into a more straightforwardly ethnocentric clarity.

Despite these similarities, there is little comparative scholarship on *The Waste Land* and the *Cahier*. It is significant that those who have compared the poems have focused on the poems' landscapes as metaphors. In Prescott S. Nichols's allegorical interpretation, the hellish landscape in each poem presages the cataclysmic fall of the colonial order and the rise of the Third World.[30] There have also been a number of valuable comparative asides in essays principally on Césaire. Abiola Irele writes in the introduction to his annotated edition of the 1956 version of the *Cahier d'un retour au pays natal* that "it is impossible not to draw a parallel here between Césaire's *Cahier* and Eliot's *The Waste Land* in their common poetic representation of a physical setting as the equivalent of a moral and spiritual condition."[31] In her comparative reading of the *Cahier* and Theresa Hak Kyung Cha's *Dictée*, Susan Stanford Friedman argues that the *Cahier* makes a return to the native land "an epic descent into hell as the precondition of another kind of return, the return of new beginnings, new hope, new life," and notes (I think wrongly) that this narrative of "inner revolution" and ultimate rebirth is "much less linear" than *The Waste Land* in its more extreme oscillations of mood and "epiphanic moments" (295). And, in a comparative chapter on Césaire and Simone Schwarz-Bart, Natalie Melas writes, "There is a long and august poetic tradition of eulogy or panegyric that extols native lands and home cities, and while there are certainly poems that evoke stultifying or corrupt cities (William Blake's 'London' comes to mind as well as T. S. Eliot's 'the Waste Land' and several poems of Baudelaire), there is little that compares with Césaire's hyperbolic inversion of the genre here."[32] It is worth emphasizing that both poems, having fixed the reader's attention on sterile and sickened landscapes their speakers inhabit, do not give any sense of those lands being repaired in ways that would have mattered earlier to those speakers: no water materializes to quench their thirst, no volcanic *mornes* erupt to revitalize the throng. Relief in both poems comes from a different source altogether, and that is a convergence of appropriated words and phrases with the nature of their bonds left unexplained and the future they cohabit left open.

The dearth of extended comparative work on Eliot and Césaire has largely to do with their manifestly different historical positions, and representations of themselves, in relation to European cultural power. Indeed, Eliot and Césaire are easily fitted into a tidy polarity of their own: white, politically conservative high modernist from a privileged background versus black Marxist surrealist from a meager background. Certainly, Eliot's ambivalent uses of black dialect, minstrelsy, and racial stereotypes in early drafts of *The Waste Land* and elsewhere constitute one of the more striking points of difference between his cultural politics and Césaire's.[33] At the same time, paradoxically enough, their elite educations at Harvard University and the École Normale Supérieure, respectively, their extensive learning in classical and modern European literature, and their complicated affiliations with European institutions of cultural authority despite their New World origins have prompted some critics to characterize them both, as well as their poetry, as complicit with an exclusive and exclusionary imperialist order. Such generalizing paradigms routinely predetermine critical assumptions about them, so that Eliot and Césaire appear too discrepant politically to be responsibly considered together, even as their perceived elitism has made them subject to some of the same criticisms.

Generalizations such as these vie with and often overpower the intimations and reverberations of the poems most closely identified with Eliot and Césaire, despite these poems' elaborate embodiments of a poetics of oblique and polymorphous suggestion that Mallarmé first advanced as definitively modern.[34] The already well-documented influence of Mallarmé and French symbolism more broadly on both poets in their early years, not to mention Césaire's own tribute to Mallarmé for, among other things, his "unintelligible sonnet" "Ses purs ongles très haut dédiant leur onyx," should make us wary of conflating discourse, with its "denominative and representative function," and the poetry that Mallarmé contends would not exist were it not for "language's deficiencies" and the ensuing need to make words "foreign to the language" (206, 210–11).[35] It is not unreasonable to include in the trajectory of this poetics James's conception of poetry as a singular language distinct from the "economics or politics" of the everyday, although the new world he found there was profoundly social, a totality of relations without hierarchy or compulsory assimilation, in contrast to the symbolists' idealized depths of dream and song. Sartre similarly distinguished poetry from utilitarian discourse in his defining tribute to negritude, "Black Orpheus," where he asserts that the Francophone black man's French is fully adequate to his needs "as long as he is thinking as a technician, a scholar, or a politician," but that for self-expression, "white words" (*les mots blancs*) do not suffice, and therefore "he will not express his negritude with precise, efficient words that hit the nail on the head with every blow. He will not express his negritude *in prose*."[36]

Despite important recent critical interventions in the interpretation of *The Waste Land* and the *Cahier*, both poems continue to be widely perceived, especially by critics who write on modernism or postcolonialism but are not specialists in the work of Eliot or Césaire, as expressing certain clearly identifiable and, in varying degrees, regrettable cultural politics.[37] It has been difficult for *The Waste Land* to escape the reputation it acquired early on, less from its initial readers' anxious bewilderment at "the poem's intransigent opacity," as Lawrence Rainey has documented, than from the ensuing New Critical readings that "turned its enigmas into something as tidy as a schoolboy's lunch box."[38] Even as New Criticism's dominion passed away, the magisterial impositions of unity on *The Waste Land* by F. R. Leavis and Cleanth Brooks continued to hold sway, not least among Eliot's detractors, who assumed *The Waste Land* to be a vehicle for the social, political, and religious conservatism that Eliot later professed and that the New Critics in turn (approvingly) found there. The dispatch of lyric specificities by generalizing paradigms can be even more extreme in the case of the *Cahier*, which has often been reductively cast solely as an expression of negritude, with negritude cast as a fixed theory coterminous with a narrow selection of Léopold Sédar Senghor's prose perfunctorily taken as representative. Consequently, as Christopher Miller argues, "widely held views of Césaire make him much more like Senghor than he should be," and their conflation "has tended to harden the reputation of the *Cahier* as an ideological statement."[39] In Césaire's case, generic claims that account little for the poetry itself span Chinweizu's and fellow *Bolekaja* critics' endorsement of Césaire's negritude as proleptically Afrocentrist and Pan-Africanist (even as they vilified Wole Soyinka and Christopher Okigbo as capitulatory "euromodernists") and the more common disparagement of negritude as a naively romantic black essentialism implicated in European colonialist racial theory.[40] The pervasive influence of such interpretations makes it difficult for even the most dedicated revisionist critics to avoid taking as given certain political implications of the poems even as we seek to reimagine them.

Reading the poems without the reassurance and constraint of these paradigms, though, it is considerably more difficult to convert them into arguments whose speakers and cultural politics are anchored in place. At sea with the poems themselves, we must contend with them as seductively unpredictable, roughly textured, musical, often bewildering adventures in narrative unfulfillment. They characteristically violate the locally meaningful—what Mallarmé demarcated as the "brute or immediate"—to suggest a more expansive and substantive import underlying, or beyond, their words ("Crise" 278; "Crisis" 210, trans. mod.). They do this through a persistent intertextuality without contextualization, a persistent multilingualism without translation, abrupt discursive shifts from the oracular to the dialogic to the elegiac to the anecdotal, and pervasive parataxis. The effects of the parataxis are multiple: on the one hand, it gestures to what is missing from a speaker's vision, and from our own vision of a speaker; on the other hand, as Souleymane Bachir Diagne explains, it has the effect of "making each image an isolate, rendering each word monadic" and thus foreign in Mallarmé's sense of the poetic word.[41] Together, all these modes of disrupting familiar meanings and patterns of thought make even the most learned and persuasive interpretations appear approximate and incomplete. *The Waste Land*, for example, in which Eliot's characteristic juxtapositions and parataxis became even more extensive as a result of Ezra Pound's editing,[42] famously closes with citations following fast one after the other, above and below the vaguely defined "I" in Eliot's own much-cited line, "These fragments I have shored against my ruins":

London Bridge is falling down falling down falling down
Poi s'ascose nel foco che gli affina
Quando fiam uti chelidon—O swallow swallow
Le Prince d'Aquitaine à la tour abolie

These fragments I have shored against my ruins
Why then Ile fit you. Hieronymo's mad againe.
Datta. Dayadhvam. Damyata.

Shantih shantih shantih.[43]

Later, in an interview for the *Paris Review*, the older Eliot attributed the difficulty of *The Waste Land* to his youthful inexperience, but this (perhaps slyly) self-effacing assessment does not begin to account for the tenacious endurance of the poem, even as Eliot's stature changed in some critical circles to that of outmoded cultural reactionary.[44] Césaire's retrospective comments on the difficulty of his own early work shed some light, while recalling the previous chapter's discussion of Wright's stockyard workers. In an interview with Jacqueline Leiner, he said that the *Cahier* is well understood by fellow West Indians who know not to approach it as "communication," that is, as an argument or information to be taken literally: "They do not understand it literally, word for word; that's not what it is, communication."[45] Notwithstanding its less culturally specific designation of an ideal community of readers and its different use of "communicate," Eliot's essay on Dante from 1929 correspondingly distinguishes discursive understanding from the "direct shock of poetic intensity": "It is a test (a positive test, I do not assert that it is always valid negatively), that genuine poetry can communicate before it is understood."[46] Moreover, Eliot contended later in *The Music of Poetry* (citing Mallarmé as an example) that it is precisely because "the poem means more, not less, than ordinary speech can communicate" that "the meaning of a poem may be something larger than its author's conscious purpose, and something remote from its origins."[47]

What these assertions about poetry suggest is that we should be attempting to experience the poems that inspired them at a greater distance from the seemingly straightforward biographies, theoretical manifestos, and entrenched textual analyses we have inherited from eras with critical assumptions and priorities sharply distinct from main currents of our own. Confronted with an elusive literal sense, we might now, in the wake of the hermeneutics of suspicion, be better able to search out meanings without imposing a unity that reduces each poem's own kinds of otherness.[48] Both interwar texts at their inception (though Eliot and Césaire wrote some passages before they conceived of the larger poems, and each poem was edited and revised after its composition as a "whole"), *The Waste Land* and the *Cahier* conjoin an already-established modernist privileging of language's "virtuality" over its "denominative and representative function" with new, radically open-ended comparative methods of evoking cultures in contact and operations of power, both local and translocal (Mallarmé, "Crise" 279; "Crisis" 210–11). In other words, these poems build on but profoundly reimagine what Glissant calls Mallarmé's "poetics of language-in-itself" (*poétique du langage-en-soi*) by conceiving poetic speakers whose historical, linguistic, and intercultural predicaments do not disappear but rather become the very source and subject of the poems' rippling evocations.[49] This conjunction of a poetics of indirection with a poetics of disjunctive, never-resolved cultural comparisons makes it possible for each poem to evoke what escapes any one speaker's vision or exemplification of foreignness, beyond the poet's intention and without the discursive will to comprehension and assimilation that would allow for a definite and stable judgment on foreignness to emerge. This is why I believe we should reconsider Rebecca Walkowitz's claim that *The Waste Land* "is not especially interested in representing patterns or fictions of affiliation, in rejecting fixed conceptions of the local, or in comparing the uses and histories of global thinking."[50] No doubt we find in Eliot's poem a "suppression of 'links in the chain,' of explanatory and connecting matter" as he found in *Anabase*, but this suppression crucially activates the reader's imaginative pursuit of relations among the seeming isolates in Eliot's explicitly cross-cultural and cross-regional assemblage.[51]

Certainly the poems differ markedly in their prevailing moods and conceptions of the personal and the communal. Eliot's partial, depersonalized speakers, with their aura of weary detached melancholy, cynical humor, and paralyzed terror, seem far removed from the seething resentment, bitter sarcasm, and burgeoning hopefulness of Césaire's witness to colonial racism and heir to diasporic displacement. Whereas Eliot imagines a series of fractured and seemingly unconnected speakers in a sinister world that lacks vital communities, Césaire imagines a highly changeable but more ostensibly integrated speaker whose imaginative labors gradually yield a vision of identity at once communal and straining against inherited or imposed definitions of community that would elide unpredictable relations. It is Césaire's explicit shift to the perspective of one victimized by a history of systemic racism, forced mass migration and slavery, and colonial exploitation that makes him, with James, a prodigious transitional figure in the evolution of modernist transnationalism. Together, though, *The Waste Land* and the *Cahier*—and more particularly *The Waste Land* when read after the *Cahier*—press us to an extent few other literary texts do to imagine poetry as a linguistic repository of intercultural traces in flux, the strange unions of which challenge the transparency of local interpretive frameworks.

Additional implications of this poetics of simultaneous connection and contradiction have come into view with postcolonial and transnational feminist insights into the complexities of imagining beyond what is literally denoted or represented. For Ranjana Khanna, "the attempt to theorize justice" entails recognizing "a necessity of reading nonpresent voice" and, more broadly, a commitment to seek out "ways of understanding how some readings are foreclosed and others opened up by political identitarian and disciplinary reading practices."[52] Like James's "drawing upon . . . subaltern knowledge to focus his reading" of *Moby-Dick* "from the standpoint of the crew,"[53] but without his conviction that he is recovering the author's intended and authentic univocal meaning ("It is clear that Melville intends to make the crew the real heroes of his book, but he is afraid of criticism"; *Mariners* 18), scholarship emerging out of transnational postcolonial studies offers methods of reading that can reorient us to interpret modernism differently than we did or could before, beyond just expanding our canon of source material. A practice of reading for unremarked, unanticipated, and even self-contradictory exercises of discursive authority within these poems whose very poetics undermine such authority creates new views into African solidarities in the *Cahier*, tradition's scope in *The Waste Land*, and how these and any number of other themes overlap. Turning now to the *Cahier*, and acknowledging but not limiting ourselves to its psychological dimension as the impassioned and multiform declamation of a poet-speaker who progresses from shame and anguish to ecstatic optimism, we can also come to see and learn from the *Cahier*'s enactment of a process of enlightenment in which dominant perspectives, including the speaker's own, become suspect in the fashioning of knowledge.

Speaking Césaire's Language

In Césaire's final and best-known version of the *Cahier*, the poetics of indirect and opaque comparison takes a turn to the explicitly political. Looking to the end of the *Cahier*, just before the heady final lines, we find a call to poetic action that immediately follows the speaker's vision of a slave ship where an undifferentiated mass of black slaves ("la négraille") is no longer identified with any native land (whether Martinique or Africa) but with their potential to stand in unison as a community. Césaire continues,

écoutez chien blanc du nord, serpent noir du midi
qui achevez le ceinturon du ciel
Il y a encore une mer à traverser
oh encore une mer à traverser
pour que j'invente mes poumons
pour que le prince se taise
pour que la reine me baise
encore un vieillard à assassiner
un fou à délivrer
pour que mon âme luise aboie luise
aboie aboie aboie
et que hulule la chouette mon bel ange curieux.
Le maître des rires?
Le maître du silence formidable?
Le maître de l'espoir et du désespoir?
Le maître de la paresse? Le maître des danses?
  C'est moi! (32)

(listen white dog of the north, black serpent of the south
who cinch your belt around the sky
There still remains one sea to cross
oh still one sea to cross
so that I may invent my lungs
so that the prince may hold his tongue
so that the queen may sleep with me
still one old man to murder
one madman to deliver
so that my soul may shine bark shine
bark bark bark
and that the owl my beautiful inquisitive angel may hoot.
The master of laughs?
The master of formidable silence?
The master of hope and despair?
The master of laziness? The master of dances?
  It is I!)[54]

This passage is somewhat more accessible than many others in the poem, especially those giving a prominent place to esoteric scientific (*calcanéum*),

Caribbean (*doudous*), African (*gris-gris*), and French slang words (*gueule de vache*); to wordplay (*likouala-likouala*); and, most distinctively, to polysemous, suggestively Latinate, but never satisfyingly translatable neologisms (*négritude*, *promission*, *verrition*). Like any number of untranslated citations in modernist texts such as *The Waste Land* or Pound and Fleming's *Elektra*, with its long passages of original Greek, Césaire's foreign diction throughout the *Cahier* stands as what has not been assimilated, whose singularity and discrepancy both invite and thwart efforts to turn it into something else.[55] Even the words in this passage, like Césaire's poetic diction generally, have multiple connotations and associations at once, well beyond what any one translation can capture. Still, these lines signal the stakes of all the disorienting words and combinations of words that by turns stop us short, divert us, and propel us forward in pursuit of a comprehension that never quite arrives. With the phrase "pour que j'invente mes poumons / pour que le prince se taise / pour que la reine me baise," Césaire links liberated self-expression (variously conceived, with *invente* from *invenio* and, in Césaire's usage, even *ventus*: "I invent / discover / take the wind into my lungs") to the transition away from old discursive hierarchies and toward new and previously forbidden intimacies. Here as elsewhere in the *Cahier*, Césaire makes the creation of an unprecedented language of self-expression, still hypothetical ("Il y a encore une mer à traverser," "pour que"), the condition for a new order of planetary politics. In this new order, or perhaps disorder, the sky, Césaire's figure for natural possibility beyond known material conditions, might no longer be confined in a *ceinturon* (the belt of a military uniform, as opposed to *ceinture*, a more standard term for "belt") by racially and geographically defined factions of the present, whom he addresses directly at the verse paragraph's outset. This is the "new world of the poet's vision" that James hails and compares to Eliot's incarnation in his appendix to *The Black Jacobins*. Even so, this polymorphous poetic world, however utopian, is still not free from old discursive hierarchies, and the unresolved tension between these expressive modes is one of the defining features of the *Cahier*'s comparative form. Having envisioned the transformation of a prostrate black mass into a proudly defiant assembly, the speaker calls for another seemingly impossible union, a poetics that is not only an assemblage of disparate images and expressive modes, but a collaboration between an aspirational imaginative logic of communitarianism beyond territories and known languages on the one hand and the discursive logics of racial identity and sovereign mastery that have constituted and constrained him on the other.

Reading for this collaboration or union of apparently antithetical logics of poetic imagination and conceptual discourse, as Eliot would have it, enables us to see political resonances beyond the explicitly thematized political sensibility of Césaire's poet-speaker. Such a collaboration is suggested by Natalie Melas's interpretation of the *Cahier* as an "untimely" or anachronistic address to a "dispatched interlocutor."[56] For Melas, the *Cahier* is dialogic but enunciated in the absence of an addressee who "is never consistently specified or personified," and who at some points "seems internalized in the speaker" but "could just as well be imagined as the white man, the master, the assimilated black man, the law, history" (574). Her insight that the imagined interlocutor seems to be an absent and unhearing representative or enabling discipline of a despised system of domination, and at the same time an ingrained presence in the speaker's own consciousness, points to the traces of the speaker's colonial formation within his poetry of revolt and metamorphosis. These traces do not appear only in his explicit expressions of alienation and shame, which over the course of the poem he will strive to overcome; they also haunt some of his most affirmative interjections and can determine the very range of possibility in his dream of liberation. If we take the speaker, as Melas does, to be "speaking to himself not with autonomy or freedom . . . but rather in the negative space formed by the wake of the dispatched interlocutor" (574), then his reverie, heavy with European literary allusion, of replacing the capitulating prince's words with his own begins to look less resolutely democratic than it might otherwise.

Césaire's prince has been read as one of several allusions in this section to Gérard de Nerval's sonnet "El Desdichado" ("The Dispossessed"), the second line of which Eliot quotes in *The Waste Land*'s final verse paragraph: "*Le Prince d'Aquitaine à la tour abolie*."[57] In *The Waste Land*, the widower of "El Desdichado," comparing his bereft state to that of the Prince of Aquitaine in his ruined tower, becomes identified with Eliot's speaker who shores Nerval's line and others against the ruins of his own spiritual dispossession. It is now uncontroversial to say that Eliot's Prince of Aquitaine is one of numerous figures of impotence in the sterile landscape of *The Waste Land*, through whom a nostalgic Eliot seems to bemoan the loss of authoritative leaders and guiding traditions without which capitalist modernity has become a moral void.[58] Reading Eliot after Césaire enables us to revisit figures of waning authority in *The Waste Land* to reconsider what they might imply about the status of authoritative and particularly canonical discourse in the poem. I will return to this in the next section.

In the *Cahier*, the prince who is a source of identification for Nerval's unconsoled widower and Eliot's solitary hoarder of poetic fragments is transformed into the incumbent power who would cede the floor to Césaire's fledgling speaker. For Césaire, the prince's old order of words should be succeeded by the new words of the black poet-rebel, united with the queen, another figure transported from Nerval's poem to the *Cahier*. Here *la reine* or "the queen" echoes an earlier passage of the *Cahier* where anaphoric uses of *reine* follow parallel uses of *race*: "ma race rongée de macules / ma race raisin mûr pour pieds ivres / ma reine de crachats et de lèpres / ma reine de fouets et de scrofules / ma reine de squasmes et de chloasmes / (oh ces reines que j'aimais jadis aux jardins printaniers et lointains avec derrière l'illumination de toutes les bougies de maronniers!)" ("my race pitted with blemishes / my race a ripe grape for drunken feet / my queen of spittle and leprosy / my queen of whips and scrofula / my queen of squamae and chloasma / [oh those queens I once loved in the remote gardens of spring against the illumination of all the candles of the chestnut trees!]") (Césaire, *Cahier* 26; *Notebook* 39-40; trans. mod.). My sense of "queen" in this richly ironic passage is of an oppressive and humiliating force figured as a feminized ruler, accumulating with others to form a series of such rulers, who exist as a result of the slave trade; therefore, I am disinclined to take Irele's view that "reine" in both passages is the speaker's *ennobling* word for his race, notwithstanding the parallelism in the earlier passage of "race" and "reine" ("Commentary and Notes," 127). The many racial masks that the *Cahier*'s speaker wears cumulatively work to undercut any assumptions we may have that any is the authentic one, and in calling his "race" a queen with whom he must couple so as to bring forth a new language, he makes tangible that his "queen" belongs to a prior regime, the very regime responsible for his racialization and the suffering that ensued from it. The queen in the later passage appears as a source of cultural authority associated with the prince's discursive regime rather than a precise equivalent to the earlier queens, who nonetheless continue to resonate with undertones of queens being agents of domination in the past.[59] Given this, her union with the speaker would signify a momentous transformation of the ruling order, and the speaker's hypothetical vision of this union conveys his wish to overcome a fruitless polarization, a wish anticipated in some of the poem's most quoted lines: "But in doing so, my heart, preserve me from all hatred / do not make me into that man of hatred for whom I have only hatred" (Césaire, *Notebook* 37-38; trans. mod.). Significantly, translations into English of *pour que la reine me baise* lose Césaire's wordplay alluding to Nerval's line, which refers to a queen's kiss: *Mon front est rouge encore du baiser de la Reine* (My brow is still red from the kiss of the Queen). Césaire retains Nerval's image of a queen showing favor for a male speaker, but by converting her kiss to sex that she instigates or directs, he accentuates the poet's attainment of power and his successful recruitment of the figure best positioned to know intimately, love faithfully, and ensure the perpetuation of the regime the speaker seeks to transform. The queen is at once the prior regime and the "race" that this regime conferred on the speaker and the collectivity he represents.

These lines constitute a powerful reimagining of an already densely evocative motif from Nerval and Eliot, itself couched in a long poetic tradition of dramatizing the accession of upstarts taking command of crown and (an often willing) queen. That the speaker uses this canonically fraught motif, however, to figure a process of self-realization made possible by the formation of a revolutionary new poetry intimates both poetic and political affiliations and negotiations rather than outright defiance. I take the "vieillard à assassiner," or the old man the poet seeks to kill, as an older version of the poet himself, still entrenched in "la vieille négritude" and not yet able to transform himself from an "I" to a "we" as he aspires to do at the poem's close (Césaire, *Cahier* 30, 33). Even when he calls for his "I" to be tied to this "bitter fraternity" as "we," his language of self-surrender and capture continue to signal the imaginative constraints of an inherited discourse of mastery, as Nesbitt suggests in his analysis of the *Cahier*'s "antinomies of double consciousness" (76–94). Addressing this new collectivity as *Colombe*—at once a peaceful messenger for the world and a discoverer of a new poetic world to come—the speaker's utopian vision of bond formation as tantamount to the poet being "strangled" by an ascendant collectivity's noose-like "lasso of stars" resonates with the tensely negotiated uses of "race," "blood," *nègre*, and an array of stereotypes associated with these concepts throughout the *Cahier*. These displays of lexical entanglement evoke not, as Nesbitt argues, a failure to envision a preferable state of imaginative autonomy, but rather the limits of autonomy and the necessary intimacy between a hegemonic cultural discourse and the poetry that contests and transforms it (82). In looking ahead to the creation of this revolutionary poetry, the speaker depends on a prevailing language of mastery ("Le maître" appears five times in the passage), masculine potency, and exceptionalism, even as he identifies increasingly with the collective. For instance, in his "virile prayer" the speaker beseeches, "and as for me, my heart, do not make me into a father nor a brother / nor a son, but into the father, the brother, the son, / not a husband, but the lover of this unique people" (Césaire, *Notebook* 37; trans. mod.).[60] This language of mastery, masculine potency, and exceptionalism can seem inapt as the basis for a newly inclusive and democratic language, but it is in this language that we can perceive the colonially educated speaker's own struggle to be the voice of a dynamic collective, without falling back into colonial discourse's dichotomy of the heroic trailblazer obliged to lead and the mass of passive dependents who must languish without him. The struggle of the poet-speaker to project himself into his ideally communal world and to merge with it, unhindered by the polarizing logic of a colonial politics of paternalism and conquest, plays out in the very contradictions of his unfolding language. The fractured and continually modulating voice of the *Cahier* is, more than any isolated example from the poem, the manifestation of this struggle, and Césaire's use of it brings communitarian *engagement* to Mallarmé's notion of free verse as the distinctly modern poetic means "not just of expressing oneself, but of modulating oneself" (Mallarmé, "Crisis" 205).

These implicit comparisons and their political resonances coexist with what Césaire makes explicit in the speaker's dream of finding his voice, namely, the mutually defining relationship of the new poetry still under construction and a new, collectively constituted self, also under construction, who accumulates power and prestige by speaking (and willfully not speaking) it. This new poetic language consists in many things other than authoritative words: "Le maître des rires? / Le maître du silence formidable? / Le maître de l'espoir et du désespoir?" and so on, "C'est moi!" In this passage, among others, the *Cahier* can seduce us into imagining its speaker as a unified subject roughly equivalent to Césaire himself and having a messianic sense of his poetry as a means of uniting and emboldening the Martinican people, "this squalling throng so astonishingly detoured from its cry" (*Notebook* 2). There is much in the *Cahier* to support this assumption, especially in the first half of the poem before he confesses to his own complicity in perpetuating a racist stereotype while riding a streetcar and concedes, "Mon héroïsme, quelle farce!" (*Cahier* 20). Early on, he imagines himself (in the conditional mood) a lone outsider appealing for inclusion in the collective on the strength of his facility with words: "I would come to this land of mine and I would say to it: 'Embrace me without fear. . . . And if all I can do is speak, it is for you I shall speak'" (*Notebook* 13; trans. mod.). And yet the poet-speaker is so abstractly and impersonally defined in the poem, and so closely and repeatedly identified with wider communities of Martinicans, the African diaspora, sufferers of ethnically based social oppression, and the natural world, that the "I" we come to know from the aggregate of paratactic, densely figurative lyric and dramatic sequences, interrupted here and there by a comparatively accessible narrative recollection (of Christmas, rue Paille, the streetcar incident), is effectively a collective speaking subject even before he imagines his "I" becoming bonded to the "we." These qualities of the *Cahier* complicate attempts to read it as the coherent expression of an integrated Césairean persona and instead suggest, for some critics, the poetic rendering of a collective unconscious. Thus, J. Michael Dash argues that "in the *Cahier* we do not find the apotheosis of the subject, more characteristic of conventional literature of protest, but the decentered subject" as "the site where the collective experience finds articulation" in an "unregimented and unedited flow."[61] Khanna finds in the poetry of the negritude writers generally a "search for an underlying and unadulterated collective unconscious untouched by the colonialist offense" but argues that Césaire was unusual in emphasizing its historical dimension: "Césaire conceived the collective unconscious as a repository of historical occurrences that continued to haunt."[62]

Without expecting any one concept such as the collective unconscious to account for the protean evocations of community in the *Cahier*, we can say that the speaker's constitutive identifications with others—others who are for the most part collectives rather than individuals—make the *Cahier*'s language appear again and again as a language of and for collectives whose unification the poem is striving to achieve. It must also be said, though, that the collective—or aspirationally collective—voice of the poem is overtly and compellingly erudite. The polyglot and allusive French proper to the poet-speaker indirectly suggests the distance between the singularity of his voice and the generality through which he imagines the collectives for whom he speaks, and whose own discrete voices are necessarily absent from the poem's register. Paradoxically, then, the voice that speaks for "this squalling throng so astonishingly detoured from its cry" aspires to be representative but, for all its diverse rhetorical modes, does not imagine itself as growing into a chorus, even in the poem's culminating images of solidarity building and cosmic union. The *Cahier* is not an expression of personal voices, even the poet's own.[63] Instead, Césaire's poet dredges up from his discursive reserves a language of racialization, colonial education, and scientific classification and transforms its definitive assertions, monologic judgments, and stereotypic personas into a poetic assemblage of images whose interplay changes what their meanings had been, or seemed to be, in unchallenged isolation. Through this counterdiscursive practice of comparatism, he pursues not only a presumed lost natural vitality of Martinicans and the larger community of racialized migrants and their impoverished descendants but a hard-won, no less natural vitality from newly recognized bonds formed through overlapping histories of suffering and stigmatized displacement.

Long before the emergence of *créolité*, Walcott's response to Césaire's language of resistance, in an essay on poetics in which Eliot and Césaire figure prominently but are never directly compared, was to suggest that the *Cahier*'s "tartness and impatience" make it sound "like a poem written tonally in Creole," but that "the language of Césaire in this great revolutionary poem, or rather a poem partially appropriated by revolutionaries, is not proletarian" ("Muse of History" 49). In an extended comparison (to which I will return) of Césaire to Perse, who was not only a white Guadeloupian poet but a French diplomat whose family owned two plantations, Walcott argues that despite their exceedingly different backgrounds and politics, "to the reader trying to listen purely to the language of either poet without prejudice, without subliminal whispers of history, they have at least one thing in common: authority" (49).

The *Cahier*'s vision of a poet-speaker using all his erudition to become the authoritative voice of others with whom he identifies is appealing insofar as it puts cultural capital to work for those who have been denied it and belittled for their lack of it; it can also, however, make the postcolonially trained reader, wary of intellectuals speaking for subalterns, wonder about the voices inaudible not just in colonial but in anticolonial languages of privilege. It is not simply Césaire's avoidance of writing in Creole, so often debated since the literary elevation of vernacular and indigenous languages after decolonization, or even his decisive role in securing French departmental status instead of independence for Martinique, that has put him at a remove politically from recent black transnationalist and creolist writers. If Walcott foregrounds racial rhetoric when he criticizes Césaire's vocabulary of the Cité, the tension between the poem's positioning of the speaker as broadly representative both within and beyond the Antilles and the learned particularity of his language likely contributes to a sense of Césaire as an idealist in an ivory tower, or, as Chamoiseau imagines it in *Texaco*, a gated garden that Martinican workers must penetrate so as to rouse him to action.[64] But as my argument suggests, to note the absence of the stories that the *Cahier*'s language does not tell, or cannot translate, need not be to contend that Césaire should have written in a different language or that the paradoxical encounters intrinsic to the *Cahier*'s collective voice would be better replaced with a more seemingly authentic and multiperspectival creolism; on the contrary, it is to recognize how the poem's form and diction endow it with an unprecedented capacity to evoke the struggle of an acculturated speaker to translate the subaltern perspectives he perceives into images and conceptual frameworks available to him. It is also to reiterate that, with the passage of time and its attendant shifts in critical methods of reading, the inconclusive and polysemous counterlanguage of the *Cahier* can generate effects beyond the explicit cultural politics of the text and its prior receptions. Now specifically, we might look more to the margins of the poem's heuristic process of enlightenment, to try to imagine what is missing from its speaker's dawning recognition of his place as representative of a wider collective of the oppressed, and from his rise as pioneering speaker for this collective who cannot yet speak. Listening for their silences in his exploratory, virtuosic linguistic conversions and imagining their alternative multivocality can move us to think more about what the possibilities were, in the years Césaire wrote the poem and since, for conceiving of collectivity and humane authority. They can move us to think more about claims of identification and representativeness in authoritative poetic language, such as that admired by Walcott, and to ask questions about the side of the equation we cannot hear, the voices represented but not representing. This brings us back to Eliot.

Modulating Voices of Tradition

The Waste Land has been persistently understood in the contexts of interwar pessimism and nostalgic critical conjunctions of comparative mythology, Christian allegory, and high literariness. Eliot's poem in such accounts amounts to the product and prize of an easily classifiable cultural mindset, marked by virtuoso learning and alienation from the alternately sinister and frivolous mentality of the masses. The burden then rests on the reader to match the poet's elite expertise in order to decipher the text. *The Waste Land*'s snatches of canonical literary and religious stories and songs come to be seen as dredged up from a modern collective unconscious so alienated from itself and its world that it can connect the fragments neither to one another nor to contemporary life. What follows from such a reading is a sense that the stories and songs from which *The Waste Land*'s remnants come could, if only their originary coherence were realized, radiate enduring meaning now sorely needed in the strange new world of modernity. By this logic, the poem's focus alternates between apparently more self-conscious and discerning, hence sympathetic, speakers—a wandering poet-speaker and the aged seer Tiresias—who seem acutely aware of the moral desolation that surrounds them, and a series of other speakers and characters who lack the coherence of voice and vision that would make us identify ourselves with them as we do with the poet and the seer. When we read *The Waste Land* after the *Cahier*, however, and consider Césaire's visionary speaker and his heterogeneous poetic language in formation and marked by its own exclusions, we can see Eliot's ostensibly authoritative speakers in a new light as well.

It is perhaps inevitable to confer authority on those speakers who seem most to resemble well-established personas of Eliot and Césaire themselves, intercultural poets who call us to imagine a broken but potentially integrated human culture in which a new poetry is needed to repair the historical consciousness of the poet's community, and thereby repair the human itself. Regardless of whether Eliot's intertextual citations directly influenced Césaire, there is a remarkable confluence of ideas between Eliot's images of speakers in a barren land fishing for transformative vision ("pearls that were his eyes") and Césaire's final, triumphantly sensual and procreant image of a countercultural poet fishing for a magical tongue/language:

> monte lécheur de ciel
> et le grand trou noir où je voulais me noyer l'autre lune
> c'est là que je veux pêcher maintenant la langue maléfique de la nuit en son immobile verrition! (*Cahier* 33)

> (rise licker of sky
> and the great black hole where a moon ago I wanted to drown
> it is there I now want to fish the sorcerous tongue of the night in its motionless verrition!) (*Notebook* 51; trans. mod.)

Differences in tone and diction aside (especially as they pertain to carnality), both poems invite us to look to the collectively constituted vision of a fisher of words for a culturally reinvigorating poetry that can tentatively unite what appear to be divided, even opposed, in the phenomenal world. With the "land" / "pays natal" looming large in both poems as a complex metonym for all the natural and cultural processes that ground human beings, the idea that these processes are disintegrating and might be restored by a lone visionary who suffers on behalf of his community is a seductive source of meaning in each poem, and no doubt an explicit one in the *Cahier*. And yet *The Waste Land*, even more conspicuously than the *Cahier*, is so far from the "denominative and representative" discourse that Mallarmé distinguished from the evocations and modulations of his ideal modern poetry that this account of prophetic authority has remained more stable than perhaps it should. To personify Eliot's speakers at all, quite aside from equating them with their author, one must tread lightly, because parataxis throughout the poem makes the identification of one speaker with another, and one line with another, an exercise in comparative synthesis based to a considerable degree on faith. As Eliot's remarks on Perse suggest, parataxis leaves the nature of coordinates—the nature of bonds, we might say—unspecified. It bears repeating that the relationship of *The Waste Land*'s "I" shoring fragments against his ruins to the "I" who addresses us just beforehand is never made explicit, though they share a sense of uncertainty in the absence of authoritative institutions and systems of belief:

> I sat upon the shore
> Fishing, with the arid plain behind me
> Shall I at least set my lands in order? (Eliot, *Waste Land* 5.424–26)

This "I" appears to be the same as the one "fishing in the dull canal" in "The Fire Sermon," but if so this does not take us far: he is both son and brother of departed kings, at once Ferdinand and not Ferdinand from *The Tempest*. And the "I" fishing in the dull canal appears, just a few lines above, to be the "I" who is mourning the nymphs' departure, though this "I," too, is at once the ancient Hebrews, Edmund Spenser, and even a despairing Lord Byron:

> By the waters of Leman I sat down and wept . . .
> Sweet Thames, run softly till I end my song,
> Sweet Thames, run softly, for I speak not loud or long. (3.182–84)

These simultaneous, overlapping and colliding I's are no longer only distinct personages from the past but an assembly of I's in the present that signify in relation to each other. Because we rarely know who precisely is speaking in *The Waste Land*, we can only contingently assign identities—usually multiple identities at once—to speakers to imagine their possible perspectives and relationships. In this way Eliot's multiply allusive "I" hints at the expected confessional psychologism of the lyric but maneuvers us instead into a world of uncertain voices in intermittent contact and implicit comparison, marked by all the risks of incomprehension and appropriative identification characteristic of comparisons between self and other, familiar and foreign. In representing (in both senses) some voices over others, *The Waste Land*'s speaking subjects, like the *Cahier*'s, are defined in relation to silent presences they may not recognize, but that become imaginable through the indefinite and inconclusive comparatism of their language.

I have argued that the *Cahier*'s process of creating a new language enacts the struggle of its poet-speaker to imagine new collectivities while constrained by inherited models of dominance. What this enactment does is enable us to acknowledge but also look beyond the poem's explicit politics of denouncing racist domination and dismantling its legitimating discourses, to acknowledge also the poem's ways of animating the poet-rebel's personal progress toward communal identification, thus simultaneously generating suspense and sympathy through a familiar trajectory of heroic romance, while also decentering and supplementing this triumphant romantic plot with a far less orderly image of poetic union whose future is neither foreseeable nor codifiable.[65] In *The Waste Land* Tiresias is the figure Eliot directly identifies with collectivity in the poem's endnotes, distinguishing him as "the most important personage in the poem, uniting all the rest" (52n218). Again we see the paradox of aspiring to create a poetic world unified by a visionary spokesman whose exceptionality makes that unity possible. Tiresias's presumed authority, earned in the classical canon and confirmed in Eliot's notes (whose explanatory function, albeit an idiosyncratic one, coexists in tension with the counterdiscursive aspects of the poem's form), may be seen as reinforced by the relative lucidity and, for the most part, metrical regularity of his narration of the typist's tryst in "The Fire Sermon."[66] Unsettling such implicit affirmations of his narratorial and moral authority, however, are crosscurrents circling around his claims to comprehension based in identification with women, and around the waning of his private lyricism into a composite singsong.

As the poem's "most important personage" ("although a mere spectator and not indeed a 'character,'" as Eliot vaguely explains; *Waste Land* 52n218), Tiresias most coherently represents the predicament and possibility of *The Waste Land*'s gatherer of fragments and the *Cahier*'s wearer of successive masks of negritude:[67] his keen historical memory and capacity to see through prophetic vision rather than physical sight make him the ideal embodiment of a poetry that transcends the narrowly local concerns of the "brute or immediate." Still resonating, then, as the underestimated truth teller and man of faith from the classical canon, Tiresias is conserved but reimagined in *The Waste Land* as a voice of cosmopolitan detachment and transcultural wisdom. The aura of authority these associations, old and new, lend to Tiresias owes itself also to Eliot's more explicit emphasis on Tiresias's body as a site of confluent male and female experiences. The implication that Tiresias's ancient sentence of living as a woman for seven years gives him unique insight into women's perspectives should, by the logic of the judgment that follows, deepen our sense of tragedy as he describes the typist from the margins of her unseeing world:

> I Tiresias, though blind, throbbing between two lives,
> Old man with wrinkled female breasts, can see
> At the violet hour, the evening hour that strives
> Homeward, and brings the sailor home from sea,
> The typist home at teatime, clears her breakfast, lights
> Her stove, and lays out food in tins. (3.218-23)

Tiresias's authority in the poem derives partly from the fact that he is "not only one side of a binary perspective," as Jewel Spears Brooker and Joseph Bentley argue, but "also the suggestion that the reader must try to imagine that *The Waste Land* is a phenomenon to be viewed from the perspective of the Absolute, or at least from a more comprehensive perspective."[68] At the same time, it is precisely Tiresias's status as one who is not merely an individual, but a figure in whom others meet to produce extraordinary insight, that makes the opposition between him and the typist so powerful as he—a mere spectator—contemplates her private life as if unaltered by his encounter with it. This encounter signifies differently in light of the *Cahier*'s poet-speaker exhorting himself, "Take care not to cross your arms in the sterile attitude of the spectator" when confronted with the suffering of those he represents (Césaire, *Cahier* 9). Tiresias is by no means an indifferent witness; his tone of sorrowful disapproval is one of the reasons the poem is often read as pitting the lost coherence of a forgotten world of transcendent authority against a morally corrupted, intellectually degraded modern world (a reading Brooker and Bentley, among others, reject; 53). And yet, if Tiresias is a poetic figure for Eliot's early philosophical position "that we can construct reliable—though never indubitable—judgments through the accumulation of many immediate perspectives," as Michael Levenson writes

("Eliot's Politics" 377),[69] then Tiresias's moral authority becomes more tenuous as readers grow attuned to perspectives missing from his account, and as his judgments come to seem more monological than the poem's own multiperspectivalism suggests its unifying spokesman's account should be. Levenson implies this possibility when he explains why Eliot subsequently sought a more stable source of authority in the form of religious orthodoxy: "A perspectival or composite authority always risks changing (or losing) its force, as new perspectives emerge" (377).

The discrepancy between the complex amalgamating consciousness that Eliot's note directs us to find in Tiresias and the uncompromising tone of judgment that colors the scene opens a space in the poem for considering how a seductively transparent narrative can work to authorize a canonical voice of tradition, selectively constituted of past perspectives, to speak for a collectivity defined as unified (however contrary to appearances) and yet marked by exclusivity. By the accepted wisdom that Tiresias's accumulated authority through the ages is unassailable, the unnamed sexually active single woman becomes a prototype, morally wayward and affectively incomprehensible, whose presence in *The Waste Land* bolsters fears of modern industry, metropolitan sociality, and women's independence. In his summation of the scene, Eliot's speaker, presumably still Tiresias but now merged with eighteenth-century novelist Oliver Goldsmith's character Olivia, who in turn is singing someone else's song, seems to anticipate the shamelessly sexual, jazz-possessed machine-woman of Fritz Lang's *Metropolis* (1927):

> When lovely woman stoops to folly and
> Paces about her room again, alone,
> She smoothes her hair with automatic hand,
> And puts a record on the gramophone. (*Waste Land* 3.253–56)

These lines conclude a narrative segment that stands out from much of the poem for its clarity, but whose humane lyricism becomes in the end conspicuously formulaic. One can read this semblance of simplicity as a reflection of the typist's own vacuousness, but of course it is only from the perspective of the narrator that we are permitted any view at all into her thoughts or character. Whatever clarity of vision Tiresias's account may suggest, the value of that clarity is not self-evident in a poem whose dominant mode of making meaning is through unresolved friction and ambiguous interconnections. As the account becomes increasingly mechanical and the speaker's identity increasingly obscure, the tightly controlled meter suggests as much a rigidly maintained partial view of the scene as it does the primitive sensibilities of the lovers on display, potentially diminishing whatever credibility might at first have flowed from the singular repute of Tiresias the visionary. Moreover, Eliot's repeated references to the decrepit, infertile body of this "old man with wrinkled dugs," one long past having any discernible sense of sexual desire as either a man or a woman, hint that Tiresias's insight into sexuality, predicated on his capacity to identify with both sexes, might not translate fully in this foreign space and time (3.228).

The seemingly stable and unified "I" that conceals within itself an indefinite number of disparate voices makes this passage, and *The Waste Land* more broadly, a poetic world not of mergings whose stability and universal import we can believe in but of intersecting perspectives whose appearance of congruency and transferability can mask considerable instability and difference. The long description of a woman and her surroundings that begins "A Game of Chess" gives an initial sense of coherence not only through its detailed lucidity and syntactic complexity but also by its merging into one authoritative voice a range of texts from what might be called the hypercanon (*Antony and Cleopatra*, *The Aeneid*, *Paradise Lost*, *Metamorphoses*). It begins,

> The Chair she sat in, like a burnished throne,
> Glowed on the marble, where the glass
> Held up by standards wrought with fruited vines
> From which a golden Cupidon peeped out
> (Another hid his eyes behind his wing)
> Doubled the flames of sevenbranched candelabra
> Reflecting light upon the table as
> The glitter of her jewels rose to meet it. (Eliot, *Waste Land* 2.77–84)

This authoritative voice and its semblance of coherence transform abruptly into a dialogue, without canonical allusions, of unidentified, mutually uncomprehending voices. Here are the last three lines of the long descriptive passage whose beginning appears above, followed by the dialogue:

> Under the firelight, under the brush, her hair
> Spread out in fiery points
> Glowed into words, then would be savagely still.
>
> "My nerves are bad to-night. Yes, bad. Stay with me.
> "Speak to me. Why do you never speak? Speak.

"What are you thinking of? What thinking? What?
"I never know what you are thinking. Think."

I think we are in rats' alley
Where the dead men lost their bones. (2.108–16)

This becomes more legible when put in the context of the young Eliot's many juxtapositions, in the early quatrain poems especially, of an order conferred by literature from the past with disorderly attempts at communication in the present.[70] While the present juxtaposition may be read similarly, it can also bring to mind the voices unheard *within* a canon of trusted stories and conventionally beautiful poetic language, voices breaking through and being heard in all their strange abrasiveness and literary novelty. Our heightened awareness of concurrent, often conflicting structures and dispensations of power in open-ended poetic comparisons such as Eliot's will then have raised the stature of *The Waste Land*'s less authoritative speakers and characters whose stories could not be comprehended through patterns of thought and imagery canonized in the past. At the same time, it will have enabled us to question the authority of the poem's apparently more comprehensible, and comprehending, speakers—the fisher of words with his fragments of erudition and the prophet displaced from his orderly canon—if only to see the gaps and adulterations of their own language in formation.

Like the *Cahier*, *The Waste Land* challenges us to imagine in the face of elusive former systems of belief, failing modes of communication in the present, and constitutively fractured speaking subjects. Both poems hint at new interpretive possibilities, however much those possibilities arise out of extraordinary loss and affective trauma. These possibilities come from the poems' ways of staging, albeit indirectly, a more interconnected and multivocal world than local or monocultural patterns of thought had recognized or accommodated. From this perspective, Eliot's Philomela, imprisoned far from home, raped, and robbed of speech, becomes a figure for what has been violently expelled from King Tereus's authoritative account. When Philomela becomes a nightingale, her silence transformed into the "inviolable voice" of birdsong, she represents what can be freed only by a radical translation of form and abandonment of the trusted language of authority (Eliot, *Waste Land* 2.101). Eliot in turn ceases to be the nostalgic seeker of lost authority he is so often assumed to be, and *The Waste Land*, like Philomela's voice, is transformed into another kind of song.

Shifting Grounds

The *Cahier* begins with a line that marks time, but ambiguously: "Au bout du petit matin" (at the end of daybreak). It is the first of a series of anaphoric phrases that give the poem its distinctive structure as a "dialectical litany," in Brent Edwards's phrase, in which the implications of the terms shift with each iteration and thus give a sense of poetic language as unbounded and continually renewed.[71] Like *The Waste Land*'s insistent anaphoric phrases for a fleeting moment of dusk, "at the violet hour," "in the violet air," and "in the violet light," Césaire's phrase suggests a speaker caught between night and day, a time that is both night and day, opposites embedded in each other with no meaning apart from the other. In these fleeting moments of dusk and dawn, neither day nor night dominates the other; in the absence of old oppositions, beginnings are also endings, and endings beginnings. From the confusion and despair of these pivotal moments, both poems build toward a sense of open futures that might include what had seemed impossible unions: narrators and the perspectives they omit, poems and not-yet-imaginable words. These futures necessitate the dissolution of the self and its others as currently conceived. Tropes of oblivion and transformation—Eliot's "death by water" and Césaire's *grand trou noir*—are at once threatening and hopeful images of the self's restorative submersion in transformative cycles of an enveloping nature. Eliot suggests the creative possibilities of this submersion in his own transformative uses of Shakespeare's "pearls that were his eyes"; Césaire suggests them in his multivalent erotic image of a womb-like black hole to be united with an upright *lécheur de ciel*, where a new language of relations (motionlessness and the turning motion of "verrition") may be conceived. The ethnocentric certainty habitually ascribed to Eliot and Césaire and, less often but still frequently enough, assumed to imbue *The Waste Land* and the *Cahier* is antithetical to the exploratory and inconclusive plenitudes the poems invoke in their closing words, never fully translatable phrases for ways of being that do not yet exist: *Shantih shantih shantih* and *son immobile verrition*.

As interpreters of the poems, we can take insight from their virtues of exploratoriness and inconclusiveness. It is usual for many of us teaching and writing on *The Waste Land* to consider alongside it Eliot's essay "Tradition and the Individual Talent," and in particular his assertion that "what happens when a new work of art is created is something that happens simultaneously to all the works of art that preceded it."[72] My reading of *The Waste Land* after the *Cahier*, and of the *Cahier* amid our ongoing scrutiny of the politics of relation, exclusion, and domination, is one way to affirm Eliot's claim, with the "creation" of a new work tantamount to each of its interpretations, its continual rebirth, in light of all the interpretations that came before, thanks to its capacity to be read in one way and then another. None of this is to say that formative readings and contexts should, or even could, be forgotten; indeed, their capacity to be augmented, contradicted, augmented, and contradicted again in an ongoing process is what best enables us to conceive readings pertinent and exciting for our present. Nor is it to say that the cultural politics of Eliot's and Césaire's poems can be fruitfully read as equivalent, only that the explicit cultural politics of the poets and their poems, to the extent that we can determine what they are, do not exhaust the implications, including political implications, that their counterdiscursive, intricately comparative poetics create and just as quickly contradict. For instance, insofar as Philomela may now be read as the brutalized and silenced subaltern, her prominence in a poetic world that abounds in fallen sovereigns makes it possible for her presence in *The Waste Land* to signal what Eliot leaves unrepresented—the mythical Philomela's violent insurgency against King Tereus with her sister Procne, who is also his wife and queen; in solidarity they avenge his crimes against Philomela by killing his son (among other colorful acts) and thereby ensure the end of Tereus's regime.[73] Thus, Eliot may not include in *The Waste Land* any image of insurgent collaboration comparable to the metaphorical slave revolt envisioned by Césaire's poet at the close of the *Cahier*, but its possibility still reverberates through the figure of Philomela, whose transformative song in Eliot's rendering is accompanied by unsounded notes of sisterly solidarity that can bring down a tyrant.

More than twenty years before his review of *Texaco*, Walcott anticipated the obvious political objections to a comparative reading of Eliot and Césaire in his own comparison of Césaire with Perse, whose incantatory poems of migration and conquest shared with Eliot, as well as with negritude poets such as Césaire, a network of literary influences including the French symbolists.[74] Without reference to James, though echoing his distinction between "economics or politics" and the poetic, Walcott writes,

> Perse sees in this New World vestiges of the Old, of order and of hierarchy, Césaire sees in it evidence of past humiliations and the need for a new order, but the

> deeper truth is that both poets perceive this New World through mystery. [. . .] If we think of one as poor and the other as privileged when we read their addresses to the New World, if we must see one as black and one as white, we are not only dividing this sensibility by the process of the sociologist, we are denying the range of either poet, the power of compassion and the power of fury. ("Muse of History" 52–53)

This definition of "poetry" as a singularly and laudably opaque kind of language has retained a privileged place in literary discourse in French and English, but it has also evolved dramatically from an ideally depersonalized "poetics of language-in-itself" to an ideally multivocal "poetics of relation." Building on the former and ushering in the latter, Eliot's and Césaire's comparative reimaginings of the poetics of simultaneity and polymorphous suggestion permitted them to build on earlier modernist uses of indeterminacy while shifting the grounds of what made that indeterminacy important: the flux of poetic speakers moving through cultures in ongoing mutual formation, even as they, and their readers, are caught in culturally isolationist, territorial patterns of imagining others. Putting the imaginative dimension of confronting the other at the forefront of his cultural theory, Glissant writes in the *Poetics of Relation* that "the power to experience the shock of elsewhere is what distinguishes the poet" ("le pouvoir de ressentir le choc de l'ailleurs est ce qui nomme le poète"; *Poetics* 29–30; *Poétique* 42). The poetic languages of *The Waste Land* and the *Cahier* effect this shock of elsewhere as few other poems have done: they enjoin the reader to experience the process of translating what escapes translation, and imagining in the face of translation's limits. For us to take from these poems stable and coherent arguments—sociological, political, or otherwise—we must considerably underestimate and domesticate their eruptions of strangeness, to us and to themselves. Such readings make the poems, as well as the movements in which we classify them, less multitudinous and less mobile than they have been and could be, by precluding intimations of relation that become apparent to us only retrospectively.

Achille Mbembe has written that "one of the functions of art and religion has been precisely to maintain the hope of escaping the world as it has been and as it is, to be reborn into life, to lead the festival once again."[75] To generate this hope, Eliot and Césaire assemble worlds that are simultaneously familiar and strange, home regimes we know too well whose juxtaposition to what they cannot comprehend impel us to ask what their alternatives could be. Each poem's utopianism consists in evoking a process of spiritual transcendence that is, at the same time, an imaginative liberation from an ostensibly divided physical world through the diversification of poetic language and the knowledge it yields. The poems present poetic language as not yet having found a way to figure the world's diversity as a collectivity, a unity and a diversity at once. But in their culminating flights of verbal imagination beyond known spatial, temporal, and linguistic frameworks, they authorize self-forgetting and ecstatic unknowing as inaugurating plenitudes where expert learning, heroic bravado, and superhuman powers of prophecy are not assured means to salvation but dynamically ambivalent relational forces among many. If collectivity has not yet been achieved in the present of the poems, *The Waste Land* and the *Cahier* do permit us to see that the future of home is elsewhere, an elsewhere open to new poetic logics and untimely, nonterritorial relations rising up from the dead lands.

3 Traversing Bounds of Historical Memory

Dethroning the Narrator and Creolizing Testimony in *A Passage to India* and *Texaco*

> The past—or, more accurately, pastness—is a position. Thus, in no way can we identify the past *as past.*
>
> —Michel-Rolph Trouillot

> Relation is learning more and more to go beyond judgments into the unexpected dark of art's upsurgings.
>
> —Édouard Glissant

Writing in 1953, E. M. Forster briefly explains that he has chosen not to include an introduction to the published edition of letters he wrote on his first visit to India from October 1912 to April 1913—the visit that inspired him to draft the first seven chapters of *A Passage to India*—because he hopes "that the reader may share my bewilderment and pleasure at plunging into an unknown world and at meeting an unknown and possibly unknowable character," the Maharajah of the Indian state of Dewas Senior, whom he addressed as Bapu Sahib.[1] In the explanatory essay that follows the letters, he recounts describing "'the curious twin States of Dewas'" to a fellow English visitor and, recalling her disbelief, mocks the imperious certainty with which she corrected him: "The arrangement must have been unique, and an authoritative English lady, who knew India inside out, once told me that it did not and could not exist, and left me with the feeling that I had never been there" (55–56).

It is not unusual for critics to take Forster's approving association of India and Indians with the "unknown and possibly unknowable" as symptomatic of a dated Euromodernist fascination with an exoticized and racialized Orient. For Edward Said, *A Passage to India* is Orientalist because it represents "the East" as unreadable, with India serving as Forster's enigmatic East just as Africa had served as Joseph Conrad's enigmatic East in *Heart of Darkness*.[2] It is an elegant analogy, one that reappears in R. Radhakrishnan's recent critique of *A Passage to India*. He, too, interprets Forster as Orientalist for imagining India as the site where coherent meaning breaks down, and he, too, links Forster's Orientalism to European primitivist depictions of Africa, including Conrad's.[3] Of course, there is no equivalent in *Heart of Darkness* of Forster's descriptions of lyric poems, religious practices, and currents of belief in India, or of his indications that there are many more such examples of India's cultural attainments than he has described. In *Heart of Darkness*, by contrast, Congolese intellectual and spiritual traditions are reduced to sinister images of head-hunting and cannibalism. On the more fundamental question of how to assess Forster's insistent depiction, over many years, of India and Indians as opaque, Benita Parry has responded more sympathetically than many of her contemporaries in the postcolonial field. She urges that "critics writing in a post-imperial era go beyond castigating its vestiges of Orientalism" partly because Forster portrays unreadability not as essential to India but as the impression of English characters whose explanatory systems are inadequate to the interpretive work they are trying to do in India.[4] My reading shares her premise that the novel's foregrounding of English characters' incapacity to understand, and of its own incapacity to represent, India's complex material realities amounts to a significant modernist divergence from, and challenge to, most British writing on India in its time. Edward Thompson's *Suttee*, for example, published four years after *A Passage to India*, betrays as much humility in the face of its complex foreign subject as Forster's "authoritative English lady."[5]

Parry's discussion of English characters' interpretive difficulties does not extend to the narrator of *A Passage to India*, however. My view is that to recognize the novel's ways of signifying beyond and even against the Orientalist implications that Anglophone postcolonial criticism has trained us to discern, we need to acknowledge the narrator of *A Passage to India* as a character distinct from Forster, and to interpret the uncertainties and opacities of his narration in relation to those of others whose stories he tells. Those others include, above all, the English visitor Adela Quested, whose entranced testimony in court overtakes the narrator's observations and suppositions in such a way as to bring to a climax the contest of competing modes of comparison running through the book. The relation of Adela's narration to that of the unnamed narrator and the significance of their interaction in the trial scene are retrospectively clarified by the conjuncture of uncertain historical narration, oral testimony, and entrancement as a means to uncomprehended truth in *Texaco*, the celebrated *créoliste* novel by Patrick Chamoiseau. My comparative reading of these novels proceeds from Forster to Chamoiseau and back again, bringing Forster's attention to the contingencies of historical witnessing and acculturated judgment to Chamoiseau's more overtly self-reflexive vision of the necessarily collaborative nature of reconstructing a communal history long marginalized and still elusive even to those who testify to it and strive to commemorate it. My reading of these novels draws from the postcolonial debates I have cited but also continues to engage with the differently situated, equally important postcolonial corpus of black transnationalist and Francophone creolist historiography, cultural theory, and literary theory already foregrounded in previous chapters, a corpus still less than fully integrated into Anglophone literary studies, even global modernist studies. This theoretical work adds to well-known Anglophone postcolonial discussions of territorial constructs (such as nation-states, "East" and "West," "center" and "periphery") and their shaping of identity a distinct attentiveness to more manifold, unpredictable, and often opaque dynamics of relation within and across cultures.

Closer attention to Forster's narrator as an English traveler on his own passage to India, an outside interpreter and chronicler whose position shifts in relation to what he describes, illuminates the novel's climactic trial scene, as well as the trial's strange catalyst, the amorphous threat to linguistic comprehensibility, physical self-possession, and social order perceived by English characters in the Marabar Caves. Two crucial questions to address are why the novel so closely associates the breakdown of language with indeterminate sexual desire and why only English tourists are made to contend with them when they visit India under the Raj. The nature of the connection between language and sexuality, and the reasons for English anxieties about the violability of their own language and sexuality, become clearer when we consider the outing to the caves not as the simple sightseeing expedition the characters expect it to be, but as an invitation, even a provocation, to intermix socially outside a British-controlled environment. Reencountering Forster after Chamoiseau, as well as other thinkers of diaspora and relation, we are newly able to consider this localized intermixing, with its power to confound and transform, as a figure for much broader processes of creolization—linguistic, ethnic, religious, cultural—made possible and indeed irresistible by sustained colonial contact and settlement.

Touching Ghosts

In *Silencing the Past*, Haitian anthropologist Michel-Rolph Trouillot prefaces his discussion of the Disney Company's aborted plan in the 1990s to build a historically themed amusement park in Virginia, "Disney's America," with a reminiscence about his own unsuccessful attempt to "touch" Mayan history in the Yucatán. Before his arrival, Trouillot had already acquired a detailed and seductive knowledge of his destination: "I knew all these stories. I had done my homework before coming to Maya land."[6] What he hoped and failed to accomplish on his trip to the central pyramid was "to communicate with a past so magnificently close" (142). Trouillot's anecdote concludes with an insight into historiographic imagination, which becomes the foundation for his ensuing critique of Disney's proposed reconstruction of African American slavery at the amusement park. He writes that he acquired this insight on subsequent travels, when his search for an abstract past gave way to a recognition of others and their relation to the past: "From Rouen to Santa Fe, from Bangkok to Lisbon, I had touched ghosts suddenly real, I had engaged people far remote in time and in space. Distance was no barrier. History did not need to be mine in order to engage me. It just needed to relate to someone, anyone. It could not just be The Past. It had to be someone's past" (142).

Published in 1924 and set in the British Raj between the First and Second World Wars, *A Passage to India* makes a well-meaning Englishwoman's failed attempts to "see the *real* India" the catalyst for a similar lesson (Forster, *Passage* 22).[7] In the novel's much-discussed but persistently enigmatic plot, the newly arrived Adela Quested resolves to "understand India" as the local English expatriate community conspicuously does not, but her resolution goes awry on an outing to the remote and ultimately overwhelming Marabar Caves (79). After Adela accuses the Muslim Indian doctor Aziz of sexually assaulting her in a cave and then recants her accusation while testifying in court, she is transported away from the clamor outside the courthouse by Fielding, a colonial headmaster and Aziz's friend, who tries to get to the bottom of what had motivated her accusation and subsequent disavowal. When they cannot compose a satisfactory note of apology to Aziz, Fielding explains to her, "Our letter is a failure for a simple reason which we had better face: you have no real affection for Aziz, or Indians generally" (288–89). She admits this, and he continues, "The first time I saw you, you were wanting to see India, not Indians, and it occurred to me: Ah, that won't take us far" (289).

The clearest point in both passages quoted above, namely that someone seeking knowledge of an unfamiliar place should care about the human beings who populate it, is tied to a more complicated idea that Trouillot develops over the course of his chapter on slavery's depiction in "Disney's America" and that also seems to me to underlie and even propel the most consequential action in Forster's plot. For Trouillot, the problem with Disney's proposed reconstruction was not that it would necessarily distort the facts of slavery, or fail to adhere to empirical standards of truth. The problem was that it would serve as a tableau of past suffering for white middle-class American tourists whose own relationship to the ongoing ramifications of slavery—continued racial discrimination and inequality in the United States and elsewhere—would be obscured by the representation of slavery as a thing of the past, a scene of horror that tourists could feel they were acknowledging and leaving behind as a clear-cut injustice already overcome. Without establishing any historical connection between the object of critique and the position of the viewer invited to witness that critique, "the representation becomes a fake, a morally repugnant spectacle" (Trouillot 149). Tourists made to shudder at a past whose relation to slavery's enduring effects has been kept safely hidden would likely feel virtuous for lamenting the past and absolved of any responsibility to search out and struggle against racism in their present. The very empirical accuracy and fabricated realism of the spectacle would validate the unexamined views of spectators already inclined to see slavery as wholly separate from themselves. While there is much to consider in this analysis and the essay more generally, what strikingly pertains to Forster's novel is Trouillot's assertion that the success of our efforts to know others will depend on our commitment to understanding what our own relation to those others entails, both for them and for us.[8]

Trouillot's insistence that to begin to know a foreign culture one must not only come to know someone from that culture but also, in coming to know them, recognize the ongoing significance of one's position of power relative to theirs suggests what is wanting in Adela's ready belief that Aziz and his account of the Marabar Caves "would unlock his country for her" (Forster, *Passage* 73, 79). It never occurs to her to reflect on Aziz's position, or the position of any Indian, in relation to her own, that of an Englishwoman who has ventured into a colonial settlement not, in fact, to learn about indigenous cultures under British control but to decide whether she will marry the local city magistrate. Her determination to "understand India" is ancillary to the real business at hand of deciphering her own desires—whether she truly desires Ronny Heaslop and the life they might share. Her investigation of India (to the extent that it is an investigation) first distracts her from the deciphering of herself she must do and then, in a roundabout way, leads to a clear verdict not on India or even Aziz but on herself and Ronny. Feeling at first detached from the English expatriates in Chandrapore and then passively dependent on them, Adela shows little awareness of herself as embedded in politically motivated relationships. She never connects her mixed feelings about Ronny (indignation at his peremptoriness, then acquiescence to it after a fleeting sense of physical attraction) with her equally mixed feelings about Aziz (unabashed inquisitiveness not about him personally but about what he, as an Indian, can teach her; dissatisfaction and boredom when he tries to do so; and perhaps an unexamined physical attraction, though the English narrator makes a point of denying this possibility). Her ambivalence about these men, however, is among the novel's more emphatic displays of her relations to cultural power. Jenny Sharpe highlights these power relations when she attributes to Adela "the double positioning of the English woman—as inferior sex but superior race."[9] Unfortunately for everyone, this insular young Englishwoman is blind to the effects of cultural power on her interactions with Aziz. Her sense of herself as an innocent newcomer, independent of the social dynamics around her, makes her fleeting quest for knowledge one we might describe, following Trouillot, as "cheap and too easy," an overconfident plunge into the other, like Disney's would-be "plunge into The Past" of slavery (150). Just as it is too easy to condemn slavery alone without also condemning "the racist present within which representations of slavery are produced" (148), so does Adela's bewildered condemnation of English colonialists for their rudeness to Indians fall short. She has not learned to question the structural relations that make this rudeness possible and even defensible in the minds of the English, or how those structural relations induce Aziz, obsequious only with the English, to offer up the Marabar Caves, of which he knows little more than his guests, as a representative exhibition of his homeland—his own fake spectacle.

If Adela appears more naive in her approach to learning than Forster's other English characters sympathetic to Indians—Fielding; Ronny's mother, Mrs. Moore; and the novel's narrator, a character often conflated with Forster—she is not alone in underestimating her entanglement in relations of power and cultural politics, or in overestimating the potential for disinterested observation and communication in the accruing of intercultural knowledge. Fielding is a case in point. He rues the political turn taken by his conversation with Aziz's Indian friends, as if the political is and should remain separate from the personal. Asked to justify England's rule over India, he thinks, "There they were! Politics again. 'It's a question I can't get my mind on to,' he replied. 'I'm out here personally because I needed a job. I cannot tell you why England is here or whether she ought to be here. It's beyond me'" (Forster, *Passage* 120). Fielding's self-assured political agnosticism, which he never loses, contributes crucially to the ultimate failure of his friendship with Aziz, as well as to his inability to understand that failure. Ian Baucom has argued that the friendship between Fielding and Aziz forms in a "moment of crisis in which intimacy is offered as war's alternative," but that with "the encroachments of the mundane," their friendship atrophies because "Fielding and Aziz's intimacy cannot cope with a present that refuses to announce itself as exhilarating and critical."[10] What this reading does not recognize is the pain that Aziz would have endured, steadily and intensely, throughout the time of his incarceration, and the extent to which that pain could alter his expectations of friends. After an extended humiliation that was at once personal and political, Aziz at the novel's end could hardly be as tolerant as he had been of Fielding's noncommittal stance on British domination or the part he has played in it as a colonial educator of boys. For Fielding, Aziz's accumulated mistrusts and resentments are a personal matter that Aziz should choose to get over and that at any rate have nothing to do with Fielding himself. Such an attitude would be hard for Aziz to abide after a trial that so baldly revealed Indians' subjugated status in the British Raj, even in supposedly egalitarian institutions such as the law courts.

It may seem paradoxical that Forster would make the remote, altogether uninhabited Marabar Caves the place to expose the dangers of assuming personal relationships and choices to be somehow independent of politics and history. The caves are so removed from the world of the social as to seem to the narrator "extraordinary," indescribably vacant of meaning or anything that might accrue meaning: "Nothing, nothing attaches to them"; "nothing is inside them"; "if mankind grew curious and excavated, nothing, nothing would be added to the sum of good or evil" (Forster, *Passage* 137–38). But these resounding assertions of the nothingness, the nonexistence of meaning, in the caves imply that the drama to come is one the characters carry into the caves with them. The meaning of Mrs. Moore's terror, and then Adela's, is not to be found there, outside themselves, in the natural terrain of India. Mrs. Moore feels she is struck in the face, touched on the mouth and elsewhere, and generally confined and overwhelmed while in a cave that Forster makes sure we know is overcrowded with Indians. The novel goes on to imply, though never confirms or explicitly proposes, that Adela's sensations in another cave are similar to Mrs. Moore's but that Adela, a young woman preoccupied with Ronny, Aziz, and sex when she enters the cave, interprets these sensations as a sexual assault. We can call it Orientalist, as Said and many other critics have, that Forster uses a cavernous wilderness of the East to serve as the exotic site where Europeans are shocked and transformed by their apprehension of a primitive reality, but it is important to see that Forster's caves function this way only in the minds of the English characters, including the narrator. The novel never confirms that the caves' mystery and disruption of linguistic coherence are intrinsic to them or universally perceived by their visitors; indeed, neither Aziz nor any other Indian tourist is shown to interpret them this way. Hence Parry's disagreement with those who take Mrs. Moore's assumptions about the cave as equivalent to the novel's: "To accept Mrs. Moore's reception of Caves as a primordial miasma, and as the dissolution of ethical meaning, is to be deaf to the valencies of the 'Nothing' emanating from Caves" (170).

The drama in the caves is one of interpretation, a historically conditioned political drama that erupts when Mrs. Moore and Adela find themselves temporarily confined in dark and intimate spaces with Indians whose physical proximity suggests new and threatening relations. They are unprepared for this because their thoughts about the event beforehand do not include any reflection on their own associations with colonial mastery, associations that make possible the sense of security and self-possession they never doubted would follow them anywhere in India as it had in England. The seclusion of the caves reinforces their sense of distance from social formations seemingly left behind in Chandrapore, not to mention imperial England, and they trust in their own autonomous explorations to yield a nonpartisan and more tolerant understanding of India. They want to connect with their new environment by observing and asking questions about it, but these methods prove as inadequate to yielding an authentic connection to what surrounds them as Trouillot's were in the Yucatán. When the Marabar Hills first come into view from the train, for instance, Adela exaggerates her enthusiasm at seeing them. As she and Mrs. Moore "awaited the miracle" of the sun rising dramatically on the hills, Forster gives us, still from Adela's perspective, a marriage analogy to convey her disappointment: "Why, when the chamber was prepared, did the bridegroom not enter with trumpets and shawms, as humanity expects? The sun rose without splendour" (*Pas-*

sage 151–52). Adela's lack of objectivity is obvious enough when she associates the sunrise with what is really on her mind—an unsatisfying fiancé and an unfulfilled romance—but even more blatant when she takes refuge in a tendentious comparison to account for what she is feeling: "Ah, that must be the false dawn—isn't it caused by dust in the upper layers of the atmosphere that couldn't fall down during the night? I think Mr. McBryde said so. Well, I must admit that England has it as regards sunrises" (152). Adela's polarizing generalization about "Indian" sunrises being inferior to "English" ones on the basis of the first sunrise she has seen in India is made even more suspect by its grounding in the offhand remarks of McBryde, the district superintendent of police and one of the novel's most politically and culturally partisan English characters. Not only in the "Caves" section of *A Passage to India* but repeatedly throughout the novel, attempts to understand the unfamiliar manifest themselves as attempts to grasp differences conceived as fixed and potentially transparent to the attentive onlooker, rather than as relationally produced. And just as repeatedly, the novel shows the misguidedness of trying to grasp differences conceived in this way.

A Contest of Comparisons

To read Forster this way, we need to distinguish between knowing as grasping (at) differences and knowing as touching ghosts, in Trouillot's phrase, which is to say, knowing as connecting with others whose potential transparency one does not presuppose, because this form of connecting requires one's mindfulness of historical contexts of relation in which connections and differences are made and remade continually. To make this distinction, I am drawing on Trouillot but also on Glissant's analysis of the French verb *comprendre* (to understand) in *Poetics of Relation*, where he distinguishes from among the word's significations a sense derived explicitly from its lexical roots (*com* + *prehendere*) and translatable as "to grasp": "There is in this verb *comprendre* the movement of hands that take what surrounds them and bring it back to themselves."[11] With this image of grasping as seizing and gathering objects of knowledge, Glissant describes a process of interpreting difference that he attributes not only to colonialist discourse, which seeks to solidify relations of domination and hierarchy, but also, less predictably, to pluralist discourse that seeks to disrupt such relations by promoting respect for difference and multiplicity. Of course, Glissant acknowledges, "the theory of difference is invaluable" for both undermining "the presumption of racial excellence or superiority" and making visible "the rightful entitlement to recognition" of minorities and their status (189). But although he acknowledges the merits of recognizing and valuing difference, he urges us to move beyond this and "agree not merely to the right to difference but, carrying this further, agree also to the right to opacity" (190). In other words, to recognize and defend others, we run the risk of rendering others transparent and comprehensible by measuring them according to our own scale of values, a reductive comparative practice that rewards sameness or its semblance, not the difference supposedly being respected. Radhakrishnan identifies a similar problem in his critique of the comparisons that inform Forster's depiction of the Marabar Caves: "Comparisons work only when the 'radical others' have been persuaded or downright coerced into abandoning their 'difference,' and consent to being parsed within the regime of the sovereign One" (16). This fundamental problem of interpreting difference does not prompt Glissant (or Radhakrishnan, for that matter) to propose that we dispense with comparisons—as if we could—but it does prompt him to emphasize that tolerance based in the pursuit of better understanding others is of limited value because that sort of tolerance tends to entail legitimating differences by demystifying them.

For Glissant, there is an alternative to appropriative processes of comprehending others. If taking hold of what is outside oneself and reducing it to what appears admissible within one's own system is "a gesture of enclosure if not appropriation" ("geste d'enfermement sinon d'appropriation"), Glissant argues, "let us prefer the gesture of giving-with" ("préférons-lui le geste du donner-avec") (*Poetics* 192; trans. mod.; *Poétique* 206). Here Glissant's felicitously open-ended intransitive locution "giving-with" (*donner-avec*) displaces the stark opposition of subjects and objects required for the maneuvers of grasping. We have seen Trouillot allude to figures from the past, or, more broadly, figures of historical difference, as "ghosts" he could not grasp from a position of separateness but later learned to "touch" by seeking out his "authentic" historical relatedness to them. Trouillot considers a sense of historicity authentic when it "engages us both as actors and narrators" rather than as narrators for whom the past is discrete from ourselves (150). In arguing this, Trouillot advocates a historiographic method that, like Glissant's theory of cultural interpretation, dispenses with the position of the interpreter as "that of the nonhistorical observer" (151). Glissant's "giving-with" similarly casts doubt on the easy clarities of polarization and detached analysis and reconceives knowledge as a cooperative practice of imparting with the help and vision of others. This emphasis on interdependency as essential to the open-ended process of coming-to-know counters the colonialist fantasy of independent investigators, explorers, and chroniclers demystifying others and their differences.

Even the least partisan English characters in Chandrapore habitually make comparisons in order to demystify differences. This is true above all of the narrator, who as a rule does not hesitate to profess his knowledge of characters and their cultural attributes. For example, he explains Aziz's unfounded distrust of Fielding after the trial in decisive comparative terms: "Suspicion in the Oriental is a sort of malignant tumour, a mental malady, that makes him self-conscious and unfriendly suddenly; he trusts and mistrusts at the same time in a way the Westerner cannot comprehend. It is his demon, as the Westerner's is hypocrisy. Aziz was seized by it, and his fancy built a satanic castle" (Forster, *Passage* 311). Sometimes the narrator professes his knowledge by ascribing it to unnamed observers whose relatively evenhanded, worldly-wise judgments seem at odds with the hostile biases of colonial administrators and other English loyalists. For example, there is a brief uproar among Indian spectators during the trial when it is suggested that Mrs. Moore might have been prevented from testifying on Aziz's behalf, followed by a pronounced state of calm when Adela comes to testify. To account for the crowd's irrationality—and, let us note, on behalf of Aziz—the narrator cites the inferences of "experts" who are clearly not Indians themselves: "Experts were not surprised. There is no stay in your native. He blazes up over a minor point, and has nothing left for the crisis. What he seeks is a grievance, and this he had found in the supposed abduction of an old lady. He would now be less aggrieved when Aziz was deported" (252). This mode of comparison, in which comparisons are starkly binary and often polarizing, assumes the possibility of a stable and discernible common ground of perceptions and values. But Forster's novel as a whole, distinct from any one character or speaker, shows this ground to be a quagmire, the soft muddy stuff where muddles lie in wait. It shows this by undercutting the credibility of the binary mode of comparison by setting it against another that governs the representation of the novel's most defining enigmas. In this alternate mode, relations are posed but left unsettled, understood only partially because of what some characters assume to be either overarching cosmic forces or deep-seated psychological ones, though the novel never validates these supernaturalist and psychologist theories. The novel strongly and pervasively implies that relations are understood only partially because they are far more dynamic and interpersonally constitutive than theories of fixed differences have led characters to expect.

The two comparative modes cross and compete with each other in the narrator's periodically shifting position from a confident chronicler and cultural diagnostician to a sidelined witness and transcriber of exchanges whose meaning he leaves obscure. This narrator receives little critical attention as a distinct character because his sensibility, like that of the narrators of Forster's earlier novels, can be taken as reminiscent of the author's own, although, as the passages quoted at the start of this chapter convey, Forster's persona in his autobiographical writings on India is decidedly less detached and definitive, and more intimate and self-reflexive, than the narrator of *A Passage to India*. Nonetheless, Forster's choice to identify him as a knowledgeable visitor to India like himself, who ordinarily expresses clear and definitive opinions about Indians and the English, allows Forster to attenuate that narrator's authority in certain kinds of situations, especially ones that even a self-assured English traveler would have trouble summing up from observation, however measured, or from prior knowledge, however extensive or carefully acquired. In contrast to his typically authoritative pronouncements about the motivations and perceptions, culturally instilled biases, and religious beliefs of Englishmen and Indians, Forster's narrator refrains from propounding comparably straightforward theories to account for the novel's most tantalizing mysteries: What actually happened in the cave to make Adela believe that Aziz had attacked her? Why is she possessed to remember the event differently, if incompletely, only while testifying in court, after having timidly doubted her memory for some time? What does it mean that some characters are haunted by perceptions of "ghosts" and "echoes"? And why, in the end, can't Aziz and Fielding be friends as they were before the trial? Whether or not we are disposed to agree with the narrator's theories, such as those that compare suspicious Muslims and hypocritical Westerners or seasoned experts and mercurial natives, is beside the point. My point is that we cannot depend on the narrator to account for the novel's most unconventional and momentous action, and the resulting uncertainty that attaches to his position as narrator has consequences for addressing the novel's central question of why earnest and liberal-minded attempts at understanding cultural difference fail.

Failures of comprehension in *A Passage to India* are often taken as evidence of Forster's own failures of imagination, in two closely related ways:

the unresolved mysteries that accumulate over the course of the text are understood in terms of Forster's Orientalism, that is, his identification of India with a negatively inflected impenetrability and a more positively inflected supernaturalism; and the novel's final impasse, in which Fielding cannot overcome Aziz's resistance to "connecting" with him and cannot comprehend why Aziz would resist, is taken as evidence of Forster's failed liberal vision, inadequate to the task of seeing a future of transformed political relations between Indians and Englishmen in the waning years of the British Raj. But if, following Glissant and Trouillot, we read this novel's comparisons as enabling a new way of coming to know others, not as bearers of fixed differences but rather as actors and narrators of relations whose changeability makes differences themselves changeable, then failures of comprehension in *A Passage to India* should not be taken to evince Forster's inability to imagine more concrete political solutions.

In a different form of multiperspectivalism than we usually consider in discussions of modernist parataxis and juxtaposition, Forster weaves a complex pattern of sometimes well-intended, other times mean-spirited, but characteristically polarizing colonial comparisons aimed at diagnostic comprehension of the other; he then interrupts this pattern at significant turning points with comparisons that cast doubt on the foundations of comprehension and contrast its certainties with views that are both partial and malleable. These alternating comparatisms interact not simply in the exchanges of multiple characters and perspectives but from the perspective of the English narrator himself. By putting into contention and comparing, as it were, a single narrator's two modes of comparison—one that presumes clear and stable polarities, and one that confronts these polarities with "muddles"—Forster suggests the ambivalence and instability underlying his narrator's self-assured pronouncements, especially those that ontologize ethnic identities and the places presumed proper to them. The novel's heterogeneous comparative form, where definitive statements about others more often betray ignorance and prejudice than reliable knowledge, constitutes a rejection of "the confident comparative ambitions" that Paul Gilroy ascribes, citing Hegel's denigration of Africans as prehistoric and prepolitical, to a modern European political imagination that justified its structures of governance and acquisition by infusing a newly "systematic race-thinking" into the conception of history and geography.[12]

This comparative dimension of *A Passage to India*, notwithstanding the novel's apparently realist coherence, aligns it with more overtly disorienting, ambivalent, and contradictory narrations, or confluences of narrations, such as those discussed in the previous two chapters. Urmila Seshagiri identifies this alignment when she lists Forster alongside T. S. Eliot, Ezra Pound, James Joyce, and others who "all remade literary forms by rejecting a vision of the world seen steadily and whole."[13] To be sure, the world is not seen steadily and whole in *A Passage to India*, even if Forster's narrator, like the narrator of *Disgrace*, cannot signal this partiality as Stein's communal chorus does by noting that Melanctha "all her life did not know how to tell a story wholly." The semblance of trustworthy univocal narration in *A Passage to India* is one of the principal means by which Forster establishes the authority of a narratorial persona reminiscent of colonial travel writers and cultural historians, only to undermine that authority incrementally, by contrasting relations of difference the narrator claims to grasp with muddled relations he only tentatively touches on.

Narrating among the Herds

The complex shifts of *A Passage to India*'s narratorial voice intimate the untenability of narrating a history from above the fray of cultural and historical relations. Much has been made of the homoerotic desire that imbues Forster's mythologizing portrayal of a physically beautiful and inaccessible punkah wallah (fan puller), poised on a platform overlooking the courtroom and improbably oblivious to all the contention and chaos that surges up within it.[14] Introduced at the start of the trial from a perspective that could be Adela's or the narrator's own, the "almost naked, and splendidly formed" punkah wallah "seemed to control the proceedings" even as he "seemed apart from human destinies" and "scarcely knew that he existed"; when the trial is over, the "beautiful naked god" remains "unaware that anything unusual had occurred" (Forster, *Passage* 241, 257). Given the blurring of Adela's view and that of the (presumably male) narrator in focalizing the punkah wallah at the start and end of the trial scene, we should note that this inhumanly untouchable character is a figure of heterosexual as well as homosexual desirability. But as compelling as the eroticism of the description is, we should also note the importance of Forster's emphatic idealization of the punkah wallah's utter detachment from the world of language and social connections. He is put on a pedestal, alone in occupying the impossible position of absolute independence from and invulnerability to external influences. In this way, he is the novel's most extreme exemplar of what the narrator, gazing up at him from the conglomerating herds of Indians and

Englishmen below, cannot possibly be—a figure of the disinterested beauty, unattainable to a self-questioning and relativizing modernism, of Flaubert's ideal authorial persona, everywhere sensed but nowhere seen, like God in creation.[15] The narrator can imagine him thus only by removing him completely from the sphere of authorial language and observational discernment. Ironically, the sovereignty the narrator desires is so alien to his own position that he associates it with the most extreme condition of subalternity in his midst.

Of course, to suggest that the narrator and everyone else in the courtroom except for the godlike untouchable are represented as enmeshed in historical relations and thus inevitably part of the conglomerating and, to an extent, intermixing herds in and beyond the courtroom may seem mischievous in light of the narrator's sharp distinctions between "the herd-instinct" and Fielding's preferable independence of mind.[16] The narrator's generalizations about "the herd" convey his disapproval of intellectual uniformity based on blind loyalty to one's communal affiliations, as well as a desire to occupy a position of intellectual independence from which to understand what communally inculcated biases prevent others from recognizing and admitting. In his essays and private diaries as well, Forster defines intellectual independence as a triumph of authentic personal feeling over broad social pressures to adapt one's views to the norm—hence his famous claim in the *Nation* in 1938, "I hate the idea of causes, and if I had to choose between betraying my country and betraying my friend I hope I should have the guts to betray my country."[17] In *A Passage to India*, Forster associates Fielding's independent thinking with his capacity for true friendship and, in Leela Gandhi's terms, a *philoxenic* friendship that brings "the disruptive category of risk" to communalist and statist positions of belonging and security, or presumed security.[18] By associating independent thinking not with self-sufficiency but with an openness to "*philoxenic* risk," Forster raises the prospect of a salutary vulnerability and susceptibility to unforeseeable transcultural bonds. Such bonds are at variance with the ominously "*homophilic* loyalties" of McBryde, who advises Fielding to stop thinking for himself on behalf of his accused friend: "But at a time like this there's no room for—well—personal views. The man who doesn't toe the line is lost" (Gandhi 29; Forster, *Passage* 190).

Acknowledging that the authority of Forster's narrator is uneven and in this way evokes his historical and cultural positioning reinforces rather than denies Forster's pains to juxtapose the flawed cosmopolitan liberalism of the narrator and Fielding to the imperious bigotry of McBryde and his colonialist counterparts. Forster's ideals of personal authenticity, exemplified by Fielding, are not incompatible with Trouillot's suggestion that an authentic sense of historicity derives from admitting one's own partiality and uncertainty as a historically situated actor and narrator, and the impossibility of acting and narrating as an impartial, nonhistorical observer. Though Forster, in *A Passage to India* and throughout his writings, invests his ethical hopes not in "vast, world historical ideas," as Aamir Mufti points out, but in the individual's capacity to make soundly reasoned judgments informed by personal bonds,[19] a distinguishing feature of his individualism is that he does not imagine anyone as unconstrained by the influence of their particular experiences of culture. On the contrary, Forster portrays even the unconventional Fielding as a creature of his distinct history: "New impressions crowded on him, but they were not the orthodox new impressions; the past conditioned them, and so it was with his mistakes" (*Passage* 64). This is no less true of the impressions of the Englishman who narrates *A Passage to India*.

A Passage to India is structured as a succession of occasions for intercultural commingling, whose moral and political significance radiates out from the mostly unwilled and unforeseeable alterations and disruptions that issue from them. For Forster's English travelers and expatriates, inadvertently transformative encounters with others interrupt the streamlined discourse of imperialist cultural history their community takes for granted, with its presumptions of English colonial entitlement pitted righteously against the menace of native insubordination. The juxtaposition of this cultural discourse's clear-cut binary oppositions to mutually constitutive interactions that contradict them implies the epistemology of grasping, whether aimed at repressive division or sympathetic connection, to be an anxious denial of volatile relations that cannot be so tidily categorized or stabilized. Forster's narrator describes the British, Hindu, and Muslim worlds as discrete on the whole, and yet in overstating the divides between them he hints at the possibility of what they deny (for example, that Adela, having "nothing of the vagrant in her blood," has no sexual desire for Aziz, or that the punkah wallah lacks the capacity to notice, much less contemplate, a spirited Indian audience's triumph over British authorities; *Passage* 169, 257). If we recognize Forster's Raj as a space of intense and ongoing encounter between white English expatriates, Muslim Indians, and Hindu Indians, then the insistent assertions, by both the narrator and other characters, of the solidity of identities and the divides that separate them appear to serve as a discursive guard against the inevitable consequence of such encounters: a state of relations in which at least some degree of intermixing irreparably changes the character of bounded communities.

Notably, it is the English who perceive new relations and their transformative potential as threats to autonomy and self-possession; these perceptions arise in a largely unexamined context in which the English have customarily assumed their political dominion to ensure their dominion over social and cultural processes in the colony more broadly, not least over the representation of colonial encounters. The narrator only lightly acknowledges the threat of these new relations, but through the women's lost sense of their autonomy and self-possession—in the caves and in court—Forster obliquely represents how the creolizing effects of coming into contact with cultural difference can insinuate themselves into conditions of dominion and, however traumatically and involuntarily for the individuals involved, work to change those conditions. We see this in the plot's most dramatic twists: the crises that Mrs. Moore and Adela undergo when they feel themselves overcome in the close confines they share with Indians in the Marabar Caves, and Adela's radical retrospective vision of the caves when she falls into a trance before a mixed audience in the courtroom and, forgetting herself, is able to tell a different history.

Through his alternately authoritative and tentative English narrator, Forster evokes a struggle to make sense of the transformation of communities and cultures in contact from the perspective of those who cannot yet admit their ongoing and irreversible effects. Thus, to connect Adela's distress in the cave to Mrs. Moore's, which is to connect Adela's sexual confusion and anxious ambivalence about marriage to Mrs. Moore's loss of faith in the linguistic and religious order familiar to her, we cannot depend on the narrator's explicit account alone. Forster puts "the personal" into unstable fields of communal and historical relation too broad, intricate, and full of unknowns for any one speaker to describe reliably. But once the authoritative narrator comes to appear as another communally embedded character with partial and changeable views, then other speakers become essential for their own partial and changeable views, which goad, constrain, supplement, and contradict each other. Forster makes these perspectival dynamics central to his portrayal of Adela's testimony, to which we will return at the close of this chapter. By bringing the constitutive interaction of differently positioned narrative views to the fore of a novel that is also a revisionist history of colonial India, Forster makes an easily overlooked contribution, both aesthetic and historiographic, to a specifically antiauthoritarian practice of multiperspectivalism that Milan Kundera has called "dethroning the narrator."[20]

Though Kundera does not discuss Forster in his theories of the novel, his readings of European, North American, and Antillean narrative interventions in imperial and totalitarian historical discourses help us to recognize *A Passage to India* as part of a broad-based and still ongoing interimperial literary rebellion against narratorial authority, especially when that authority is claimed in contexts where cultures or communities coexist in asymmetrical relations of power. Notwithstanding the differences between French colonial policies of assimilation in the Antilles and the British Empire's frankly separatist "indirect rule" policies in India, these policies' shared basis in expansionist rule by force,[21] as well as their shared deployment of racial categories to justify the perpetuation of that rule,[22] makes Francophone literary challenges to imperial narrative and historiographic conventions more pertinent to the interpretation of *A Passage to India* than either Anglophone or Francophone literary critics have acknowledged. Though French colonialism, slavery, and their legacy in the Antilles may seem distant from Forster's British Raj, Martinican *créoliste* Patrick Chamoiseau's exuberant dispersion of narratorial knowledge and responsibility to evoke a demotic counterhistory offers, like Trouillot's historiography and Glissant's cultural theory, retrospective insight into Forster's more circumspect modes of dethroning the colonial narrator. Embodying Kundera's multiperspectival ideal and building on—but also with—Glissant's anti-universalist theories of difference as essential to dynamics of relation, Chamoiseau's fiction attenuates narratorial authority to make possible a politically engaged creolist aesthetics that overtakes his well-known exegeses on *créolité*.[23] Reading *A Passage to India* in relation to Chamoiseau clarifies what is new about Forster's earnest and well-meaning chroniclers of history—his English narrator and Adela Quested, more briefly—whose knowledge of what they are narrating becomes unsettled and uncertain in "mixed" company. Through their vacillations Forster enacts a dawning European awareness of creolization, with its unpredictable mixtures and dispersions of cultural memory, as the inadvertent consequence and unruly threat to imperial aspirations to coherence.

Dethroning the Narrator and Creolizing the Story

"Tearing through the curtain" of preconceptions, Kundera argues in *The Curtain: An Essay in Seven Parts* (*Le Rideau: Essai en sept partis*), novelistic aesthetics can uniquely disrupt intellectual uniformity (comparable to what

Forster calls the "herd-instinct"): "it is *the identifying sign of the art of the novel*" to replace unquestioned myopic views (views from behind "the curtain") with multiple juxtaposed and interconnecting views (*Curtain* 92). The multiperspectival structures characteristic of the novel are for Kundera what mark the genre as both modern and worldly: "For narration as it had existed since the dawn of time became the novel when the author was no longer content with a mere 'story' but opened all the great windows onto the world that stretched out in every direction. Thus were joined to a 'story' other 'stories,' episodes, descriptions, observations, reflections, and the author was faced with very complex, very heterogeneous material onto which he was obliged, like an architect, to impose a form" (153; trans. mod.). To develop his theory of the novel, Kundera traces two kinds of comparison—the comparison of perspectives within novels and the comparison of novels across cultures and eras—whose "echoes" are the novel's means to move beyond "individual psychologies" and "introspective memory" for their own sake in order to "plumb the enigma of identity" in "super-individual" (*sur-individuel*) terms: "To understand we must compare," he writes, citing Austrian novelist Hermann Broch; we "must put identity to the test of comparisons" (161). As an example of the comparative work that novels can do to relate the individual to larger collectives, so that even exceptional personalities and relationships are understood in more broadly expansive relational terms than the characters involved can grasp, Kundera points to the "trailing echo, the light tread of memory growing faint" at the conclusion of *Anna Karenina*. What seems for a time the monumental tragedy of Anna's suicide and Vronsky's despair is relativized by Tolstoy's final shift into Levin's prosaic days on his farm (152–53). In comparative narrative forms such as this, Kundera sees a solution to the novelistic tradition's own frequent overestimation of individuality to the neglect of a broader "existential problematic" of historical relations, affiliations, and interdependencies. This neglect, at once a literary and a historiographic matter, is connected to "the problem of the abusive power of the single narrator" (161, 166). Pervasively multiperspectival novels in particular, such as Pierre Choderlos de Laclos's *Les Liaisons dangereuses* and William Faulkner's *As I Lay Dying*, "are caught up in the same desire to break that power, to dethrone the narrator [*détrôner le narrateur*] (and their revolt not only takes aim at the narrator in its literary-theory sense; it also attacks the atrocious power of that Narrator who, from time immemorial, has been telling mankind one single approved, imposed version of everything there is)" (*Curtain* 166; trans. mod.; *Rideau* 202).[24]

Kundera's distrust of the single narrator, endowed with an abusive and atrocious power, coincides with his view that dominant historical narratives foreclose the narration of other histories by fostering a false sense of certainty about past events and experiences. We can extrapolate from Kundera's prior reflections on the transformative nature of memory and his subsequent reflections on the value of narrative multiperspectivalism that multiperspectival novels have the potential to unsettle "our certainties about the past" and "History itself" by making us mindful that speakers who narrate past events as they remember them are not simply recording those events but transforming them into their own creations (*Curtain* 148, 166). Novels that put the transformative nature of memory and narration on display cast doubt on any historical narrative that excludes from consideration not just contending historical narratives but its own fictionalizing nature, the fictionalizing nature of the memories that constitute its own vision of history. Kundera writes that "beyond the slender margin of the incontestable (there is no doubt that Napoleon lost the battle of Waterloo)" lie the myriad approximations and untruths of "all the testimonies that historiography relies on" (148–49). In highlighting this distinction, he suggests the political value of novels that confront us with irresolvable and opaque aspects of remembering and narrating memories to others (148–49).

Reflecting on a persistent European imperial bias in historical accounts of the Haitian Revolution (not only by Europeans and North Americans but by Haitians as well), Trouillot poses the question, "Can historical narratives convey plots that are unthinkable in the world within which these narratives take place? How does one write a history of the impossible?" (73). For Kundera, it would seem that the answer to this is multiperspectival comparatism, a narrative practice that confronts readers with the political dynamics of relation and their impact on processes of personal memory and public commemoration. It is in the twentieth-century novel that he finds the most politically subversive comparative forms and modes, "previously unthinkable" methods of relating cultural histories separated by vast distances and discrepant positions in dominant canons of historical knowledge (Kundera, *Curtain* 161). Again, Kundera's theory of multiperspectival comparative narration matters because he shifts the discussion from multiperspectivalism as a means of exploring individual perspectives and psychological dispositions for their own sake to its possibilities for disrupting isolated worldviews and territorial ontologies of identity that undergird imperial and totalitarian configurations of power.

Of course, though Kundera does not refer to it, the transformation of personal and cultural memory in the comparative narration of an intercultural history is a central theme of *A Passage to India*. Some of Forster's images of this transformation are depersonalized, as when Esmiss Esmoor's legend spreads through the crowd and into Indians' collective memory of the trial. Others appear at first peculiar to individual characters, like those who contend with "echoes" and "ghosts" they cannot explain, though these echoes and ghosts resemble (and indeed echo) those of other characters, so that even private demons such as these signify points of connection rather than psychological or historical idiosyncrasies. Forster's echo is a figure for what remains of a past experience that someone is struggling to remember and understand, an experience incomprehensibly foreign in the moment and therefore all the harder to recall and recount without confusion. Kundera's echo is not the sort that continues to haunt someone already confounded; his interest lies in the metamorphosis of what is recognized and assimilated smoothly in the present into traces that resonate with what has been forgotten, but that inescapably alter it in the process. Despite this difference, Forster's portrayal of memory's fallible but transformative effects in the narration of history anticipates Kundera's framing of novelistic form within a broader discussion of historical narratives' inevitable alteration of the past. Both attend closely to the struggle waged within historical narratives between forces of obliteration and, if not unmediated conservation, at least transformation that might commemorate perspectives made minor by conquest. If "the perpetual activity of forgetting gives our every act a ghostly, unreal, hazy quality," as Kundera argues, a more particular kind of forgetting threatens to follow imperial and totalitarian conquests: the obliteration of cultural identities cast out of new expansionist regimes of knowledge and history, or made marginal and ultimately unrecognizable within them (*Curtain* 149, 155-58). The twentieth-century novel's increasingly radical and wide-ranging juxtapositions of cultures push against the forces of this obliteration.

To illustrate how literature might thwart the forgetting of the nondominant in imperial histories, Kundera offers a juxtaposition of his own. He compares his native Czech literature's struggles to define a distinctly Czech communal identity in the wake of Russia's invasion of Czechoslovakia in 1968 with black Antillean literature's struggles, beginning with Césaire's *Cahier d'un retour au pays natal*, to answer the question "*Who are we?*" after the "*fundamental and foundational forgetting*" of ancestral languages and traditions that Africans' deportation, enslavement, and colonial subjugation in the Americas entailed (Kundera, *Curtain* 158). Extrapolating from Kundera's comparison and his subsequent discussion of multiperspectivalism, we can elaborate this reference to Césaire by noting that it is in the *Cahier* where we first see, from the comparatist perspective of an amorphous speaker who is racially nondominant in France but verbally and intellectually privileged in Martinique, a polemical lyric encounter of narratorial perspectives, memories, aspirations, and languages. Kundera does not discuss Césaire in this respect but praises intercultural juxtapositions in Antillean novels such as Jacques Stephen Alexis's *L'Espace d'un cillement* (*In the Flicker of an Eyelid*), which portrays Haitians living under US occupation alongside Marines who occupy the country,[25] and Alejo Carpentier's *El siglo de las luces* (*Explosion in a Cathedral*), which removes the French Revolution's new technology of the guillotine from an exclusively French metropolitan context to explore its social and political effects in the Caribbean (162).[26] To Kundera's examples of twentieth-century Antillean novels whose comparative structures situate individuals' actions and affective experiences within far-reaching "super-individual" and intercultural dynamics of relation, we could also add two earlier Antillean nonfiction narratives, both contemporaneous with Césaire's *Cahier*, that boldly juxtaposed dominant and nondominant histories: C. L. R. James's *The Black Jacobins* (1938) and Eric Williams's *Capitalism and Slavery* (1944).[27] James's and Williams's early global comparatist histories departed from the preponderantly nationalist and Eurocentric histories of French Enlightenment and British abolitionism, respectively, tracing these revolutionary developments to political and economic imperatives in Europe, the Antilles, the United States, and (in Williams's case) India.

Comparative forms that Kundera takes to be distinguishing features of both modern novelistic aesthetics and world literature have had a heightened presence in Martinican literature, no doubt partly due to the formative influence of Césaire's highly comparative poetics. The importance of comparatism, both intratextual and intertextual, to Martinican literature may also be due to Martinique's geographic and cultural position, as Kundera argues in another, contemporaneous essay republished in his collection *Encounter* (*Une Rencontre*). "Martinique: a multiple intersection (*intersection multiple*); a crossroads among the continents; a tiny slip of land where France, Africa, the Americas meet," though the beauty of this multiple encounter, he writes, is lost on France, Africa, and America because of Martinique's diminutive size and relative powerlessness.[28] I want to bring together Kundera's discussion of Chamoiseau, whom he considers repeatedly when theorizing the novel, with his general conception of narrative multiperspectivalism as a form of political and historiographic defiance.

Kundera implies in the passage above that Martinique's particularity consists in the heterogeneity of its cultural memory. In *The Curtain* he champions novelistic comparisons that keep a heterogeneous cultural memory alive by replacing monologism with a vision formed of disparate perspectives, and whose purview extends to the structural relations that make these perspectives possible; in this regard, Kundera's theory of the novel may be read as closely aligned with Trouillot's historiography. In *Encounter*, his characterization of Martinique as a multiple encounter (alluding, as I noted in the previous chapter, to a line from Césaire's "Corps perdu") suggests why the concentrated diversity of a former colony might be fertile ground for producing such novelistic comparisons. Martinique, like the novels Kundera admires, is a site where distant and endangered pasts contend with forces that would suppress them, persisting as echoes with the potential to invoke histories worth narrating.

The Curtain and *Encounter* both include essays from the early 1990s that put Chamoiseau's narrative art in wide-ranging comparative literary contexts. Kundera's readings of Chamoiseau's novels in both essays center on *Solibo magnifique*, published in 1988 and before the appearance of *Texaco* (1992),[29] the Prix Goncourt-winning novel that Chamoiseau dedicated to Kundera's wife, the musician Véra Kundera, as well as to Glissant.[30] Though he did not revise these essays to include analysis of *Texaco* before republishing them, much of his discussion of *Solibo magnifique* is directly relevant to what has become Chamoiseau's most celebrated novel. Cautioning against reading *Solibo magnifique* as "an exotic, local novel, focused on a character unimaginable elsewhere: a folk storyteller (*un conteur populaire*)," Kundera argues that "Chamoiseau's novel deals with one of the greatest events in the history of culture: the encounter between oral literature in its last hours and written literature as it is being born" (*Rencontre* 135; *Encounter* 95). Chamoiseau's literary persona has two designations: the *Marqueur de paroles* or Marker of Words, which Réjouis and Vinokurov memorably translate as the Word Scratcher; and Oiseau de Cham, a play on his surname and *oiseau de champ*, or bird of the field. Oiseau de Cham appears in *Solibo magnifique* as the writer who transcribes the words of the *conteur* or oral storyteller named Solibo, and he reappears in *Texaco* to transcribe the words of Marie-Sophie Laborieux, the oral storyteller and community leader who founded Texaco, a Creole squatters' settlement on land abandoned by the Texaco oil company at the margins of Martinique's upscaling capital city, Fort-de-France. Kundera reads *Solibo magnifique* as an "encounter across centuries," a quintessentially modern novel that revives the *conteur* but regards him as a figure from the past in a way that novels prior to the nineteenth century were not yet poised to do: "from Rabelais to Laurence Sterne, the echo of the oral storyteller's voice continued to sound in novels; writing, the writer was *speaking* to the reader, addressing him, insulting him, flattering him; in turn, reading, the reader was also *hearing* the novel's author" (*Encounter* 95; trans. mod.). To consider how Chamoiseau revives the *conteur* but also significantly complicates her authorial and narratorial status, let us start with a brief summary of *Texaco*.

Sprawling and intricate, *Texaco* is a finished novel by a single author that presents itself, through shifting frames of reference and self-reference, as a multiauthored, self-reflexive history still in the making; it is a metafiction in the guise of a metahistory. In the fictional world it inhabits, it is the Word Scratcher's painstakingly transcribed, edited, and revised account of the oral history narrated to him by an aged Marie-Sophie Laborieux shortly before her death. The novel begins near the end of this history with the arrival of an invader—a young urban planner who has come to raze the Texaco settlement "for a modernizing city council that wanted him to rationalize and expand the city's space, and conquer the pockets of insalubrity which were a crown of thorns around it" (Chamoiseau, *Texaco* 26; trans. mod.). The urban planner is felled by a stone thrown by an unidentified squatter and then, by local accounts, "resurrected," first revived by a medicine man named Papa Totone and then converted by Marie-Sophie, whose narration to him of the long history of struggle that led up to Texaco's founding miraculously transforms his initial mission of destruction (or "renovation," as he had thought) into a passionate resolve to preserve this colony of the dispossessed. Marie-Sophie's narration to the urban planner, which she calls her "sermon," constitutes an additional narrative layer: the history that Marie-Sophie narrates to the Word Scratcher is an attempted reconstruction of the history she has already narrated to the urban planner to save Texaco. Thus, the novel unfolds as the written version of Marie-Sophie's oral account to the Word Scratcher of her prior oral account to the urban planner. These three narrative layers are supplemented by the Word Scratcher's inclusion in the written version, coextensive with Chamoiseau's novel, of various other texts: a historical outline at the start of the book, extending from

3000 BCE to 1989, entitled "Milestones in Our Attempts to Conquer the City"; the Word Scratcher's excerpted letters, notes, and final reflections (which conclude the book) on his literary and historiographic project, especially his efforts to conceive a writing that might convey the mesmerizing poetry of Marie-Sophie's spoken words; excerpted passages from the many notebooks (*cahiers*) in which Marie-Sophie has recorded her thoughts, memories, and inherited stories, and which she entrusts to the Word Scratcher before her death; and excerpted passages from the urban planner's notes to the Word Scratcher after his conversion. We never learn the precise words that Marie-Sophie used in her "sermon" to the urban planner; what we have is an approximation of the vibrancy and abundance of its collective vision through a collage-like conglomeration of juxtaposed and overlapping fragments of texts and testimonies, each of which would be indecipherably partial had the Word Scratcher not positioned it in comparative and dialogic relation to the others. This gives a figurative form to the interdependent communal relations of the characters narrating and testifying, characters who, far from presuming themselves to be detached observers, repeatedly identify themselves as members of the Texaco community or in relation to it; as Marie-Sophie remarks at one point, "saying 'me' is like saying 'us'" (314; trans. mod.). Even the French urban planner, after his conversion, identifies himself as belonging to this same "us": "I suddenly got the feeling that Texaco came from the deepest reaches of ourselves and that I had to learn everything. And even: to relearn everything" (165–66).

Chamoiseau's narrative practice is rare in its characteristic emphasis, especially in *Texaco*, on the communal and interdependent nature of the personal. Texaco's residents have little power individually, but as a coalition of idiosyncratic, intermixing but never merging voices, they manage to hold their ground against the centralizing and standardizing forces of *l'En-ville* ("the In-city," Fort-de-France's privileged center) that would expel them from the city as nonconforming public nuisances. Chamoiseau makes a strong and willful woman, a poor black woman, the visionary founder, the people's historian, the indispensable narrator Oiseau de Cham calls "the source" (*l'informatrice*), who guides and galvanizes not only her fellow squatters but also a man who designs cities and civic spaces and another man who writes about them. And yet Marie-Sophie's exceptional displays of courage, fortitude, and eloquence typically arise out of her encounters with others and the guidance and assistance they provide. She is a master *conteur*—"I had never felt such profound authority emanate from anyone," the Word Scratcher writes of her (Chamoiseau, *Texaco* 387)—but the nature of her authority is different from that accorded to migrant and exilic men, from Aeneas to the Buendías, who found communities and shape histories through solitary inventions and individual military prowess. The stories Marie-Sophie tells are the stories of her neighbors and ancestors, and her purpose is one of relating (in the intertwined senses of narrating and connecting) these stories to audiences who also figure in those stories (notably, the urban planner, the Word Scratcher, and the mayor, Aimé Césaire), whose reception matters not, primarily, in individual terms but in communal ones, not as means of developing their characters or laying bare their psychological interiority but as means of inspiring them to give what they can to defend and fortify Texaco.

The raconteur's narration takes form in response to an audience of listeners; in this lies the ethico-political significance of Chamoiseau's raconteur. By reviving the figure of the raconteur and endowing her with the gift to relate the Martinican people's own versions of their history, Chamoiseau directly contests an ethos of possessive mastery with an ethos of negotiation and collaborative creation. In *Texaco* (as in *Solibo Magnifique*) the dialogic and mutually defining relationship of the storyteller to her audience converges with that of the oral storyteller to the writer because the writer is also part of the oral storyteller's audience. Oiseau de Cham's own authority as a storyteller and occasional narrator is relativized by his dependence on the oral storyteller's improvised narration, which forms the bulk of his book; he subordinates his own narratorial position to hers as he struggles, in vain he fears, to translate the beauty of orality into a literature that does it justice. In a resounding evocation of nothingness reminiscent of Forster's, he looks at Marie-Sophie's aging body and fears the day her extraordinary speech will disappear: "I felt weak, unworthy of all of it, unable to transmit so much wealth. Her memory would go with her like Solibo's, and there was nothing, nothing, nothing I could do except make her talk and put some order into what she churned out" (Chamoiseau, *Texaco* 389). However, his humble position as a "marker of words" or "word scratcher" is at the same time the indispensable position of conservator: the whimsical *conteur* depends on the writer's methodical, preservationist efforts to translate her visionary talk into a text that might survive in legible form: "She told me her stories in a rather difficult way. Sometimes, though she hid it from me, she had memory gaps, repeated or contradicted herself. . . . From time to time, I consulted [her notebooks] in order to compose what she had told me, to compare what I thought I had heard, and, if need be, correct a voluntary omission, a reflexive lie" (387–88; trans. mod.). Chamoiseau's storytellers, both *conteur* and writer, thus build the story of Texaco (and *Texaco*) together, while also building with the supplementary, sometimes contradictory accounts of other *conteurs*, writers, speakers, and interlocutors. Marie-Sophie's oral history is suffused with the reminiscences of slavery and plantation life passed down to her by her father, the former slave Esternome; Oiseau de Cham describes her as having "all her life chased after her father's words" (387; trans. mod.). Neither Marie-Sophie nor Oiseau de Cham claims to understand fully what all these stories mean, separately or together, nor do they accept them all as fully accurate, but comprehensibility and coherence are not the measure of Texaco and its history. Chamoiseau represents both narrating and coming to know the cultural history of a people as a messy and continual process of mixing and building that cannot be tidied up into a transparent and conclusive state of certainty.

Chamoiseau's revival of the narratorial personage of the *conteur*, improvising before a reactive audience whose presence and imagined perspectives inform the narrative, is closely associated with his elaborate creolizing of the French language. His French is creolized less in the sense that it resembles Creole as actually spoken in the Caribbean—"no Martinican talks like that," Kundera writes—and more in the sense that it takes inspiration from Creole's colloquial conversational tone and amalgamating lexical inventions (*Encounter* 94). Kundera values Chamoiseau's literary ingenuity (which Oiseau de Cham portrays as the ingenuity of the *conteurs* whose stories he records) for the authorial freedom it asserts, "the liberty of a bilingual writer who refuses to grant absolute authority to one or the other of his languages, and has the courage to disobey" (94). This freedom is not one of detachment, however; the verbal and diegetic liberties Chamoiseau takes afford a novelistic multiperspectivalism in which narrators continually amalgamate other viewpoints, in particular viewpoints other than ascendant or conquering ones, into their own. Even as he transgresses linguistic rules and literary norms whose culturally privileged status he identifies with the centralizing regimes of French imperialism and a globalizing US corporatism, he shows, pragmatically and compassionately, how those rules and norms have come to be trusted, if also transformed, sources of meaning for many French Antilleans. In *Texaco*, for instance, the Word Scratcher's friend and rival, the Francophile Haitian squatter Ti-Cirique, aspires to write in "a French more French than that of the French," while Marie-Sophie, the novel's foremost advocate of Creole culture as exemplified by the Texaco settlement she founded, does not see the aesthetic merit of what she calls her "poor epic"—the very model of the language the Word Scratcher yearns to set down on paper—and begs him "to 'fix up' her speech into good French" (Chamoiseau, *Texaco* 9, 388). Both displaying the disorderly poetic beauty of Creole-inspired wordplay and narrative structure and rendering it unrecognizable to characters acculturated through a universalist discourse of French humanism, Chamoiseau suggests how deeply ingrained in the prevailing common sense of a linguistically plural French Antilles is the notion that French is the preeminent language of humanistic expression and that "there is a 'right' way to use the language," as Glissant writes in his critique of "apoetical" monolingualisms (*Poetics* 114, 112). In Chamoiseau's fiction, it is the dynamic commingling of an authoritative French and a demotic Creole, rather than the literary privileging of authentic Creole over French (as in the creolophone novels of Chamoiseau's fellow *créoliste* Raphaël Confiant), that works to upend the authority of an elite and exclusionary humanistic French by adulterating its reputed purity and order.

Chamoiseau's refusal to leave intact the colonialist dichotomy between a literary French and a colloquial Creole is inseparable from his refusal of related, similarly politicized and racialized dichotomies: the realist novel and the fantastical folktale, documentary history and oral testimony, and writing and orality more broadly. As the literary enactment of a Creole *conte* being turned into book, *Texaco* throws these dichotomies, and the fixity of their opposed concepts, into a muddle, a messy state of *emmêlement* (intermixing, entanglement) that elsewhere, in his critical essays, Chamoiseau contrasts with the oppositional thinking intrinsic to domination. In the following passage, he credits the *conteur*'s characteristically plural and inclusive narratorial voice with mixing up and relativizing authoritarian power relations, making the *conteur* not the glorified spokesman for a community that cannot speak but a medium of their multivocal expression: "In the seething world of human beings, races, and violence that was plantation life; among these human scraps deprived of their Being and their speech by the condition of dominating or being dominated, there will rise up one who will express the language of all, who will make us speak together. That one is the Creole storyteller. And the speech of the Storyteller, gushing out in the world of Diversity, is always foundational. It mixes up and relativizes."[31] This passage is part of a larger commentary on the figure of the *conteur* in St.-John Perse's poem *Anabase* and on what Chamoiseau takes to be the alliance of the *conteur* and the poet who, perhaps inadvertently in Perse's case, relativizes cultural divisions presumed by *le conquistador*. Chamoiseau has described his own intellectual journey as one from waging opposition to one of searching out interrelations, so that he can now propose extricating Césaire and Glissant from the "identitarian irons" that have long held them fast in opposition to Perse, a white Guadeloupian poet and diplomat who espoused French universalism (135). Chamoiseau develops this point in a chapter structured as a direct address to Perse (who died in 1975): "We opposed you to Césaire. Césaire was the slave in struggle. And you were the Master. That created dynamically stimulating poles. We needed these very poor readings to serve as fuel in the struggles we were waging. We didn't know how greatly this reading impoverished Césaire, just as much as it impoverished you. We didn't understand that, in the work of great poets placed by misfortune in a colonial land, testimony would always be comprehensive (*entier*)" (188). Chamoiseau argues that the poetic vision of Perse, a "conqueror but with a different consciousness" ("conquistador mais dans une conscience autre"), combines the author's aspiration to universalism with his Creole consciousness of diversity (202). The intermixing of these opposing perspectives culminates in a "beautiful testimony" in which a speaker pursues "a new immanence in what moves, gets mixed up, modifies itself without end" (203, 202).

When we consider Chamoiseau's novelistic revival of the storyteller as a raconteur explicitly addressing an audience, together with his ideal of poetic language as a kind of super-individual testimony able to supersede isolated personal views, including those of the one testifying, by evincing a creolized consciousness of contending views in relation, we are probing how Chamoiseau, and hence also Forster, reimagines the relational dimensions of narration in contexts of social stratification and sustained intercultural contact. Chamoiseau's irreverent mixing of standard French with Martinican Creole so that French becomes more receptive and less prescriptive is one of the ways *Texaco* announces itself as a new kind of history for a new kind of community, a history and a community not founded on the domination of others. Another, closely related way, and one that receives less attention, is its creolizing of narratorial relations so that storytellers and their audiences, no longer polarized, make and remake history through intimate exchange, a kind of *donner-avec* or giving-with. Chamoiseau reconfigures the relations between narrators and audiences in such a way as to replace an ethos of possessive mastery, both imperial and narratorial, with an ethos of interdependent and collaborative building. This reconfiguration entails a surrender of narrators' presumed mastery of their subjects and a consciousness of their relative positions within an ongoing dynamic of intermixing, with all the muddles and mix-ups that intermixing brings.

Ecstasies of Dethronement

Throughout *Texaco* and in the climactic trial scene in *A Passage to India*, the fitful overcoming of identitarian divisions is linked to a productively uncertain and self-questioning mode of narration figured as testimony, given to audiences whose own words and views animate and enter into it in unpredictable and mutually constitutive exchanges over which narrators and audiences have only limited control. In *A Passage to India*, the potentially constitutive influence of an audience on the story told to it is the subject of an exchange between Fielding and McBryde, in which Fielding requests to see Adela after Aziz's arrest. Fielding tells McBryde that he believes Adela is "under some hideous delusion" and that he wants "to ask her if she is certain, dead certain, that it was Aziz who followed her into the cave" (Forster, *Passage* 186, 188). When McBryde offers to have his wife confirm this with Adela, Fielding persists:

> "But *I* wanted to ask her. I want someone who believes in him to ask her."
> "What difference does that make?"
> "She is among people who disbelieve in Indians."
> "Well, she tells her own story, doesn't she?"
> "I know, but she tells it to you." (188)

Of course, McBryde dismisses Fielding's argument and denies his request, but the exchange has an important narrative function in quite directly preparing us for Adela's recantation later in the courtroom, where for the first time she must tell her story to a mixed audience of Indians and Englishmen—skeptics, believers, and, most important, the supremely indifferent punkah wallah, whose presence disrupts the adversarial trial structure and relativizes Adela's understanding of her own position in the world: "Something in his aloofness impressed the girl from middle-class England, and rebuked the narrowness of her sufferings. In virtue of what had she collected this roomful of people together?" (242). Already in Fielding's exchange with McBryde, Forster prepares us to anticipate a story changing when its narrator's perceived audience changes. What makes Fielding's suggestion a daring one is that the story in question is a historical account whose narrator (Adela) makes truth claims that are credible only so long as she appears independent of her audience's desire to hear one story and not another.

Forster and Chamoiseau question the independence of narrators and other speaking subjects at their novels' most pivotal points by juxtaposing presumptions of certainty to unexpected encounters with difference that culminate in radical learning. What distinguishes characters who learn through such encounters from those who, like McBryde, never do is their receptivity to being unsettled and guided by elliptical meaning that escapes the interpretive frameworks familiar to them. On entering into unknown and unexpected territory, the learning invader is unmoored from the conceptual comforts of home and, once ecstatic (in the fundamental sense of being mentally out of place), consents to an exchange that transforms the story they tell. In *Texaco* these pivotal events of transformative learning include the momentous conversion of the French urban planner to the cause of Creole squatters he had intended to displace. He accounts for his own conversion by pointing to the edifying unclarity and disorderliness of "the Word" (*la Parole*) given him by Marie-Sophie, hailing her as "the Old Woman who gave me new eyes" through "the chaos of her poor stories" (Chamoiseau, *Texaco* 165-66).[32] It is the urban planner's lack of certainty in the first place that makes Marie-Sophie try to relate her community's history to him: "And most of all, I didn't feel in him that inner stiffness that establishes certainties. He was a questioning guy. There was yet a chance" (26; trans. mod.).

In another transformative encounter, a despondent and increasingly apolitical Marie-Sophie hears the *Cahier d'un retour au pays natal* read aloud and then reads it herself, her "matador demeanor" restored by "the magic of words which flew from a tomtom" (Chamoiseau, *Texaco* 366). Marie-Sophie's revival by Césaire's poem echoes (in Kundera's sense) her account of the urban planner's revival by Marie-Sophie's *conte* (the event with which Oiseau de Cham opens the book but that occurs after Marie-Sophie's encounter with Césaire). In both instances, a polyvalent, aspirationally demotic writing figured as testimony displaces certainties not by imparting new ones but by making an audience recognize the value of mystification in the process of learning to unlearn a dominant common sense. Marie-Sophie recounts being enthralled on hearing Ti-Cirique read aloud from Césaire's *Cahier*, imagining herself magically transfused by the poem's spirit of negritude: "A sentence suddenly took possession of me. I asked him to repeat it for me. Then I took the book from him and read by myself, without understanding squat, letting myself be carried by the invocatory words that turned my blood nègre" (366; trans. mod.).[33] This encounter with difference through poetic testimony sparks another: the unlikely dialogue and collaboration between a reinvigorated Marie-Sophie and the solitary Césaire himself, whom she must persuade, like the urban planner, to support the cause of Texaco. Emboldened by her reading of his poem, Marie-Sophie rallies a group of women from the settlement (while the men, including Ti-Cirique, are too timid to join them) to seek out "Papa Césaire" in what Chamoiseau pointedly portrays as his gated garden. When Césaire bristles at the intrusion, she recites back to him the words that had taken possession of her, but whose precise meaning still eludes her. In this way, she gives back to Césaire the words he gave her, winning his trust by sharing in their power without feeling fully in command of the words she speaks or deferring to their author's authority either. The *Cahier*'s most important meaning in *Texaco* is generated by its communal exchange: its recitation to her, the Creole storyteller, by the Francophile Ti-Cirique, and then to the illustrious Césaire by the squatter Marie-Sophie, is a sharing, a giving-with, that instigates further collaboration among characters and texts whose significant differences do not polarize them but, on the contrary, enable them to supplement each other's efforts. Their collaboration does not necessitate a strong or secure sense of identification (based in an appropriative practice of comparison) so much as an awakened sense of how each relates to the other, and what each might do differently from the other's point of view.

Near *Texaco*'s conclusion, Oiseau de Cham takes over the narration from Marie-Sophie after her death, describing his "scribbling of that magic chronicle" as a transformation of her multitudinous speech into writing and, in the process, a transformation of himself that reveals the limits of his learning (Chamoiseau, *Texaco* 390): "She mixed Creole and French, a vulgar word with a refined word, a forgotten word with a new word. . . . Her voice, like that of some great storytellers, dipped into unclarity. In such moments, her sentences whirled at a delirious pace and I would not understand squat: the only thing left for me to do was let myself (shedding my reason) plunge into that hypnotic enchantment" (388; trans. mod.). The Word Scratcher's account of his incomprehension and need to surrender his preconceived ways of thinking to a new language echoes (again in Kundera's sense) his rendering of Marie-Sophie's account of her surrender to Césaire's poem, as well as the urban planner's conversion. Through transformative encounters such as these, Chamoiseau shows the clarities of certainty to be overtaken by a mysterious onset of receptivity to difference. History becomes an intimate and ongoing oral and written exchange among individuals unable to make sense of it on their own, but whose receptivity to what their explanatory frameworks cannot contain makes them newly susceptible to ecstatic learning. That he figures learning through a series of interlocutions between narrators and their audiences helps us better understand what *Texaco* and *A Passage to India* together contribute to a multifarious modernist literary tradition of evoking narratorial self-doubt in spaces of intercultural complexity. These novels, separated by sixty-eight years and responding to particular but interrelated practices of domination, are part of this tradition but exceptional within it. They are exceptional in envisaging—overtly and pervasively in *Texaco*, fleetingly but climactically in *A Passage to India*—narration to a heterogeneous audience as effecting, often inadvertently and beyond a narrator's comprehension, a propitious negotiation and internalization of difference from which new relations might emerge.

The juxtaposition of certainty to receptivity, so consequential in Forster's trial scene, brings us back to the two contending modes of knowing that run through *A Passage to India*: knowing as grasping (at) differences, and knowing as "touching ghosts," that is, knowing as connecting with others whose potential transparency the knowledge seeker does not presume. Forster contests the epistemology of grasping not just through Adela's failure to gain knowledge by assiduously gathering information but through the evolution of her learning process into an unexpected confrontation with her own relation to others in the climactic courtroom scene. She must confront her relation to a godlike punkah wallah who is elevated, both literally and figuratively, above the action she has precipitated, and she must also confront her relation to a mixed audience in front of whom she chooses to accompany her English allies when they are made to descend from their own elevated platform. In both cases, shifting physical relations evoke shifting relations of power as they did previously in the Marabar Caves, but now, Adela's fearful resistance to what she and Mrs. Moore had felt in the caves changes into a captivated openness to what is beyond her grasp.

When Adela looks up at the punkah wallah on his "raised platform near the back," she begins to reassess the merits of her case; soon afterward, when Aziz's barrister is sustained in his objection to the seating of English spectators on a raised platform because "a platform confers authority," she chooses to descend from the platform along with the others, even though he has not objected to her being seated there (Forster, *Passage* 241, 245–46). Losing "the battle of the platform"—a dethronement that, again, is compulsory for the others but voluntary for her—initiates a process in which Adela's growing consciousness of herself relative to others in the courtroom appears to free her from the well-established part her audience, both allies and opponents, expects her to play (247). She testifies as if possessed by a magical force, uncharacteristically able to cast aside the story that McBryde had sought to solidify through their careful rehearsals of her testimony before the trial. Adela's salutary, if quickly concluded, state of possession, and the new self-possession that comes with it, is less revealing of what actually happened in the cave than it is of her break away from the monologic narrative she is expected to repeat, and against which Aziz, as an Indian, cannot speak in a way that will be heard by those presiding over "the flimsy framework of the court" (256). Before a heterogeneous audience, Adela forgets the polarizing certainties she is expected to reaffirm and transformatively remembers past events as if above the fray, like the punkah wallah whose position she has just contemplated for the first time in relation to her own.

And this is where we come to one of the more striking instances of Forster's attenuation of his principal narrator's authority. Adela's testimony, quoted directly and described indirectly by the Englishman who witnesses it, counteracts the binary comparatist mode of knowing most characteristic of that Englishman's narration. The competing comparatisms that run through the novel come to a head in the trial scene, where the oppositions that both necessarily and excessively govern the trial itself are overtaken by Adela's alternative mode of relating, and relating to, what is foreign and incomprehensible to her. Her testimony not only stands apart from the bigoted discourse of McBryde and his allies who expect to hear a certain story and, with it, to secure both Aziz's conviction and a confirmation of the British Empire's entitlement to rule India; it also stands apart from the narrator's ostensibly trustworthy pronouncements about Indians and their fixed differences from the English, pronouncements that identify the narrator's position as decidedly not above the fray even as he professes to dispense independently and dispassionately acquired intercultural knowledge. At this point in his narration, the uncertainty of Adela's testimony insinuates itself into the narrator's own explanatory account: "She didn't think what had happened or even remember in the ordinary way of memory, but she returned to the Marabar Hills, and spoke from them across a sort of darkness to Mr. McBryde. The fatal day recurred, in every detail, but now she was of it and not of it at the same time, and this double relation gave it indescribable splendour" (Forster, *Passage* 253). Forster's notion of a "double relation" allows him to portray Adela as seeing herself and others as if from more than one position; this allows uncertainty to creep in and complicate views, presumed knowledges that are expected and imposed from within communities. The multiplication of Adela's views leads directly to her unexpected and indeed uncharacteristic embrace of an uncertainty she had previously sensed but discounted:

> Her vision was of several caves. She saw herself in one, and she was also outside it, watching its entrance, for Aziz to pass in. She failed to locate him. It was the doubt that had often visited her, but solid and attractive, like the hills. "I am not—" Speech was more difficult than vision. "I am not quite sure." . . .
>
> Something that she did not understand took hold of the girl and pulled her through. Though the vision was over, and she had returned to the insipidity of the world, she remembered what she had learnt. (254, 256)

Although afterward Adela "remembered what she had learnt," the nature of her trance and what precisely "pulled her through" is one of the novel's defining muddles, and one that the Englishman recounting her testimony knows, or perhaps learns from her testimony, not to resolve.

When Adela, Mrs. Moore, and Fielding casually debate the meanings of "muddle" and "mystery" during their first social engagement with Aziz, none of them hesitate to disparage "muddles," the unresolved problems of social and political relations, philosophical and religious concepts, aesthetic forms, and narrative accounts that interrupt and undercut the pursuit of clarity, coherence, and predictable symmetry that Fielding explicitly identifies with Englishness, and later Europeanness, itself:

> "I do so hate mysteries," Adela announced.
>
> "We English do." (Forster, *Passage* 73)

Ronny Heaslop regularly has the function of reducing complex social interactions and the mysteries that inhere in them to easy explanations and formulas, but, more subtly, the tolerant humanist Fielding is inclined to do this as well. In the exchange cited above, he presumes that Aziz will agree "India's a muddle," and then, touring Venice after the trial, he imagines his Indian friends unable to appreciate the "joys of form" he sees in this "civilization that has escaped muddle" (73, 314). At this point, though, the narrator's perspective deviates from Fielding's to a degree it does not with regard to "the herd-instinct" he describes prior to the trial. Soon after narrating, through free indirect discourse, Fielding's thoughts on "Mediterranean harmony," the narrator relativizes Fielding's assumed hierarchy by describing an alternative beauty of disorderly abundance in the Hindu temple where Godbole worships, even as he recognizes, like Fielding, that the musical and visual "frustration of reason and form" is "a muddle (as we call it)" (314, 319).[34]

Postcolonial literary critics have often questioned the political merits of *A Passage to India*, arguing that Forster's long-praised indictment of English colonial racism is compromised by its inadvertently ethnocentric depiction of India as lacking the social cohesion, philosophical pragmatism, and emotional discipline that would make Indians' political self-determination possible and desirable. Of particular concern, as I noted at the start of this chapter, has been Forster's emphasis on India's incomprehensibility. Elleke Boehmer, for example, grants that "*A Passage to India* remains a historically important novel for its scathing exposition of social and ethical calcification under the Raj," but, echoing Said's objection in *Culture and Imperialism*, she sees a missed opportunity in Forster's reliance on "colonialist tropes of unreadability," arguing that his recurrent image of "India's tenebrous immensity offers no viable alternatives to the novel's agonized liberalism."[35] Said's critique of the novel also extends to the trial scene. He credits Forster with recognizing that a fair trial for Aziz could not have been maintained without undermining British colonial dominance, but he also implies that Forster does not quite know what to do with this recognition: "Therefore he readily (even with a sort of frustrated impatience) dissolves the scene into India's 'complexity'" (Said 75). These readings assume that unresolved complexities associated with intercultural experience and with differences that cannot be repressed or appropriated mark Forster's failure to imagine politically viable solutions, or any solutions at all.

But Adela's testimony may also be read as a triumph over exactly this solution-oriented way of thinking, which Forster and Chamoiseau both unambiguously identify with a European imperialist mindset. Her testimonial freedom arises out of her willingness to be dethroned—figuratively when she voluntarily relinquishes her elevated platform, then narratorially when she acknowledges her uncertain and fallible memory. She has learned to see herself and her history from more than one position at once, and that learning cannot be reduced satisfactorily to the "nervous breakdown" Fielding imagines, or to any of the sensible explanations he proposes to her later to make sense of the discrepancies in her story (Forster, *Passage* 255, 266). That the narrator must leave open the reasons for Adela's accusation and subsequent recantation suggests the learning that his narration manifests and potentially effects: the novel's many unsolved mysteries and the narrator's silence on their meaning train the reader to accept that we cannot grasp everything and that trying to do so distracts us from the encounters that matter most, those that enter us unpredictably and change us, moving us from a pursuit of possessive mastery to a resolve to try to imagine our positions relative to others, even if their viewpoints are not transparent to us. The English in *A Passage to India* are not converted to a creolist perspective as Chamoiseau's French urban planner is; they are not even able to attain a sufficiently durable connection to each other to imagine that they might begin to build a history, or how they might begin to do so. But it is a mark of their learning that Forster's novel ends with a muddle, in which a narrator lets a well-meaning but self-assured colonial educator's question go unresolved before an audience of readers who may address it from different positions, transforming it as we speak.

Supernaturalism and the Approximation of Newness

In 1909, several years before drafting the first seven chapters of *A Passage to India*, Forster wrote of death and the final unrecorded moments before a particular friend's death as "worlds into which the literary imagination cannot penetrate."[36] By the time he completed the novel in 1924, Forster had turned his attention from impenetrable worlds of death to unresolved and perhaps irresolvable mysteries of life, experiences that defy the explanatory logic of liberal-minded but culturally embedded narrators attempting to chronicle intercultural history in an age of imperialism. We have considered how such narrators, in *A Passage to India* and *Texaco*, are liberated through distinct practices of multiperspectival comparatism from having to comprehend all that they narrate or else, like Conrad's Marlow, having to bewail their inability to do so. What liberates them is an ideal of knowledge building across differences that supersedes "knowing" as the profession of certainty. Narratorial credibility is reimagined as deriving in part from intellectual humility and a timely receptivity to the unknown. This brings us to some final reflections on the novels' shared preoccupation with supernaturalism as a means of summoning forth—without resolving—the lived experience of strangeness.

A Passage to India and *Texaco* both draw continually on a "language of theology," in Forster's own phrase, without authorizing any one dogma or belief; both attend to notions of the supernatural that are locally meaningful within culturally heterogeneous contexts (Forster, *Passage* 357). Forster's three chapter headings, "Mosque," "Caves," and "Temple," signal a juxtapositional comparative structure similar to those Kundera admires in Antillean novels by Alexis, Carpentier, and others, though Forster's juxtaposition of three discrete religiously affiliated sites (the Jain affiliation of the caves is briefly touched on in court, when the British misidentify the caves as Buddhist) and, by extension, three religious traditions is another way the novel guards against the possibility of seemingly independent practices or bodies of belief becoming creolized and otherwise transformed by external influences over time (247). By contrast, creolization is *Texaco*'s guiding star, not only linguistic and narrative but religious creolization as well.

Texaco's spatially and chronologically organized chapters together appear under the heading "Le Sermon de Marie-Sophie Laborieux," which is framed by a prefatory section titled "Annonciation" and a brief conclusion titled "Résurrection." Despite the apparent prominence of this Christian framework, most of the novel's biblical allusions appear in the brief "Annonciation," where the urban planner is transformed in Marie-Sophie's eyes from *le Fléau* (the Scourge) and *l'ange destructeur* (the angel of destruction) to *notre Christ* (our Christ). The "Résurrection" section does not revisit the urban planner's prior "resurrection" by Papa Totone but instead recounts Oiseau de Cham's anxious efforts to bring new life—literary life—to Marie-Sophie's words after her death. In *Texaco*'s final paragraph, the Word Scratcher acknowledges that it was he who imposed this Christian framework on Marie-Sophie's testimony, thus closing the book by accentuating its distance from the elusive oral history it seeks to translate: "I reorganized my Source's burgeoning word around the messianic idea of a Christ; this idea respected the community's dereliction prior to the urban planner who managed to decipher it" (Chamoiseau, *Texaco* 390; trans. mod.). By the time Chamoiseau reveals this latest evidence of the text's fabricated nature, he has already cast doubt on its dichotomy of savior and saved in a range of ways, not least by conferring the epithet of Christ on a character who must first be saved physically, ethically, and politically by those whose settlement he in turn saves from being razed. (Even then, he saves it only as part of an ongoing cooperative effort.) In confounding the usual hierarchical definitions of savior and saved, and in depicting the relation between a people and their representatives as one of mutual exchange rather than indebtedness, Chamoiseau further attenuates the authority of the messianic leadership that Césaire already recast, if ambivalently, as a collective labor and uncertain pursuit in the *Cahier d'un retour au pays natal*.

These framing metaphors of Christian metamorphosis (resurrection, conversion, salvation) are implicit comparisons with an important translational function, one to which my next chapter will turn: they translate for a largely distant and privileged readership the life-changing momentousness of events in a poor community unaccustomed to being heard or having its way. At the same time, the novel reimagines (even resurrects) Christianity not as the supreme Word of God but as one of many creolized sources of spiritual meaning, explicitly subordinated to the "Word" (*la Parole*) passed from Marie-Sophie to the Word Scratcher, the elusive poetry of Texaco/*Texaco*. Christianity is also less intrinsic to the novel than the ancestral figures called Mentohs ("les Mentô"), "simple, insignificant-looking" black men invested with superhuman powers, whose covert presence and magical dispensation of justice on slave plantations in the Americas was, Marie-Sophie believes, the foundation of Texaco's spirit of defiance against neocolonial and corporate forces of territorial domination (Chamoiseau, *Texaco* 95, 54). She does not consider Christianity to be at odds with her belief in Mentohs, of whom she says (in a vernacular difficult to translate), "Not many blacks still suspect their existence. Yet only the Good Lord knows how we could ever have done without them" (52; trans. mod.).[37] Even so, Chamoiseau makes clear, these mystical black men of the past and the "traditional resistance" they embody are not what Martinicans need (386). Having sought a modern-day Mentoh in Papa Totone, Marie-Sophie finds herself propelled toward Texaco instead: "I suddenly felt his too great solitude. I began to listen to City" (295).

By reducing Christian redemption to an expedient metaphor and ancestral "slave power" to a valued historical remnant, *Texaco* trades the idea of otherworldly truth, and especially the compensatory "heaven" and "natural order" bestowed by Christian colonialists, for an affectionate rendering of faith-in-the-world, where wondrous stories can expediently meet and, as if by magic or some miracle, spur political action (52). With its multiple layers of narration, each manifestly partial and subjective, Chamoiseau's "history" of Texaco excludes from its stories of supernatural transformation any that could be credibly read as omnisciently told or literally true. History in *Texaco* is always a tale that mixes with other tales and situated beliefs, and in mixing with them both revives and revises them.

And this returns us to Forster's language of theology. Even as the chapter headings in *A Passage to India* dignify the diversity of India by according equal recognition to three of its religions, each as distinct as the sanctum that symbolizes it, traces of a more untidy diversity become visible as characters mingle and perspectives multiply. From early in the novel, institutionalized religions are shown to coexist and sometimes even coalesce faintly with alternate belief systems. When Aziz mistakes Mrs. Moore for a ghost while worshipping in the mosque, he sees no contradiction between the Islamic faith and his belief in ghosts (Forster, *Passage* 17). In moments of uncertainty, the Nawab Bahadur, Mrs. Moore, and Adela Quested also express an openness to nondenominational explanations involving spirits. Such explanations are discrepant with the novel's general stance of agnosticism and so all the more powerfully convey the magnitude of a character's bewilderment. Forster never quite disproves and sometimes seems to condone this supernaturalism as an explanatory discourse, as when Mrs. Moore, hearing that a car had collided with an animal on the road, instinctively exclaims, "A ghost!" without knowing that the Nawab Bahadur, usually a critic of superstition, fears that the car had hit a ghost from his past (104, 106, 99–100). Supernaturalism's unresolved coexistence with a sometimes belittled but for the most part narratively privileged rationalism makes the question of whether otherworldly forces are indeed an authentic cause of the novel's action an unanswerable one.[38] We can discern, though, that Forster's intimations of ghosts and miracles suggest a connection between Indians and Englishwomen, however vaguely and noncommittally. Because Chamoiseau not only admits but celebrates the transformative reality of creolization, he is freer than Forster to represent connections across cultures as occurring not in a supernatural sphere that transcends the constraints and divisions of the cultural, but within cultures themselves as they are lived physically, through languages, stories, and bodies in close and adulterating contact.

4 Traversing Bounds of Solidarity

Poor Analogies and Painful Negotiations in *Three Guineas* and *The Farming of Bones*

> I know how fallacious historical parallels are, particularly the one I am about to draw.
>
> —Aimé Césaire

> I started, in a conscious way, to seek connections in phenomena even in the seemingly unconnected.
>
> —Ngũgĩ wa Thiong'o

Within a month of the January 12, 2010, earthquake that left much of southern Haiti in ruins, Edwidge Danticat returned to her native Port-au-Prince to find, amid homes and public buildings collapsed, "piles of human remains freshly pulled from the rubble" and appearing, outside the city's General Hospital, to be "stuck together in two large balls."[1] She remembers her impulse to imagine these unrecognizable balls of flesh as the remnants of nursing and midwifery students clinging to each other in their final moments of shock and terror. But her friend Jhon, a resident artist, explained otherwise: "'These are all body parts,'" he said, "'legs and arms that were pulled out of the rubble and placed on the side of the road, where they dried further and melded together'" (165). Danticat recounts this return to Haiti, her first since the earthquake, in an essay she calls "Our Guernica," where interlaced images of a devastated landscape and the Haiti that came before are superimposed, briefly but significantly, on two other sites of communal devastation: "a destroyed Hiroshima" and the Basque town of Guernica, bombed in 1937 by Nazi Germany in support of Franco's Nationalist campaign against the Spanish republican government (164, 170). She knows these sites through the visual arts; the "destroyed Hiroshima" she remembers is from an unspecified film she has seen—leaving us to compile the sources of our own mental images of Hiroshima—while the Guernica she contemplates with Jhon is the one many of us know best:

> Misty-eyed, he whispers, "Like Picasso and *Guernica* after the Spanish Civil War. We will have our Guernica."
>
> "Or thousands of them," I concur. (170)

Coming to terms with an earthquake's aftermath by comparing it to wartime sites of catastrophic violence against civilians is, in a sense, not unlike imagining the prior compassion of living bodies now reduced to inanimate flesh: it directs us elsewhere, to another place and time, in the face of an overwhelming image of trauma in the present. Both are deflections of sorts, variations of what Bruce Robbins describes, in an essay published the same year as Danticat's, as the narratorial practice of "looking away" from "large-scale historical violence" (for instance, in the form of an aside about a character's future) at the very moment when that violence is unfolding most vividly and unbearably in the story.[2] But while Danticat might allow her narrator, and us, some distraction from the scene's horrors when she reminds us of prior calamities that inspired art, or when she transforms disfigured corpses into people huddled together, mutually giving and taking comfort in the face of death, she does so by pressing on readers remote from Haiti a different sort of burden: the imperative to care about Haitians' suffering because it resembles something they already care about, or think they should. To reach this audience, Danticat incorporates into her essay's documentary description both a fleeting historical fiction—the imagined suffering of a few that encapsulates the suffering of Haiti's earthquake victims en masse—and a guiding analogy that links these few and the community they represent to other civilian casualties already deemed important on the world stage. I will return to historical fiction as a fleeting figure that interrupts larger discourses of which it is part, and as a narrative genre through which more extended stories might respond to other, prior discourses. I want to proceed first, though, to the idea of analogies as a means of making do with inadequate resources, with "inadequate resources" denoting a scarcity not of locally meaningful evidence but of the attention and sympathy of distant readers who could intervene if only they had the will to do so.

Danticat's gentle, democratizing corrective to her friend's yearning for a singularly monumental artwork like Picasso's *Guernica* that will crystallize and authorize the singularity of the Haitian earthquake's destructive impact is not incidental to her comparative mode of portraying that impact to a distant audience, her turn to analogies to impart some broadly recognizable meaning to the grotesque lumps of flesh she sees in the unbearable present of her return.[3] A hope for thousands of *Guernicas*—thousands of artworks comparable to *Guernica*, each comparable in its own way—is a hope for a collaborative, rather than authoritative, vision of the earthquake's significance. So, too, does her own art become collaborative to the extent that its image of the Haitian dead is constituted in part by its references to other artists' images of mass slaughters. Both the essay collection where "Our Guernica" appears and its introductory chapter are named for Albert Camus's 1957 lecture "Create Dangerously," in which Camus asserts that "art cannot be a monologue."[4] Danticat develops Camus's assertion into an idea of writers as intensely responsive, and responsible, to the world around them, a world of injustices and inequalities where "bodies are littering the street somewhere. People are buried under rubble somewhere. Mass graves are being dug somewhere. Survivors are living in make-shift tent cities and refugee camps somewhere, shielding their heads from the rain, closing their eyes, covering their ears, to shut out the sounds of military 'aid' helicopters" ("Our Guernica" 18).

Given Danticat's emphasis on the communal and cross-fertilizing character of art, especially the politically engaged art she herself creates and admires by others, we may wonder if another literary source might not also underlie her exhortation to "create dangerously": Aimé Césaire's *Discourse on Colonialism*, the best-known version of which dates from two years before Camus delivered his lecture at Uppsala University.[5] To break through the presumptions and pieties of European humanist justifications of colonialism and to expose its actual effects—"all this wreckage, all this waste, humanity reduced to a monologue"—Césaire launches his polemic with, among other things, a rallying cry to do the dangerous work of questioning received definitions: "the essential thing here is to see clearly, to think clearly—that is, dangerously—and to answer clearly the innocent first question: what, fundamentally, is colonization?"[6] What connects Césaire's call to see and think dangerously with Danticat's call to create dangerously is not just the value both put on politically contrarian thinking that entails risks to writers like themselves. It is that both explicitly address an audience of readers whose cooperation, indeed collaborative dialogue, in this risky thinking they make a point of encouraging. At the same time, their dialogues with these audiences are risky in themselves in that they portray injustices so as to unsettle the moral certainties and unconsidered assumptions of a powerful segment of their audience whose trust and support they need if they are to effect systemic change. It is worth remembering that neither Césaire nor Danticat is merely, or even primarily, addressing the marginalized and oppressed.

With this in mind, what may at first seem innocuous comparisons of the earthquake's dead to war victims in Guernica and Hiroshima begin to appear as more pointed indictments, defiant of borders not only between politics and a presumed "nature" but also between governments usually represented in global North discourse as strictly separate from each other and even morally opposed with respect to human rights.[7] Danticat's skeptical reference to "military 'aid' helicopters" in the passage above similarly challenges readers sympathetic to purportedly humanitarian military interventions in foreign lands, without regard to their invasiveness and potentially destructive consequences. This is the "danger" that politically engaged writing poses to its author and audience alike, this risking of the writer's most potentially influential readers' esteem by putting their own values at risk, that makes the use of translational fictions such as analogies in literatures of *engagement* and social protest a more parlous and complicated business than one of simply capturing an audience's attention and sympathy. The question becomes, how might the writer seduce readers into caring about injustices not just distant from themselves but with which they might be complicit, and how then might the writer unveil this complicity while sparking a sense of solidarity that makes those readers want to change? Bearing in mind the strategic aims and perceived audiences of such translational texts of *engagement*, we can better see their displays of earnest investment in the evidentiary power of analogies and other forms of comparison as both performative and compensatory, a kind of poor theater.[8]

Manifestos for Justice: Making Do with Analogies

"I know how fallacious historical parallels are, particularly the one I am about to draw"—thus Césaire, in the final pages of the *Discourse on Colonialism*, briskly qualifies his idea that "colonial enterprise is to the modern world what Roman imperialism was to the ancient world" in its short-sighted assaults on cultures whose flourishing could have helped it to rebuff threats to its own civilization (*Discourse* 74-75). While Césaire concedes the limits of analogies like this one, he makes it the basis of his concluding appeal for "a new policy founded on respect for peoples and cultures," a pluralistic "policy of *nationalities*" ("politique des *nationalités*") to replace the imperialist work of fortifying and augmenting "the nation" at other cultures' expense (*Discourse* 77; *Discours* 59). As Gary Wilder has pointed out, Césaire envisions "a mutualist modernity without colonial domination" by simultaneously looking back in time and looking forward; Wilder links this treatment of temporality in the *Discourse* to Césaire's "poetry of untimeliness where conventional distinctions between past, present, and future do not obtain; memory and futurity, reality and imagination, are dialectically entwined."[9] Like Danticat's appeal for transnational sympathy and solidarity with Haitians in "Our Guernica," Césaire's appeal for a postimperial partnership between colonizers and colonized peoples makes use of historical fictions that conjure prior forms of cooperation and solidarity to begin to imagine what future forms might be (and, in the case of the Roman Empire, should not be).

A manifesto of Marxist internationalist humanism from the early years of decolonization, Césaire's *Discourse* anticipated transnational postcolonial discourse's defining critiques of ethno-nationalism and neo-imperialism as dominant sources of personal identification and communal affiliation. Robert Young has argued that postcolonial writing "offers a different model of comparison" from prior literary traditions of "comparison in the West," notwithstanding their shared propensity to undermine nationalist ideologies.[10] "Postcolonial literature is the first literature that is a comparative literature rather than a *littérature comparée*," Young proposes, because its "comparing takes place in the literature itself, through form and content, not just in subsequent critical acts of comparison" (688). Written by those already pressed into a state of comparison by colonialist discourse, who "had no choice" but to conceive of themselves and their work comparatively and "in dialogue with other literatures," it is "a literature, as Édouard Glissant puts it, of *relation*" (688). This requisite comparatism, as it were, which affects scholars of nondominant literatures no less than the writers whose work they study,[11] is also characteristic of feminist texts that, since well before postcolonialism, have also questioned hegemonic formulations of identity and belonging in defense of those ill served by such formulations. Feminist writers have long had to think comparatively in defense of (at least some among) the nondominant.

Césaire's recourse to analogies and other comparisons to both seize the attention and unsettle the assumptions of an audience prone to denounce some forms of cultural violence while dismissing others as unimportant may remind us of Virginia Woolf's own persistently comparative strategy of persuasion in her feminist anti-war polemic from 1938, *Three Guineas*.[12] Like

Danticat after the earthquake, Woolf makes the Spanish Civil War an occasion for contentious comparative critique in the interests of building new collectivities, more equitable and humane by virtue of their provisionality and dialogism. She is explicit that comparatism, in the reading of histories and the viewing of paintings, is a means to dispel the unexamined patriotism that would make one believe that the men of one's country "are 'superior' to the men of other countries" (128; though it must be noted that she looks to Europe alone as a source of the texts and paintings she would have us compare to dispel patriotism). To be sure, this anti-manifesto manifesto dispenses with the declamatory tone of avant-garde manifestos that Césaire would later adopt in the *Discourse*. But the two works are very much aligned in their marshaling of comparisons, dialogic structure, and an aspirational rhetoric of internationalism and universal humanism to rouse a readership they characterize as having, at best, historically ignored the rights and dignity of those their manifestos for justice seek to defend.

Woolf's long-underrated polemic against patriarchal repression and the patriotic myths undergirding it has met with resurgent, and largely positive, interest since the turn of the century, probably because its dialogic structure and anti-nationalist themes coalesce productively with those of an increasingly influential transnational literary field. In a general sense, the book's pacifist cosmopolitan feminism has aged well, its speaker's memorable contention that "as a woman my country is the whole world" an appealing rejoinder to the military interventions and deficient cross-cultural understanding that US patriotism after 9/11 came so widely to represent (Woolf, *Three Guineas* 129).[13] Like the *Discourse*, *Three Guineas* polemicizes in frequently analogical terms, and, also like the *Discourse*, it circles back repeatedly to what at the time of its publication was a highly provocative analogy involving fascism. The drive to dominate women in England, writes Woolf as World War II fast approaches, is fundamentally the same as the drive to dominate women, Jews, and others deemed outsiders in Franco's Spain, Mussolini's Italy, and Hitler's Germany. Colonialist racial violence, writes Césaire as postwar decolonization is beginning its fitful spread through Africa, Asia, and the Caribbean, is fundamentally the same as fascist racial violence. Not only are the analogies reminiscent of each other, but certain rhetorical tactics used to substantiate them recur from Woolf's text to Césaire's as well: both juxtapose isolated, often unattributed quotations by respected intellectuals, statesmen, and other male public figures to uncannily similar statements by despised fascists and war criminals with whom they would customarily never be compared.

The multiform comparatism of both texts confronts a readership explicitly identified as local with its unsuspected comparability—its moral likeness—to another collective whose autocratic and discriminatory values they want to impugn but, in some disavowed area of their own jurisdiction, inadvertently share. Quoting from a *Daily Telegraph* article from 1936, for example, Woolf aligns the remarks of an unspecified commentator on the evils of women's employment with a like-minded passage she leaves unattributed, but which comes from Hitler's speech to a Nazi women's association that same year. She concludes, "One is written in English, the other in German. But where is the difference? Are they not both saying the same thing? Are they not both the voices of Dictators, whether they speak English or German, and are we not all agreed that the dictator when we meet him abroad is a very dangerous as well as a very ugly animal? And he is here, among us, raising his ugly head, spitting his poison, small still, curled up like a caterpillar on a leaf, but in the heart of England" (Woolf, *Three Guineas* 65). Césaire similarly concludes a discussion of Hitler with a quotation that begins, "'We aspire not to equality but to domination,'" and surprises us with the revelation that the speaker is not Hitler but Ernest Renan: "Who is speaking? I am ashamed to say it: it is the Western *humanist*, the 'idealist' philosopher. That his name is Renan is an accident" (*Discourse* 37). When Césaire compares colonialist aggressions against neighboring cultures with the unneighborly aggressions of the Roman Empire, his appeal is the culmination of an extended analogy of Nazis to French apologists for colonialism, only one of whom is Renan. He introduces the analogy in perhaps the book's most frequently quoted passage:

> Yes, it would be worthwhile to study clinically, in detail, the steps taken by Hitler and Hitlerism and to reveal to the very distinguished, very humanistic, very Christian bourgeois of the twentieth century that without his being aware of it, he has a Hitler inside him, that Hitler *inhabits* him, that Hitler is his *demon*, that if he rails against him, he is being inconsistent and that, at bottom, what he cannot forgive Hitler for is not *the crime* in itself, *the crime against man*, it is not *the humiliation of man as such*, it is the crime against the white man, the humiliation of the white man, and the fact that he applied to Europe colonialist procedures which until then had been reserved exclusively for the Arabs of Algeria, the "coolies" of India, and the "niggers" of Africa. (36)

In neither text is the analogy to fascism the only prominent comparison, though in both it is the most frankly controversial for its time and probably still the best known. Readerships, of course, change, and it is other comparisons that put Woolf and Césaire at greater risk now of seeming out of touch, comparisons, usually couched in universalizing humanist terms but involving some notable conflation or exclusion, that seem at odds with the inclusivity their cultural critiques invoke as their end and ideal.[14] Their bold promotions of freedom from some form of politically and economically motivated social oppression have eased Woolf's and Césaire's passage to current critical debates in which they are generally treated as congenial interlocutors, but their precise conceptions of freedom and its relationship to justice have also incurred a share of skepticism. To my knowledge, *Three Guineas* and the *Discourse on Colonialism* have not been considered together comparatively, but each has benefited from important interpretations that resist the temptation to treat them as either laudably radical or lamentably elitist in their visions of emancipation and instead consider the intricacies of their ambivalent articulations of resistance. Usually these interpretations emphasize innovations that came up against the limits of the writer's own vision. One such interpretation is Laura Winkiel's analysis of Woolf's salutary disruptions of progressive models of history even as Woolf seemed unable to recognize colonized communities and people of color as fully modern (an analysis Winkiel concludes by supplementing Woolf's gender critique with anticolonial critiques by Césaire, as well as Suzanne Césaire and C. L. R. James).[15] Another is Michael Rothberg's analysis of Césaire's own salutary disruptions of progressive models of history, even as Césaire "sometimes subordinates historical particularity to linear narratives of progress and regression," especially Marxist ones (70).

A few critics have also attended to the *value* of ambivalence in these writers' articulations of resistance, or to what might be the advantage of a discursive tension between what now appears as prescient insight and what alongside it can seem oddly complicit with countervailing powers. Françoise Vergès, for example, gives an account of discourses of emancipation in the formerly colonized French overseas departments, to explain how anticolonialists such as Césaire used a "strategy of borrowing" from "the 'French book of republicanism' and its motto of liberty, equality, fraternity."[16] She argues that this borrowing "was not a gesture of pure mimesis, of alienated colonized who credulously endorsed the Enlightenment project," but rather a process in which anticolonialists advanced their emancipatory goals by positioning themselves between "suspicion toward the ideals brought by Europe and the Enlightenment and the recognition of a filiation toward those ideals" (16–17). Vergès urges that we attend more closely and sympathetically to the "*heterological* position" of these anticolonial thinkers, "a position 'in-between': citizen *and* colonized, worker *and* citizen, member of the colonized community *and* member of a subethnic group, *and* women" (17). In his study of negritude between the First and Second World Wars, Gary Wilder argues that Césaire and fellow negritude poets Léopold Senghor and Léon Damas "linked a liberal discourse grounded in republican rights and rationality to a postliberal discourse grounded in racial alterity and irrationality."[17] Though they did not avoid reproducing antinomies of colonial humanism, he writes, their integration of "rational-critical interventions in the republican public sphere" with alternative modes of critique inspired by contemporary countercurrents such as vitalism, Marxism, primitivism, and modernist aesthetics enabled them to make reasoned critiques of colonial modernity while also pointing to the limits of reason as a means to knowledge (256–57).

These critical theories of anticolonial Francophone negotiations with legitimating discourses of imperial state power impress on us the historical exigencies informing ambivalent or heterological articulations of resistance. They also signal the interdependence of these articulations with the thought they critique, by demonstrating "that the entwined histories of slavery, imperialism, capitalism, republicanism, and modernism had bound metropolitan and Caribbean peoples to one another within a shared if asymmetrical modernity."[18] In this way, these studies coalesce with those that bring postcolonial and diasporic theoretical insights to bear on the complex mix of allegiance and nonconformity, subversion and complicity in writing by European modernists such as Woolf. Laura Doyle warns us not to "consider the pursuit of freedom the primary aesthetic or political project of authors" such as Woolf because in doing so "we may overlook literature's more sustaining and dialectical movements—not heroically onward and upward, but rather back and forth in call and response within and among readerly communities."[19] Anna Snaith similarly cautions that our "desire for 'pure resistance'" prevents us from recognizing the value of Woolf's exploration, in novels such as *The Years*,[20] of "the plethora of motivating and interdependent forces—familial, sexual, political—that determine the individual, class or society's capacity for change."[21] We would do better, such readings suggest, to envision writers not as conquering heroes who have freed themselves and might still free others from a hegemonic culture's conceptual chains (with all the virile colonialist overtones of that ideal) but as "mere persons forever in encumbered relation" (Doyle 454). Allowing for the subversive value of principled forms of cooperative negotiation extends feminist and postcolonial writing sensitive to "forms of resistance and struggle by the subaltern that escaped notice in the heroic narrative about resistance" (Vergès 77).

For all this, we could still productively complicate readings of *Three Guineas* and the *Discourse on Colonialism* by taking seriously the possibility that ideologically fraught, sometimes self-contradictory formulations of freedom and identity are not simply expressions of their authors' own ambivalent, inadvertently conservative, and not always consistently theorized positions. The forms of the texts signal to us that the arguments advanced and the evidence supporting those arguments are not straightforward responses to the inheritance of invidious comparisons that Young rightly identifies as formative of a postcolonial literature focused more on relationality and its historical contexts than on the moral, physical, and intellectual compass of unique personalities, with their tragic fates, fatal flaws, and masterful overcomings of wretched circumstances. Both *Three Guineas* and the *Discourse* are polemics, but both are also fictions, explicitly addressed to fictive audiences of powerful men. This is particularly obvious in *Three Guineas*, where Woolf retained the structure of a speaker addressing a sympathetic audience from its initial context of a public lecture she delivered to the National Society for Women's Service in London in 1931, first in the fictive public addresses of *The Pargiters* and then in the fictive letters of *Three Guineas*, whose speaker must address her correspondent, a barrister, in his absence. Significantly, her shift was from an actual audience of women, present and listening to her speech, to an imaginary audience of one gentleman, absent but, in the fiction, a willing listener who has invited her to address and advise him. The speaker of *Three Guineas* is one who repeatedly modulates her voice in an imagined dialogue with her professionally accomplished male reader, including for his perusal two letters she has written to women correspondents also seeking her help. Césaire's more ostensibly confident and inflammatory speaker in the *Discourse* is less openly adaptive to his fictional audience of legislators who resemble the Assemblée Nationale, of which Césaire was a member from 1946 until 1993. But here again we have a fiction, because although Césaire did periodically address his fellow *deputés* in frank and passionate language, he never delivered the *Discourse* in that forum, or in any comparable forum. The *Discourse* was never, as Daniel Delas puts it, "declaimed on high from a platform" until more than thirty years after its publication on the day of the French Revolution's bicentennial in 1989, when it was read in the presence of Césaire in the gothic cloister of a former convent in Avignon (Delas 1443).

As fictional addresses to powerful men who are already listening, when in fact no such dialogue has yet begun and it is the task of the writing to usher in that dialogue, these works signal to us that their authors are closely attuned to who their audiences are, or more precisely, who among their potential readers must hear them and recognize the legitimacy of their appeals in order to help them effect the change they want. Even a polemicist as openly defiant as Césaire's speaker in the *Discourse* needs to be heard and, ultimately, trusted by that segment of his audience. In some sense, Césaire's inclination to give voice to others who cannot speak for themselves, so important in his *Cahier d'un retour au pays natal*, endures here to an extent that little resembles Woolf, who fashions her speaker's voice to a considerable extent out of other texts by and about women, from fellow letter writers and diarists to Sophocles's *Antigone*. But even Césaire, who positions himself as alone in an assembly of hostile Frenchmen whom he must berate as well as enlighten, still makes communication a central trope in his essay, however aggressively he may be communicating. Both *Three Guineas* and the *Discourse* are, at bottom, negotiations with mainstream discourses from which they are not just departing but also, to a certain extent, drawing in order to make themselves credible. It is with this in mind that we should read their comparisons of fascist practices that their audiences are certain to find repugnant with what are largely locally accepted practices of social domination, exploitation, and exclusion. At once provocations to debate and rough translations that might educate complacent citizens who assume they occupy a moral and political high ground, both texts insistently remind us that their speakers are engaged in a process of communicating with an elite, clearly delimited group of people whose opinions matter to public policy and public opinion. In doing so, Césaire and Woolf—Woolf with particular explicitness—make the *communicability* of a speaker's vision central to the vision itself.

With this in mind, we can better account for the apparent peculiarity, amid Woolf's brave analogies between "the tyranny of the patriarchal state" and "the tyranny of the Fascist state," of her extended comparison of the English "educated class" (and "daughters of educated men" in particular) to slaves who are either generically defined or located in the ancient Near East, while victims of the more glaringly apposite transatlantic slave trade are obliquely suggested but nowhere explicit points of identification (*Three Guineas* 121).[22] This can seem downright bewildering in light of the significant contributions that several of Woolf's paternal ancestors made to English abolitionism in the previous century.[23] Even Eric Williams, whose seminal history *Capitalism and Slavery* represents English abolitionism as driven by competing political interests and a closer relationship to economic imperatives than its proponents' humanitarian rhetoric suggests, writes favorably about the Stephen family's efforts on behalf of emancipation. Williams's account is especially laudatory about Sir James Stephen, Britain's undersecretary of the Colonial Office and Woolf's grandfather, who drafted the Slavery Abolition Act of 1833 after writing disgustedly of West Indian planters: "The deprivation of a mansion or an equipage painful though it may be is hardly to be set against the protracted exclusion from those common advantages of human life under which from the admitted facts of the case the slaves are proved to be labouring."[24] Woolf's omission is not so bewildering, though, if we take her comparative mode of argumentation in *Three Guineas* as part of the fiction of a speaker addressing a particular audience for whom she must roughly translate and render imaginable a perspective she acknowledges is foreign to theirs. It follows that she would favor analogies and other means of translation likely to reach that audience, who, living in England in 1938, were demonstrably more open to recognizing in themselves and their families a potential affinity with victims of fascist attacks in Spain than to identifying with the traumatic histories of black African slaves.

Particularly off-putting, no doubt, would have been any direct suggestion of a link between the ugly history of racial exploitation and slave trading in Africa and the Americas—culpability for which most cultivated Englishmen in the 1930s were likely to have considered far removed from themselves—and England's waning but persistent colonization of those same regions throughout the years in which Woolf was writing *Three Guineas*. In her elaborate use of analogies and comparative quotations, the embattled interwar feminist can obliquely characterize women of her class as an exploited and underestimated resource of rivalrous male autocrats scrambling for ever more control, thus indirectly making "daughters of educated men" a national analogue to the colonized abroad. Further analogizing women to African slaves would have made the connection between racism and colonialism difficult to ignore, and so inflammatory for the time as to have distracted from her primary focus on women's education and its role in preventing war. Challenging old comparisons with new ones in a time of heightened competition among nations was, for Woolf, a reaching out as much as a resistance and a contestation; it was a translational performance for others who did not yet share her speaker's faith in collaborative enunciations of justice but who might be persuaded, if she could make herself comprehensible, and credible, to them.

Knowing When to Look Away from a Massacre

Woolf's performance of what we might call, building on Vergès's argument in *Monsters and Revolutionaries*, a heterological humanism that entails a strategic selection of universals for a carefully defined local audience is nowhere more evident, or more easily misunderstood, than in her description of photographs from the Spanish Civil War. What interests me about this portion of the text is the way that Woolf's speaker makes what would have been familiar and commonsensical truth claims about evidence and human instincts so as to win her audience's trust sufficiently that they might eventually reevaluate those very truth claims as currently conceived, for instance, in their nationalist and patriarchal formulations. These photographs of war, the speaker insists, will provoke her reader's humane response as soon as she displays them, but as anyone who has read the illustrated edition of the book already knows, she never does display them. Part of the fiction of *Three Guineas* is that she is laying them out before us and that we are looking, with her, at Spanish civilians' "dead bodies and ruined houses," a phrase that recurs many times after its introduction in the following passage. The repetition of this phrase forms a refrain that stands in for the photographic evidence Woolf's speaker claims to include with her letter to prove that her gentleman correspondent shares her instinctive understanding that "war is an abomination," when, on the contrary, a shared understanding is precisely what the refrain is designed to bring into being:

> This morning's collection contains the photograph of what might be a man's body, or a woman's; it is so mutilated that it might, on the other hand, be the body of a pig. But those certainly are dead children, and that undoubtedly is the section of a house. A bomb has torn open the side; there is still a birdcage hanging in what was presumably the sitting-room, but the rest of the house looks like nothing so much as a bunch of spilikins suspended in mid-air. . . . When we look at these photographs some fusion takes place within us; however different the education, the traditions behind us, our sensations are the same; and they are

> violent. You, Sir, call them "horror and disgust." We also call them horror and disgust. . . . For now at last we are looking at the same picture; we are seeing with you the same dead bodies, the same ruined houses. (*Three Guineas* 14)

Woolf's speaker here appears to predicate her elaborate pacifist argument on the assumption that unveiling factual evidence of war trauma, such as photographs of casualties from an ongoing, not-too-distant war, will unite "sons and daughters of educated men" in opposing war in general. Susan Sontag, taking Woolf and her speaker as one and the same and attending little to the formal and evidentiary complexities of *Three Guineas*, takes this universalizing humanist argument at face value and disputes it in no uncertain terms. For cursory readers of *Three Guineas*, who find themselves seduced by its professions of faith in the power of an image to activate its viewers' compassion simply by making war's violence visible, regardless of who might be the victim of that violence—for those readers, Sontag's exasperated correctives to Woolf are valuable. "Photographs of an atrocity," Sontag objects, "may give rise to opposing responses."[25] On this point, she contrasts *Three Guineas* with Ernst Friedrich's 1924 book *Krieg dem Kriege!* (*War against War!*), a more worldly-wise text, in Sontag's view, whose use of captions in multiple languages reveals that Friedrich, unlike the apparently credulous Woolf, "did not make the mistake of supposing that heartrending, stomach-turning pictures would simply speak for themselves" (15). As others have pointed out, Sontag's argument does not adequately contend with the intricate conceptual and formal frames around *Three Guineas*'s assertions about human instincts, and with the ironies that this framing produces.[26] First is the simple, or not so simple, fact that Woolf never does rely on "heartrending, stomach-turning pictures" to "simply speak for themselves." Contrary to her speaker's claims to show the photographs in full confidence of what her reader's response will be, Woolf withholds those photographs, from him and from us, and goes to the trouble of instead writing a book whose argument is so multilayered, so deeply researched and carefully documented, that it took her seven years to write it. Why did she go to such trouble if she believed that simply showing a few pictures would persuade her readers to join her in opposing war? Why indeed does her speaker refer so often to the differences and difficulties of understanding between men and women of her class, especially in matters of war and competition, if she believes that looking at photographs will unite them in a shared horror of war?

My point is that Sontag too readily trusts in Woolf's show of earnestness, without sufficiently considering the relationship of that show to the manifest fictions of the text, first and foremost the fiction that she is showing her reader war photographs. Their absence is accentuated by the presence of the photographs that Woolf does include in *Three Guineas*; it is only a few pages after the passage above, in a book of over two hundred pages, that the first in a succession of comparatively banal, locally significant photographs appears. These five photographs, entitled "A General," "Heralds," "A University Procession," "A Judge," and "An Archbishop," are most directly a means of undercutting the authority of Englishmen by linking their ostentatious ceremonial dress to their self-aggrandizing and competitive politics. More fundamentally, though, the presence of these photographs, amid references to dead bodies and ruined houses that we never see, suggests what the British ruling class does see and consider important. The five photographs represent public faces of nationalist institutions whose domination of the pictorial spaces of the text elides outsiders—foreigners, women, and the lower classes, most obviously, but also the casualties of patriotic violence—reducing them to specters that haunt the public discourse. Taking these specters into account requires an ability to look away from what is pervasively seen and considered important, and to imagine what is not yet visible to the public.

Here we return to the idea with which this chapter began: the narratorial movement of "looking away" in Danticat's essay "Our Guernica," both in the form of transnational analogies of Haiti's earthquake victims to civilian casualties of aerial bombing in Guernica and Hiroshima and in the form of a fleeting historical fiction that interrupts, and in the process intensifies, an ostensibly documentary or "fact-based" discourse. The latter, Danticat's briefly imagined transformation of lumps of flesh into nursing students embracing in terror, is in a way reminiscent of Woolf's imagined snapshot of carnage, with its speaker's speculations into what the disfigured bodies and scattered remnants might once have been. Both are historical fictions that break the conventions of the nonfiction prose accounts where they appear, so as to translate the abstract suffering of the too-many-to-count into the wrenching suffering of a vivid few. In this sense they train the reader to look away from factual evidence that supposedly has the potential to be known by sight, and to look instead to what is not currently or usually visible. *Pace* Sontag, Woolf in effect discourages readers from taking unmediated seeing as the means to reliable knowledge. It is the very assumption that we can know "facts" from just looking at the evidence before us that her ironic applications of the word "fact," amid the many analogies, comparative quotations, and assemblages of divergent opinions in *Three Guineas*, belie.

If Woolf casts doubt on the notion that compassionate feeling and just action follow instinctively from a confrontation with readily available photographic evidence, the value of doing so becomes clearer when we consider Woolf's position in the context of a war culture of aerial bombing whose development she had witnessed years before during World War I, and whose reemergence she was again facing as she wrote *Three Guineas*. Rey Chow has analyzed this culture in *The Age of the World Target*, arguing that the early to mid-twentieth century's new technologies of aerial bombing depended on a dichotomous structuring of the relation between viewers, empowered by their capacity to know by sight, and the viewed, whose visibility makes them susceptible to being targeted as objects of knowledge and, possibly, of destruction. Chow criticizes what happens to conceptions of unknown civilians, remote cultures, and knowledge as such when the maintenance of national supremacy becomes a matter of needing to gain a clear-cut view into elsewhere, an elsewhere that comes to be understood first and foremost as a potential target. Like *Three Guineas*, Chow's book closely associates prevailing aims of scholarly knowledge production with military practices and their self-legitimation: "Often under the modest and apparently innocuous agendas of fact gathering and documentation, the 'scientific' and 'objective' production of knowledge during peacetime . . . became the institutional practice that substantiated and elaborated the militaristic conception of the world as target" (40). Woolf's artfully indirect way of making us see a bombed-out home and family and her refusal to let us think we know the victims once and for all by making them photographically, "factually" visible to us appear in light of Chow's argument to be Woolf's means of countering the assumption that what one needs most to know is what one can see, the very assumption that made their targeting possible. Woolf's analogies, comparative quotations, and historical fictions are all figurative means with which to make her audience look away from what they can see from their privileged positions for viewing the world, and to begin to imagine the ethical import of relational patterns beyond and apart from stable polarities of viewer and viewed, self and other, us and them.

Woolf's conceit of claiming to display photographs whose unveiling can have only one effect, while in fact keeping such photographs out of view and persuading her readers with language alone, suggests the allure of arguments that assert the spectacular singularity and exceptionality of trauma, and the rhetorical value of shifting, once the sympathetic reader's shocked indignation and self-righteousness are aroused, to put those lures of the spectacle into much wider and more complex historical networks of relation than universalizing theories of human instincts in the face of trauma have done. Even where Woolf appears to be using verbal images of traumatized bodies to induce in her fictional correspondent (and actual readers) an epiphanic realization of war's brutality, she builds her essay around these images in such a way as to educate the reader not about extraordinary wrongs done by a particular faction (as propaganda would do) but about how those mutilated bodies came to be, and why we should conceive of them in the way she slyly claims to be instinctive. The contest at the heart of *Three Guineas*, as historicizing theories of trauma by Sibylle Fischer and Lauren Berlant, among others, have prepared us to see,[27] pits two modes of responding to trauma against each other. The first is a familiar and, no doubt for many readers, initially appealing humanist lament over the wanton destruction ("dead bodies and ruined houses") that tyrannical regimes wreak—a lament that ostensibly unites the speaker and her gentleman correspondent in a self-congratulatory moral stance of recognizing evil when they see it. The second is a subtle and quietly seductive argument by illustration of sympathy as implicated in discursive patterns of consensus building that are necessarily politically motivated, adaptive, and arbitrarily constituted with the tools (that is, texts) at hand. Because it is collectively produced discursive training, *not* innate human instinct, that makes some visions of justice outweigh others in the public sphere, *Three Guineas* turns not to photographic "facts" to prevent war, but to education.

The Value of a Poor Education

A point of difference between the *Discourse on Colonialism* and *Three Guineas* is that *Three Guineas* openly questions itself; it is, paradoxically, a monologue whose speaker frequently stops to imagine how her correspondents might respond to her words. Rather than smooth over the doubts and deflations that ensue, Woolf displays them, making the reciprocal process of contestation and amendment, the reorienting of oneself in the persuasion of others, a constitutive feature and implicit ideal of her discourse, while its explicit focus is the unjust destructiveness of patriarchy and its ethos of competition and belligerence. Complementing the essay's cardinal theme, then, but considerably expanding its scope, is a mode of disputation that performs its difference from the confident proclamations of the tyrant by presenting itself as uneasy in its authority, answerable to others, and making do with what evidence it has, as best it can.

In this way, *Three Guineas* exemplifies what Ngũgĩ wa Thiong'o has called "poor theory." "Poor theory," Ngũgĩ writes at the outset of *Globalectics*, seeks "to accord dignity to the poor as they fight poverty, including, dare I say, poverty of theory."[28] Taking "poor" to mean "the barest," and "poor theory" as thought that maximizes the barest, Ngũgĩ defines poor theory in light of his past experience of writing plays in the "poor theater tradition, the traveling and community theater movements in East and Central Africa" (2, 5). Just as "the poor person's unintentional daring and experimentation comes from necessity," poor theater "does with whatever is handed to it, making an aesthetic under circumstances not chosen" by its practitioners (4, 6). In this way, Ngũgĩ implies that constraint and deprivation become enabling conditions of the pursuit of intellectual freedom. Ngũgĩ's discussion of poor theory is unusual in its recasting of what "theory" has come to mean for many of us in interdisciplinary cultural studies: the theory he advances is not rarefied, not the province of the academically educated, and neither more knowing than the arts it seeks to analyze, contextualize, and critique nor even discrete from them. On the contrary, "poor theory" takes its ethos from the theatrical practice that inspired it and is exemplified in Ngũgĩ's argument by fiction itself. He anticipates our surprise at this: "Fiction as theory? Can we in fact think of fiction, the novel, as writing theory? We have to go back to the original meaning of theory in Greek, *theoria*, meaning a view and a contemplation. View assumes a viewer, a ground on which to stand, and what is viewed from that standpoint. A view is also a framework for organizing what is seen and a thinking about the viewed. Fiction is the original poor theory" (15). Ngũgĩ conceives of fiction, both the reading and writing of it, as a way to understand experiences such as traumatic shock, politically motivated terror, and the institutionalized devaluation of one's native language and culture, when discursive prose cannot accommodate their many layers of sense and feeling: "How could an article really capture the complexity of what I had experienced in colonial Kenya? The blood in the streets; the dead guerrillas hung on trees as a public spectacle; the horror stories of white officers collecting ears, noses, eyes, genitalia, or even heads of the vanquished as trophies!" (17). His yearning to "order the chaos" of his most acute childhood loss, his discovery on arriving home from boarding school that British forces had burned his village to the ground and relocated his family and community to a concentration village, drew him eventually to the novel as "a theory of felt experience" that "reaches out to beyond the space and time of its location" (18, 19).

Ngũgĩ's transnational postcolonial account of poor theory and its alignment with historical fiction is remarkably reminiscent of *Three Guineas*'s movement from the fiction of a war photograph, which impels distant readers to imagine a scene of carnage they might otherwise explain away through partisan arguments, to the utopian envisioning of a revolutionary "poor college," an "experimental" and "adventurous" new college "founded on poverty and youth" (Woolf, *Three Guineas* 43). In this section of *Three Guineas*, what begins with impassioned, Marinetti-esque demands for a wholesale overthrow of one women's college curriculum gradually yields to a very different stance of negotiation and compromise. The speaker comes to acknowledge that she alone cannot solve the problems of women's education and its complicities with a competitive patriarchal culture that promotes international rivalry and war. The way to solve these problems, she suggests, is by conversing together and revaluing what cannot culminate in unilateral power and profits. Like Ngũgĩ, Woolf advocates an alliance of poverty, collective action, and narrative imagination for affording views that challenge tyrannical regimes of knowledge and governance. Anticipating the question of "what should be taught in the new college, the poor college?" she replies, "Not the arts of dominating other people; not the arts of ruling, of killing, of acquiring land and capital." Instead, "the poor college must teach only the arts that can be taught cheaply and practised by poor people; such as medicine, mathematics, music, painting and literature. It should teach the arts of human intercourse; the art of understanding other people's lives and minds" (43). Ngũgĩ, too, wants to usher in a post-nationalist conversation through curricular reform, more particularly in literary studies, that will replace a long-standing hierarchy of dominant and peripheral texts with "a mutually affecting dialogue, or multi-logue" of far-flung works of literature and orature imagined as points on a globe, where "there is no one center; any point is equally a center" and all the points are "balanced and related to one another by the principle of giving and receiving" (*Globalectics* 8, 61).

Like Ngũgĩ's earlier, widely read book *Decolonising the Mind*, *Globalectics* challenges nationally and ethnically elitist theories of literary and cultural value inherited from colonialism, by arguing that perceptions of centrality are changeable and shaped by educational structures that are also changeable; both books urge us to ask, "from what base do we look at the world?"[29] "With Africa at the centre of things" in the African university curriculum,

Ngũgĩ predicts in *Decolonising the Mind*, another shift can occur: "after we have examined ourselves, we radiate outwards and discover peoples and worlds around us" (94). *Globalectics* indeed shifts from the earlier work's focus on the politics of writing, teaching, and giving curricular priority at African universities to literatures in indigenous African languages, to the enduring promise of postcolonial perspectives in the reimagining of global relations among people and their cultures. This turn echoes another that Jacqui Alexander notes in transnational feminist pedagogy and critique: whereas "there was a time we believed history to be incomplete, erroneous even, in its evisceration of feminist standpoints," now "we need to develop a similar urgency around relational curricular projects that put us in conversation, not domination, with a range of relational knowledges."[30]

However different their immediate political foes or delineations of "the poor," Woolf, Ngũgĩ, and Alexander build their appeals for radical educational reform on a shared belief in the potential power of the systemically disempowered to decenter and ultimately discredit worldviews that authorize state-sponsored violence. They share, too, a belief in the potentially subversive force of the "poorly" (read "heterogeneously" rather than "minimally") educated to supplement and, when necessary, contradict apparently factual evidentiary discourse with creative fictions of various kinds and from various points of view. Woolf's arresting verbal image of abject, state-ravaged bodies, to the extent that her speaker identifies this image as a photograph on display in her text, is a fiction, like the letter she purports to be writing and the sympathetic male correspondent eagerly awaiting it. But it is also, she insists, a "fact." Her hope is to reeducate the public to see this fact—a fact narrowly interpreted in the English public sphere as evidence of the fascist enemy's brutality—as evidence also of even well-meaning Englishmen's complicity in a dehumanizing system of nation building and war making.

I have said that *Three Guineas* models a way of envisioning justice that is experimental and self-correcting, responsive to an audience its speaker learns from by imagining herself in their place over the course of her enunciation. That she learns equally from "facts" found in the "history and biography" readily available to an upper-class Englishwoman in the 1930s and from those excluded from such public archives of evidence is one of the more remarkable features of the process of learning that *Three Guineas* enacts. Its speaker, faced with an accumulation of prior discourse, never forgets for long that her voice is one of many, and that to be heard she must build a dialogue with published texts that enjoy the status of evidence but also with other, unheard, hypothetical voices whose potential to be imagined shapes the very terms of the debate:

> The letter broke off there. It was not from lack of things to say; the peroration indeed was only just beginning. It was because the face on the other side of the page—the face that a letter-writer always sees—appeared to be fixed with a certain melancholy. . . . "What is the use of thinking how a college can be different," she seemed to say, "when it must be a place where students are taught to obtain appointments?" "Dream your dreams," she seemed to add, . . . "fire off your rhetoric, but we have to face realities." (Woolf, *Three Guineas* 44–45)

In this passage, the speaker's impassioned appeal for a utopian poor college where "society was free" and "learning is sought for itself" is stopped short not so much by her own pragmatism as by her exercise of that neglected art of understanding she would have the poor college teach (44). Woolf maintains a relentless dual focus on the uneducated, ill-equipped, poor speaker's need to draw from texts that happen to be available to her and the imperative she feels to stop and take account of others who do not appear in those texts but whose points of view haunt them and any response she might make to them. It would seem to be her very poverty that makes her disposed to do this imaginative reckoning, to stop and doubt herself along the course of her argument, and to adapt that argument accordingly. She thus establishes a bond between her deficient access to source material that a better education might have afforded her and her compensatory, adventurous and experimental use of sympathetic imagination to fill in the gaps of the material she can secure. At the same time, the speaker of *Three Guineas* is profoundly concerned with how to guide her reader to imagine as she does, her reader who is not poor in the ways she is.

Woolf's argument alerts us to the discursive and historical contingencies not only of her audience's position but also of her speaker's own, and of the fictions she can imagine from that position. The speaker's potential as an effective translator depends on her capacity to anticipate which stories, and which comparisons, will be recognized by the privileged readership she hopes to persuade. This is where their shared class identification becomes essential to the staging of their conversation, and where her avowed status as an "outsider" should be treated as a strategy for being heard, rather than a truth, however appealing, about her cosmopolitan intellectual independence. For all her utopian demands on the women's poor college and then, seeing that her demands cannot be met, her calls for it to be burned to the ground, she makes a rhetoric of cooperation and self-deprecation her most disarming instrument of persuasion. When she decides to support the college as best she can, notwithstanding its necessary participation in a professional system marked by competition and social hierarchy, she makes clear her preference for conversation and negotiation over imperious coercion and unyielding rage. This commitment to conversation and negotiation entails openly acknowledging her selective attention to members of her own class (while leaving race unmentioned) when she calls for an "Outsiders' Society" of women like herself: "It would consist of educated men's daughters working in their own class—how indeed can they work in any other?" (Woolf, *Three Guineas* 126).[31]

The dialogue that Woolf imagines in *Three Guineas* does not include everyone. But it does give us a method for imagining what her speaker cannot yet translate to her audience, by modeling a process of conceiving justice that is as much a measure of the book's enduring pertinence as any of its isolated claims. I know of no other essay that so explicitly enacts the moralist's obligation to participate in a contentious communal process where "we continually challenge each other to enunciate our vision of justice," to borrow Alexander's phrase (116). Woolf, in putting before a fictional audience of epistolary correspondents one speaker's principled enunciation of justice, makes the imagining of a distant audience's perspectives formative in the unfolding of that enunciation. This is the real poor college of *Three Guineas*, the fiction of a dialogue or even, in Ngũgĩ's terms, a "multi-logue," where voices in contention—some heard or read, others anticipated, and still others not yet imaginable but en route to the debate—goad, reorient, and supplement each other unpredictably to model a collective imagining of social change. It is a college where Woolf teaches readers to search out the face on the other side of the page; she makes no claims to be able to search out every face herself.

This brings us back to Danticat.

Amabelle and Antigone: Noticing Collaborations

The texts considered above have in common that they urge readers to notice and learn from neglected perspectives; they also have in common that they are structured as addresses to easily identifiable audiences assumed to be listening. *Three Guineas*, initially a lecture that Woolf delivered to an audience of academically educated professional women, takes the form of an epistolary reply (consisting partly of other epistolary replies) to an imaginary correspondent who has sought out her help; Césaire's *Discourse on Colonialism* mimics the oratories he and fellow *deputés* were accustomed to present to each other in the Assemblée Nationale; *Globalectics* originated as Ngũgĩ's prestigious Wellek Library Lectures in Critical Theory at the University of California, Irvine; and Jacqui Alexander's essay on "teaching for justice" began, like *Three Guineas*, as a lecture to professional women.[32] In all cases, the speaker assumes the position of one whose views, however politically oppositional or aligned with the disempowered, are at the very least being heard, and are expected to be heard. Reading these texts together facilitates the recognition that a speaker's expectation of having an interested audience, even just one willing listener or reader, is an inaugural step toward the kind of collective action Woolf envisions for her utopian poor college and her Outsiders' Society for daughters of educated men, both of which are ideas that grow out of her book's fictional starting point, where a woman addresses a man of influence who has already expressed a desire to listen to her. What happens, then, when this conversation of texts admits another kind of first-person declamatory performance, one in which the speaker testifies but has no audience in the fictional world she inhabits and no expectation of finding an audience; what happens when the speaker herself is the face on the other side of the page, and we, her distant and unmentioned readers, become the only conceivable audience who could respond to her protest?

"Our Guernica" was not Danticat's earliest or most extensive use of the Spanish Civil War as a source of analogies to cast light on a collective Haitian trauma largely unknown to her international readers. While Woolf uses Franco's Nazi-backed uprising to help her tell the story of an Englishwoman who feels frustrated that she does not have better options for influencing educational and professional reforms and thereby preventing war, Danticat uses the same war to help her tell the story of a poor Haitian migrant woman who has no influence on public policy, nor any hope of ever influencing it. Published twelve years before the 2010 earthquake, Danticat's novel *The Farming of Bones* puts Dominican dictator Rafael Trujillo's genocidal massacre of Haitian immigrants and Afro-Dominicans in 1937 at the center of a historical landscape of spreading fascism, with the Spanish Civil War raging in the distance.[33] Living in the Dominican borderlands, Amabelle Désir has worked as a domestic servant to an affluent Spanish expatriate she calls Papi since she was orphaned as a child, and she watches sympathetically as he sits by his radio each night, listening with dread and helplessness, as so many progressive-minded news consumers did in those years, to reports of Franco's progress and fascism's ascendancy.

The novel recurrently evokes analogous patterns of social and political relations of which Amabelle, the novel's narrator, seems unaware, but which Danticat's readers are obliquely guided to recognize and reflect on. As one uprooted from her homeland and occupying, like other Haitian migrants in Trujillo's Dominican Republic, a precarious social position with few apparent rights,[34] Amabelle feels an affinity with Papi even though her subordinate status is only too clear from her extreme reserve with him, her deferential mode of address, and her austere living accommodations. She imagines that her sense of identification with Papi may be mutual: "Like me," Amabelle tells us, "Papi had been displaced from his native land; he felt himself the orphaned child of a now orphaned people. Perhaps this was why he often seemed more kindly disposed to the strangers for whom this side of the island had not always been home" (Danticat, *Farming* 78). Danticat links the sense of exile that Papi and Amabelle share to their distance from militarized nation building, preceding this statement of affinity with Amabelle's narration of an exchange she overhears between Papi and a privileged young creole named Beatriz, the family doctor's proudly "liberated" daughter: "'Do I like the way things are conducted here now, everything run by military men? Do I like the worship of uniforms, the medals like stars on people's chests?' he asks her. 'No,' Papi said. 'I don't like any part of it'" (77–78).

Through Papi, Danticat criticizes militarism's self-justifying trappings, which, like Woolf, she associates with despotic abuses of power and their culmination in military violence and civilian support for war in the name of ethnic and nationalist loyalty. Amabelle overhears Papi's remarks about Trujillo's military dictatorship, made in response to Beatriz's persistent questions, within a larger conversation about the Spanish Civil War. Papi does not share Beatriz's idealistic interest in fighting for the cause—she expresses interest in the International Brigade's admittance of women fighters (Danticat, *Farming* 77)—despite what Danticat repeatedly shows to be his intense preoccupation with the Spanish republic's struggle against Franco's rebel forces, and his worry that "the good side does not always win" (43). Notwithstanding his rapt attention to radio broadcasts on the war's discouraging course, which Amabelle describes as his "fighting a year-and-a-half old civil war in Spain by means of the radio," he says little about war (including his own fighting, years before, in Spain) apart from his abhorrence of its destructiveness—hence the irony of his daughter Valencia's marriage to one of Trujillo's most obedient and ambitious soldiers, and of Valencia's patriotic portrait of Trujillo in the family parlor, where "she had made him a giant in full military regalia, with vast fringed epaulets and clusters of medals aligned in neat rows under the saffron braiding across his chest" (43). The "oddly tender" eyes and "coy gentle smile" with which Valencia endows the notoriously corrupt and brutal tyrant make him a picture of humaneness nobly embodying the national motto Valencia reinscribes in the painting, "DIOS, PATRIA, LIBERTAD" (43). Danticat's ekphrasis in the context of Trujillo's reign of terror and Valencia's submissiveness as both a wife and citizen not only supports Papi's explicit criticism of militarism but also achieves something of what Woolf's actual photographs of ostentatiously clad English leaders and public officials do: it analogizes what Woolf, in her initial lecture from 1931 that eventually grew into *Three Guineas*, called the master of the house—whose mastery over women in the house is allied with his competitive practices of acquisition and self-aggrandizement outside the house—with decorated and repressive men in positions of authority, including, finally, the fascist dictator who would enslave women and men alike, across classes and nations.[35] But for all Papi's critical distance from Trujillo, Franco, and his own daughter and son-in-law's perpetuation of sexism, social division, and authoritarianism both in their home and beyond, Danticat's critique does not stop here. That a patriotically rendered tyrant's portrait overhangs Papi's ardent nightly occupation of listening to news reports of the Spanish war, and that "Papi seemed unaware of the Generalissimo's enormous presence" as he listens, suggests more than an old man's sense of exile and isolation (43).

Any suspicion we may form from Amabelle's sense of identification with Papi that he will oppose the massacre and protect Amabelle or anyone of Haitian descent from his son-in-law and the other soldiers proves to be unfounded. On the contrary, Amabelle loses track of Papi completely once the massacre commences and she must flee, losing her beloved fiancé Sebastien in the process. The portrait's proximity, unsuspected by Papi, as he immerses himself in news of Spain's losing battle with fascism, suggests something quite different from Amabelle's sense of their likeness and mutual understanding: it suggests the irony of a kind but privileged European's preoccupation with a vicious tyranny in his native land, while overtaking his home is another vicious tyranny, which he dislikes but largely ignores because its impact is on people he does not see as his own, in a country he does not see as his own. Here again we see an analogy, this time implicit in the structure of the historical fiction, used to capture a distant audience's interest and at the same time to hint at this audience's possible complicity indirectly enough that they might want to change. Specifically, Danticat's juxtapositions suggest an analogous relationship between Spanish Civil War casualties—already points of interest and sympathy for much of her international audience—and the more obscure, little-known victims of the Kout Kouto or Parsley Massacre of 1937; *at the same time*, Danticat hints at the ineffectuality and inadvertent inhumanity of one of the book's more appealing characters, a character with whom a European or North American reader might easily identify, whose understandable and widely shared worries about the struggles and atrocities in Spain blind him to the full significance of the racist dictatorship in his present environment, and the danger it poses to a servant who has devoted her life to serving him.

Patriotism in *The Farming of Bones*, then, is not just the manifest evil of Trujillo's ethnic cleansing; it is the banal evil of distraction that allows Papi, and Beatriz as well, to look away to European fascism as the dark enemy to be overcome while attending so little to Trujillo's violent and repressive regime, even as its agents of propaganda (Valencia) and brute force (her husband, Pico) reside in Papi's own home and Beatriz's own neighborhood. Indeed, through Amabelle's characterization of Beatriz, Danticat is unusually explicit in exposing the limitations of a certain kind of cosmopolitan feminist intellectual, portraying her as the callow bearer of white European privilege: "Beatriz spent her days pounding her fingers on a piano in her mother's parlor and speaking Latin to herself. She wanted to be a newspaper woman, it was said, travel the world, wear trousers, and ask questions of people suffering through calamities greater than hers" (*Farming* 39). At no point does Beatriz ask questions of the Haitian women who serve and observe her, nor does she ever appear to ask questions about the forced travels, widespread illiteracy, and terrible sufferings of the Haitians and Afro-Dominicans all around her. What Danticat implies that Papi and Beatriz share, notwithstanding Amabelle's sympathy with one and not with the other, is that their attention is generally elsewhere. Like so many politically engaged writers circa 1937 (including, of course, Woolf) whose work leaves little doubt as to what was seen to matter on the international stage at the time, Papi and Beatriz turn their gaze almost exclusively toward Europe and the metropolitan United States, hardly noticing the narrator who observes them and wants to identify with one of them.

The Farming of Bones, with its understated depiction of interconnected tragedies, does not resemble *Three Guineas* in tone or style but shares its critical tactic of bringing fiction to the writing of an otherwise elusive history. In this, Danticat, like Woolf, challenges a familiar hierarchy of "factual" documented evidence over communal remembrance, private conversation, and the imagining of the unverifiable that such remembrance and conversation inform. Among the ways that Danticat shows fiction and nonfiction to be potential collaborators, each radiating outward and illuminating each other like Ngũgĩ's texts on a globe, is her selection of a narrator who is not, in the story, a tale-teller or, in general, a woman of words. She is a woman of observations, memories, and enigmatic dreams she has little inclination to share with other characters or to explain, either to us or to herself. At one point in the book, her attempt to testify about the massacre, along with more than a thousand others waiting in the same line, comes to nothing: there is not one official who will listen to her or to most of the others, and Danticat leaves little doubt that even the testimonies heard and duly recorded by the priests will have scant effect aside from offering some solace to the testifying survivors, however brief and inconsequential that solace must be. After this, she does not seem to believe that words expressed to others, words made public, will make a difference. In what are at first alternating chapters of Amabelle's narration of the public world she inhabits and of more lyrical and cryptic expressions, typographically differentiated in boldface print, of her private world of reminiscence and dream consciousness, Danticat consigns Amabelle's emphatic repetitions of Sebastien's name to her private world alone. Although Amabelle opens her story with a call for her lost lover's name to be remembered, a call she will repeat later on, nothing in the story gives us a sense that Amabelle has the means to pass on this story herself. After her attempts to testify publicly about their story are frustrated, her resolve to keep Sebastien's name alive seems ultimately directed at herself only. Though she is among the few literate members of the Haitian migrant community, Amabelle never appears to write their story down; remembering, and faithfully guarding her memories against external distractions and competing stories, is her way of passing the story on:

> It is perhaps the great discomfort of those trying to silence the world to discover that we have voices sealed inside our heads, voices that with each passing day, grow even louder than the clamor of the world outside.
>
> The slaughter is the only thing that is mine enough to pass on. All I want to

> do is find a place to lay it down now and again, a safe nest where it will neither be scattered by the winds, nor remain forever buried beneath the sod.
>
> I just need to lay it down sometimes. Even in the rare silence of the night, *with no faces around*. (Danticat, *Farming* 266; my emphasis)

There was a time when Amabelle did have access to listeners and interlocutors who formed a kind of audience of which she was part, but they did not include Papi or his family, or, notably, anyone who identified with a foreign or cosmopolitan community, but "wayfarers" with a shared homeland: Sebastien, and to a lesser degree Father Romain, who, before the massacre, "always made much of our being from the same place, just as Sebastien did. Most people here did. It was a way of being joined to your old life through the presence of another person. At times you could sit for a whole evening with such individuals, just listening to their existence unfold, from the house where they were born to the hill where they wanted to be buried. It was their way of returning home, with you as a witness" (Danticat, *Farming* 56, 73). Quiet and intensely private, Amabelle does not say that she herself ever let her existence unfold before others as they listened; her only confidant appears to have been Sebastien. Still, the massacre destroyed these networks of listeners, killing many, including Sebastien; destroying the mental health of others, like Father Romain, who for a long time loses his memory; and so traumatizing others, like Amabelle, as to leave them hopeless with respect to building new networks of interlocutors. When she resettles in Haiti, she is left with a private world of dreams and memories that she shares with no one in the world of the novel: "My dreams are now only visitations of my words for the absent justice of the peace, for the Generalissimo himself" (265).

Such a history, representative of many such neglected histories, is one that would likely never reach the public sphere outside of fiction, not, at least, in such affective depth and detail, because its speaker lacks an audience who will hear it. And yet through historical fiction Danticat translates elusive histories like Amabelle's beyond bounds of private memory, showing their relevance at once to documented histories of the Haitian massacre and to histories of racialized political violence elsewhere in the world. She translates them, in other words, not just by giving the subaltern Amabelle a voice but also by investing that voice with a transregionally and transculturally representative power. For this, Danticat needs a different kind of declamatory fiction from that of the *Discourse on Colonialism* or *Three Guineas*, one that can function as, among other things, a testimony of one woman's traumatic witnessing of a genocide, its contexts, and its lifelong outcomes for herself and other survivors, but that can also represent the absence of an audience for this testimony within the world of the one speaking. We, the *novel's* audience, are a different matter. Amabelle lacks Danticat's means of anticipating her own potential readership, and so Danticat's challenge is to use her "novelist's prerogative," as Woolf puts it in her 1931 lecture, to imagine a solitary poor woman's determination to make her lover's story endure by holding fast to her private world of reminiscence, a woman so poor she has no sense of possibilities for mobilizing collectively like Ngũgĩ's poor theater, or Woolf's poor college, or Woolf's Outsiders' Society (Woolf, "Speech" xli). Danticat's testimonial fiction can achieve in fiction what even a fictive address cannot: it presents us with an audience—ourselves—when none appears in the world of the fiction.

What all this suggests is that Danticat, not her narrator Amabelle, is the one seeing and inviting readers to see parallels between Trujillo's slaughter of migrants and Dominicans of Haitian descent and the slaughter of Basque and other Spanish civilians memorialized by Picasso and Woolf. As she hints at these parallels, she also shows the massacre of Haitians as having no parallel for its victims; for Amabelle, who is beaten, maimed, and bereft of Sebastien, her only remaining loved one, no event abroad is comparable or even of interest. Danticat is able to make us look outward from the local just long enough to be critical of those who, like Papi, look away from the looming disaster nearest them for too long and with too little effort at drawing connections and acting on them, however humane and enlightened their professed politics. With the juxtaposition of massacres, one well publicized internationally, the other virtually ignored, Danticat guides us to see the injustice of not recognizing the essential comparability of European fascist atrocities and the atrocities of Trujillo's military dictatorship. That the novel is capacious enough to draw us into these two apparently contradictory movements simultaneously—looking away to Spain to find affinities that warrant the attention of those of us not usually attuned to Haitian suffering but highly attuned to the horrors of the Spanish Civil War, while at the same time exploring the risks of looking away because it distracts from the specificities and urgencies of the local—testifies to the unions of contradictory elements a story can create through an aesthetics of comparatism and indirection. These tense, difficult poetic unions powerfully evoke the unsatisfactoriness of simplistic politics of polarization, undermining the dichotomizing logic that drives *antihaitianismo* and anti-immigrant racism more broadly, just as surely as it drives nationalistic violence, and colonial genocides, and the use of bombs and other weaponry that made these injustices possible.

The analogies are for all of us who read more territorially, our ethical imaginations more circumscribed by ethnic and regional identitarianisms (even ostensibly cosmopolitan ones), than we could and should. Whereas Amabelle cannot and would not try to craft a heterological language to sway the dominant or to align herself with others, Danticat does, and in so doing she heightens our awareness of the layers of address and the functions of analogy in Woolf's earlier feminist protest against a repressive and enduring nexus of nationalism, sexism, militarism, and authoritarianism. It is tempting to identify the figure of Antigone in *Three Guineas* as the representative *par excellence* of a courageous female outsider who stands alone speaking truth to power. But it is Woolf's use of Antigone in comparative connection and collaboration with the many other women's voices in the book, both fictional and nonfictional and including the speaker's own continually adaptive and modulating voice, that distinguishes *Three Guineas* from what would have been a more predictably monologic and oppositional contribution to the modernist manifesto tradition.[36] Noticing that Danticat defines herself in the book's concluding acknowledgments as one who is passing on stories she has heard from others such as her mother, whose own, orally transmitted stories were transmitted to her by others, attests to the collaborative mode of creation and learning of Danticat's writing. Amabelle seems alone but is in fact joined—outside the novel—by a collective of oral storytellers including Danticat's mother and Danticat herself, not only to pass on her story but also to translate it into a language that distant readers will trust enough to allow it to transform them.

Where Despair and Open Futures Converge

In this book's second chapter, I considered how the prospect of open futures that concludes *The Waste Land* and the *Cahier d'un retour au pays natal* is one of ambiguous and unforeseen connections, at once threatening and hopeful. The poems' evocations of a time that is both night and day, and of a natural expanse into which the self as previously known might be submerged and transformed, constitute a motif that returns in Danticat's fleeting description of a secluded cave in *The Farming of Bones*, a cave whose significance to its narrator becomes inseparable from that novel's richly ambiguous, hopeful and threatening conclusion. "Behind the waterfall," explains Amabelle, "at the source of the stream where the cane workers bathe," is "a grotto of wet moss, coral, and chalk that looks like marble," where once inside "all you see is luminous green fresco—the dark green of wet papaya leaves" (Danticat, *Farming* 100). Martin Munro has rightly pointed to the novel's portrayal of the Haitian-Dominican borderlands as menacing,[37] but here is a space that stands apart from the human systems of dominance that have rendered that landscape a menace—the plantation economy and its vast fields of razor-sharp cane leaves that scar the bodies of the impoverished workers who harvest them, and the international, neocolonial allegiances that made Trujillo's militaristic dictatorship possible—a space where Amabelle and her lover Sebastien make love for the first time and where the laws of day and night do not seem to apply:

> When the night comes, you don't know it inside the cramped slippery cave because the waterfall, Sebastien says, holds on to some memory of the sun that it will not surrender. On the inside of the cave, there is always light, day and night. You who know the cave's secret, for a time, you are also held captive in this prism, this curiosity of nature that makes you want to celebrate yourself in ways that you hope the cave will show you, that the emptiness in your bones will show you, or that the breath in your blood will show you, in ways that you hope your body knows better than yourself. (100)

Like other memories narrated in the present tense that interrupt the novel's main action to reveal Amabelle's haunted inner life, the cave is not remembered once but continually in a state of reliving lost experience and yearning for its return. The remembered cave stands apart from all other spaces in the novel because it is a space of mergings in a world marked by strict social divisions and antagonisms. Even Amabelle's hut, also a site of physical and verbal intimacy with Sebastien, is so ascetic in relation to the plush bedroom of her mistress, Papi's daughter Valencia, and so regularly the place where Amabelle and Sebastien relive their childhood traumas as they sleep, that it resonates far more darkly than the cave behind the waterfall in search of which Amabelle, as an old woman, will return one day, without success. I close with this easily overlooked image of a lost cause and thwarted return, the nostalgic search for a vanished cave where light continues to shine into the night, to acknowledge that Danticat puts at the summit of her story about a borderland in literal and figurative senses a space and way of being that overcomes the consequences of those borders, a space that suggests lush natural growth in clear contrast with the man-made fields of cane where

Sebastien once worked and the ornate, alien enclosure where Amabelle once worked. The cave is the novel's exceptional space of serene seclusion, protected from all human agency apart from that of the undisturbed lovers.

And yet, taking refuge in a space protected from human penetration and influence is not, and cannot be, the long-term solution for migrant Haitians who must earn their living as best they can, or for a writer protesting their victimization. The novel's next most optimistic, and more pragmatic, means of envisioning justice for the future is the dialogic (or multi-logic, as Ngũgĩ would have it) collaboration it enacts through its own narrative development, between the narrator Amabelle, who has a story but no one to hear it, and Danticat, who can imagine and tell that story thanks to her overlapping communities of interlocutors and readers. A place of harmonious mergings is not possible at the end of *The Farming of Bones*, but there is a kind of impossible union in this story that is both a fiction and a lost history from whose telling the writer appears to remove herself as an authority, to make of herself an amanuensis. The story's fraught dialogism, its guarded embrace of representation as a means of healing notwithstanding representation's dangers, is what most closely approximates Amabelle's final submersion of herself in the Massacre River. Lined with border police between Haiti and the Dominican Republic, it is a place of intersecting histories and languages that have harmed her, but that might also, through their contact, begin to change with her. Amabelle's submersion of herself in these dangerous and potentially healing waters is an image of painful negotiation with no certain end, an image that supersedes but also coexists with the novel's earlier, aspirational glimpse into an impossibly protected place of mergings behind a waterfall.

Conclusion

The Beauty of a Trembling World

> There was something strange in the shadow that the flicker of her eyes cast, something which (as anyone can test for himself by looking now at the sky), is always absent from the present—whence its terror, its nondescript character—something one trembles to pin through the body with a name and call beauty, for it has no body, is as a shadow without substance or quality of its own, yet has the power to change whatever it adds itself to.
>
> —Virginia Woolf

When Virginia Woolf defines modern poetry as a poetry of difficult comparisons, she suggests a mode of comparative reading that works not only to reveal the margins of cloistered communities but to give a sense of the difficulty that differences pose to personal and collective self-knowledge. Neither assimilable nor fully excludable, figures of coexisting and interpenetrating difference in the comparisons that launch *A Room of One's Own* move the focus outward to a larger world not quite grasped by the speaker, who is discerning enough to know she does not grasp it. The known and trusted are positioned in relation to what cannot be reconciled with them, and out of that relativizing comparison emerges a never quite specified vision of totality that Woolf, here and elsewhere, calls "the beauty of the world." This phrase recurs in Woolf's work at moments when language fails to explain or resolve a problem. After the beautiful Mrs. Ramsay dies in *To the Lighthouse*, the artist Lily Briscoe senses the world's elusive beauty at night and hopes that she and her housemates will be able to translate it into a sovereign grandeur they can understand, but she also assures herself that even in the absence of this translation, meaning will yield itself up in the song of the sea:

> Through the open window the voice of the beauty of the world came murmuring, too softly to hear exactly what it said—but what mattered if the meaning were plain? . . . They would see then night flowing down in purple; his head crowned; his sceptre jewelled; and how in his eyes a child might look. And if they still faltered . . . , if they still said no, that it was vapour, this splendour of his, and the dew had more power than he, and they preferred sleeping; gently then without complaint, or argument, the voice would sing its song.[1]

Yet Lily awakens to find she cannot secure this significance, asking herself, "What does it mean then, what can it all mean?. . . Nothing, nothing—nothing that she could express at all" (145). And earlier in *To the Lighthouse*, Woolf treats Mr. Ramsay's self-aggrandizing fantasies with dry mockery, but his visceral recognition of "the beauty of the world," embodied in his family, is what interrupts these fantasies: "Who will not secretly rejoice when the hero puts his armour off, and halts by the window and gazes at his wife and son, who, very distant at first, gradually come closer and closer, . . . who will blame him if he does homage to the beauty of the world?" (36).

Our response to these images of incomprehension in the face of the world's totality cannot now, nearly a century after Woolf wrote the words, be neatly separated from the critical imaginative training imparted to us in the years since by transnationalist revaluations of poetic opacity as a democratizing political force. This revaluation of poetic opacity is indispensable for Glissant in approaching what he, too, has repeatedly called *la beauté du monde*. For Glissant and in turn for Woolf, the political power of this necessarily oblique and indefinite phrase inheres in its recognition of the difficulty of imagining what is strange to us, in others and in ourselves, without dominating it through assimilation or exclusion. It implies an intractable diversity within the totality that encompasses us all. Before considering the implications and value of Glissant's concept in more detail, it is worth noting that the nonterritorial global orientation it reveals both developed out of his recognition of the Caribbean as a distinct site of historically particular communal and linguistic relations and has provoked criticism for the role that poetic alterity came to play, with its implications of what supersedes positive discourse, in Caribbean creolist theory as transnational processes of creolization became its central focus.

In *Local Histories/Global Designs*, Walter Mignolo credits the authors of the *Éloge de la créolité* with distinguishing among *créolité*, *nègritude*, *Americanité*, and *Antillanité* in such a way as to "uncouple" both "language from ethnicity" and "language from territoriality."[2] For Mignolo, the epistemological potential of Creoleness is as a "border thinking from the perspective of the subaltern," one that formed in response to the nineteenth-century discourse of borders that assumed a "natural correlation between language, territory, and race" (247, 240). He writes, "Creoles, Caribbeanness, and Creoleness are still categories that overlap but which belong to different levels. Being or defining oneself as Creole means identifying a group of people, differentiating them from others. Thus, to say [as the *Éloge* authors do] that 'neither Europeans, nor Africans, nor Asians, we proclaim ourselves Creoles' . . . is an identification in relation to a territory, and to the historical processes that created that territory" (241–42). At the same time, Creoleness challenges this "territorial epistemology," because even as "Creoleness is defined from the mode of being engendered by French colonization in the Caribbean, it is also projected beyond it to characterize Creoleness as a world experience" (246, 242).

By the time Mignolo wrote this in 2000, the Caribbean territorial dimension of *créolité* was already giving way to more globally oriented creolisms in Glissant's *Poetics of Relation* and the new theoretical work it helped to inspire by Chamoiseau, among others. This new work developed the idea of Caribbean and other archipelagic configurations as models of highly differentiated and uneven world processes of creolization rather than as the proper geographic sites of creole identity as such. By the time Chamoiseau wrote *Frères migrants* in 2017, translated the following year as *Migrant Brothers: A Poet's Declaration of Human Dignity*, it was not uncharacteristic of him to write, "Whether consciously or not, Relation deterritorializes."[3]

The increasingly global orientation of Glissant and Chamoiseau has been criticized by some scholars who see their emphasis on poetics and broad relational dynamics as overly abstract and insufficiently attuned to historical and political contexts. Chris Bongie, for example, contends that "notwithstanding the remarkable consistency of Glissant's vision over the past five decades when it comes to championing a cross-cultural poetics of Relation, his most recent work is characterized by the concerted attempt to 'desuture' that poetics from any and all oppositional politics of the sort with which he himself had once associated it."[4] Although he wrote this in 2008, before the appearance of some of the essays considered below, Bongie has reiterated this position more recently, and he is not alone.[5]

More broadly, Bongie has expressed skepticism of the political efficacy and self-consistency of numerous other critics, such as Gayatri Spivak and David Scott, whose sometimes tortuous, implicitly modernist practices of literary and cultural comparison, representation, and critique helped to inspire this book's own uncertain comparisons. Clearly, Bongie is more confident than I am about the superiority of a dependably concrete "conflictual politics," which he appears to consider sufficient for transforming readers' diverse ways of imagining their relations and responsibilities to each other and to a shared but resiliently divided environment (Bongie, *Friends* 329–30). What such critiques in the name of a materialist historicism do not take seriously enough, in my view, is the generative value, both for political and social critique and for representations of cross-cultural relations and possibilities of relation, of transnational modernist comparisons to acknowledge and respond responsibly to that most threatening other: the representing subject's own inadequacy to secure transcultural knowledge from the culturally situated position they necessarily occupy. The forms these comparisons take, and the value they hold for our ongoing rethinking and representing of planetary relations, interpenetrations, and often unspoken, unrecognized, and unrealized bonds, are what this book has followed, from Stein's intermixing in a time of blood politics to Glissant's and Chamoiseau's trembling in a time of border thought.

I want to address such critiques by reflecting on what comparatists and scholars of transnationalism may gain from taking seriously Glissant's abstract notion of "the beauty of the world" in contexts of widespread political polarization and ready access to misleadingly transparent disinformation. The concept appears repeatedly in Glissant's work since *Poetics of Relation*, including the pamphlets he coauthored with Chamoiseau on politically topical subjects, still lesser-known essays that form a basis for Chamoiseau's recent vision of "a *global politics of hospitality*" in *Migrant Brothers*. I take this concept as representative of a number of such attempts in this developing body of Creole and creolist transnationalist work to conceive language as a means of linkage, decidedly not a means of reassuring incorporation into a presumed unity any more than it is a means of blockage and repulsion from that same unity. Lyrical and abstract as these attempts have been, they have been generative for comparative scholarship not because they effectively reiterate and reinforce an aesthetic and political status quo, as their opponents imply, but because their articulations of political responsibility in the face of interpenetrating material conditions across localities offer something other than, and at least as valuable as, the definitively stated political diagnoses and prognostications that their critics seek.

Against "territorial intolerance" and "plunder in the name of the unique root," Glissant writes, "the wanderer, who is no longer the traveler, the discoverer, or the conqueror, seeks to know the totality of the world and already knows he will never accomplish this—and in this, he knows, the threatened beauty of the world resides."[6] In this passage from *Poetics of Relation*, Glissant conjoins an aspiration to imagine the totality of the world's relations with a recognition of its impossibility and a committed resistance to defining totality in any way that would obscure the diversity and dynamism of that totality.

Literary and cultural comparatists can take several insights from Glissant's association of a vaguely defined "beauty of the world" with the recognition of opacity in "the thought of wandering" (*la pensée de l'errance*; *Poétique* 32–33). Wandering in search of a totality one realizes one will never know is a comparative practice that is open-ended but not aimless, a pursuit, but one not driven toward a nameable destination, or even by an expectation that any destination will be reached. Wandering is thus imagined as a practice of comparison that keeps moving, and keeps searching. A second, related insight is that points of opacity and inconclusiveness have epistemological value; they are vital to what makes this practice of comparison valuable, and what differentiates it from other practices that treat opacity and inconclusiveness as problems to be resolved or flaws to be concealed. "The beauty of the world" is a continual movement of seeking to comprehend the world's totality of relations through a comparative practice of relating them to each other, while remaining undeterred by the impossibility of arriving at this comprehension. What threatens this beauty is any force that would block its movement. Clearly, "beauty" for Glissant is not a rarefied, transcendent quality of the world and its worthiest writing divided off from politics. The political power of the phrase "the beauty of the world" derives from Glissant's refusal, when confronted with institutionalized repression and polarization, to settle on a conflictual mode of imagining alternatives.

In 2009, in the early months of the Obama presidency, Glissant and Chamoiseau coauthored a political pamphlet called *L'Intraitable beauté du monde* (or, loosely, *The Unvanquishable Beauty of the World*), by turns a direct address to Obama and a meditation on his historical significance and future promise. Its title brings to the fore of their reflections the obliquely defined concept from Glissant's earlier work, "the beauty of the world," this time modified by a word (*intraitable*) whose standard usage in French approximates "intractable" or "unyielding" but whose further intimation of an imperviousness to bondage comes from its stem *traite*, or "trade," a common abbreviation for the Atlantic slave trade. The outrages and sorrows of the Middle Passage periodically surface in lyrical and somber passages that interrupt the essay's meditations on the diversifying force of creolization, lest we forget, as we affirm long-standing but increasingly visible forms of creolization in the United States, their historical basis in forced migrations and intermixings, as well as voluntary ones. Glissant and Chamoiseau see in the history of transatlantic slavery, ethnic and state violence, and the global consolidation of vast economic inequities the naturalization of another kind of bondage, an enculturated subservience of mind to the ethos of thinking oppositionally, dividing and conquering. In keeping with Glissant's *Poetics of Relation*, they marshal against this ethos an antithetical "beauty," indirectly and indefinitely defined by what it is not: "There is not beauty in selective memories, fundamentalisms, isolated national histories, ethnic purifications, the negation of the other, expulsions of immigrants, enclosed certitude."[7] That this enumeration of disparate, contextually distinct forms of statist and sectarian division culminates in the phrase "enclosed certitude" signals the epistemological import of a motif that runs through their address to Obama: the building of walls, both literal and figurative. Efforts to wall off intruders are bound up with efforts to repress doubts, gaps, and contradictions in ideals of community; all are efforts to foreclose potentially transformative relations that could produce new collectivities.

Glissant and Chamoiseau's address to Obama occasionally quotes from their earlier essay from 2007, *Quand les murs tombent* (*When the Walls Fall*), a meditation on identity written in protest against then French president Nicolas Sarkozy's controversial creation of a "Minister of Immigration, Integration, National Identity, and United Development," or a "Minister of Walls" (*mur-ministère*) as they contemptuously put it.[8] They call for a world where present-day nation-states, with their "borders that separate" each from the other, will have become nation-relations with "borders that distinguish and link together, and that distinguish only to link together."[9] Here, too, they define the world's beauty through negation: a Minister of Walls who works to accommodate us to the fortification of borders, making us complicit in thinking of ourselves as independent rather than connected and mutually constituted, is "precisely the opposite of beauty" (*tout le contraire de la beauté*; 26).

When Glissant and Chamoiseau advise Obama that "there are more pathways and horizons in trembling and fragility than in full command," they associate freer movement and more expansive futures with a refusal of unmitigated political power, but also with a refusal of secure knowledge and fearless belief, or the appearance of them (*L'Intraitable* 55). Pathways and horizons opened up "in trembling and fragility" diminish the authority of the socially dominant and indeed of any untroubled and inflexible worldview, any unshaken conviction. "The thought of trembling" (*La pensée du tremblement*), Glissant writes in his contemporaneous *Philosophie de la relation*, "takes us beyond rooted certainties" to see fragility not as a finite condition (which could be opposed to a norm and mastered, presumably) but as a continual, sinuous attunement "to the vibrations and earthquakes of this world, to the cataclysmic convergences of sensations and intuitions."[10] The thought of trembling in these recent works and the thought of wandering in *Poetics of Relation* are the metaphorical (poetic) terms Glissant offers for envisioning alternatives to a definitive (discursive) ethos of walling-off, alternatives whose *pursuit* constitutes the beauty of the world.

"Beauty" is a word that appears often in Woolf's writing, and its meanings shift considerably from one appearance to the next. Her usage can seem conventional, as when she endows Mrs. Ramsay with a manifest and unanimously acknowledged physical beauty in *To the Lighthouse*, although even then Woolf connects this appearance of beauty with a frustrated yearning for comprehension: "But was it nothing but looks, people said? What was there behind it—her beauty and splendour?" (28). In view of her more conventional uses of the term, there can seem little reason to question whether others denote anything apart from extraordinarily lovely spectacles, so that "the beauty of the world" would seem a straightforward testimonial to the visible glory of nature. But in *A Room of One's Own*, the worldly vision that develops out of an unbeautiful Manx cat's interruption of complacency at Oxbridge is not of a universalizing pastoral variety, nor does the narrator view the natural world passively. At "the time between the lights," she writes, on a day in October amid the flowers of spring, "when for some reason the beauty of the world revealed and yet soon to perish (here I pushed into the garden, for, unwisely, the door was left open and no beadles seemed about), the beauty of the world which is so soon to perish, has two edges, one of laughter, one of anguish, cutting the heart asunder."[11] The beauty of the world that fleetingly reveals itself in the wild untended garden at Fernham, or, for that matter, the beauty of the world that murmurs in the night as Lily tries to make sense of Mrs. Ramsay's sudden death in *To the Lighthouse*, or that briefly lifts Mr. Ramsay out of his self-absorbed quest for a more conclusive philosophical knowledge, is precisely not a beauty of consensus, visible and comprehensible to all. It is a trope for what eludes systems in which consensus and comprehension are possible, what is too vast and various to be imagined at once, but whose rhetorical power lies in its intimations of what escapes such systems. Lily and Mr. Ramsay fail in their determined efforts to demarcate and stabilize meaning, but these efforts are not accorded centrality in the novel; they coexist in an open state of comparison with the characters' vague intuitions of more momentous worldly connections.

Woolf's trope prefigures a similar comparison in *A Room of One's Own*: the narrator relegates to an aside the disciplinary authority of the beadle who chased her off the lawn earlier that day, and juxtaposes it to fiction's power, like the world's, to admit of contradictions and make us try to imagine their concurrence, like laughter and anguish on the horizon of possibility, or the events of a single October day that somehow unfold in springtime. Woolf's exuberantly self-contradictory description of the seasons directly distinguishes the rigid realm of "facts" from fiction's far more extensive fields of vision. With this distinction, Woolf allies her poetic language's robust capacity for difficult concurrences with the very beauty of the world, against which culturally sanctioned territorial divides—doors to the garden—appear arbitrary and impermanent. No longer subject to Oxbridge's rules, which in the person of the beadle had curtailed her thoughts as they did her movements, she is freer in this time between times, a time of intermixing seasons and periods of day, to see "phantoms only, half guessed, half seen" (Woolf, *Room* 17). This is not a rejection of temporal categories—she is after all brought back to a realization that it is October—but an illustration that there is aesthetic and political power to be found in poetic practices that flout discursive norms, covertly and indeterminately.

Reading modernist texts such as Woolf's in light of Glissant's conception of the beauty of the world and his theorizations of anxious modes of narration and figuration illuminates transatlantic modernism's own uneasy, obliquely self-questioning modes of narrating difference and shifts the discursive context in which to assess their cultural politics. Glissant and Chamoiseau's aspirational calls for social transformation are most fairly read together with their many reflections on particularities of slavery, immigration policy, and migrancy. It is equally important to consider the politics of their poetics in its close relation to their own readings of particular literary texts whose significations they show to surpass and sometimes even contradict the political positions of their authors. As we have seen repeatedly in this book, there is a variously articulated but coalescing literary practice characteristic of transnational modernist comparatisms to counter repressive culturalist and communalist ideologies through a strategic vagueness and implication through negation, rather than through a fictively definitive and restrictive affirmation. I have argued that a comparative practice of reading that attends to the confluent and interactive relational dynamics of comparative literary techniques itself participates in modernism's ongoing transnational and anti-imperial challenge to the ethos of walling off the new. This challenge amounts to an intercultural textual exchange, in which diversely situated and articulated poetries and theories increasingly appear as interdependent and defined through fluctuating mutual relations, rather than as rooted, discrete, and politically static.

Taking "the beauty of the world" as a figure for the expanse of dynamic relations that exceed the comprehensive mastery of any one speaker, culture, state, or empire, we can read Glissant and Chamoiseau's creolist images of the world's beauty and Woolf's cosmopolitan feminist images of it as mutually supplementing each other, amounting to a reclaiming of "world totality" once totality has been salvaged from idealizations of sovereignty and reconfigured through a poetics of shared vulnerability. "Any one of us can, in the wake of a fire, a tornado, a tectonic fury, a job loss, be forced to leave home and ask for asylum," Chamoiseau writes in *Migrant Brothers*, his poetic appeal for "a *global politics of hospitality* that states once and for all, in the name of all, for all, that in no place in this world, for whatever reason, will there be such a thing as a foreigner" (xviii). For there to be no such thing as a foreigner in any place in the world, Woolf's vision of the beauty of the world, experienced as a result of gendered exclusion from fraternal solidarities, suggests that we must also remember ourselves as foreigners, all of us, to the totality of the world that is home and necessarily exceeds our comprehension of home.

The passage from *Orlando* that serves as the epigraph to this conclusion culminates, or for an instant seems to culminate, in Woolf's protagonist "heaving a deep sigh of relief" and assuring herself, "I am about to understand . . . " But instead of arriving at "something tolerable, comprehensible," her inchoate thoughts of what "one trembles to pin through the body with a name and call beauty" take her beyond "the visible world" to where "everything was partly something else, and each gained an odd moving power from this union of itself and something not itself."[12] Eighty-five years later, Chamoiseau would write that the poetry of his Antillean predecessor St.-John Perse, long confined in "identitarian irons," "will always escape our explanations, and still more my meditations. But I produce them gladly . . . to keep company with an open beauty" (*pour la fréquentation d'une beauté ouverte*).[13] Neither transparently nor unequivocally, but anxiously and aspirationally, the nonterritorial comparisons I have pursued in these chapters cast doubt on enclosed certitudes with what they show, often murkily on the horizon, to be a far more copious, creolized, and intractably unsettled world, an open beauty. Recognizing its openness to forces of contingency and transformation that do not proceed progressively and, barring apocalypse, have no endpoint is not at all to give up the pursuit of linking collectivities without claiming them as territories. On the contrary, it is the pursuit that precludes surrendering to a posture of disengagement.

Notes

Introduction. Anxious Mastery and the Forms It Takes

Epigraphs: Ranajit Guha, "Not at Home in Empire," *Critical Inquiry* 23, no. 3 (1997): 484; Édouard Glissant and Patrick Chamoiseau, *L'Intraitable beauté du monde: Adresse à Barack Obama* (Paris: Galaade, 2009), 55. The latter phrase reappears with slight modifications in Chamoiseau's monograph *Césaire, Perse, Glissant: Les liaisons magnétiques* (Paris: Philippe Rey, 2013), 106.

1. Wendy Brown, *Walled States, Waning Sovereignty* (Brooklyn, NY: Zone Books, 2010), 26, 125.

2. Édouard Glissant, *Poetics of Relation*, trans. Betsy Wing (Ann Arbor: University of Michigan Press, 1997), 122, 123, trans. mod.; originally published as Édouard Glissant, *Poétique de la relation* (Paris: Gallimard, 1990), 136, 137.

3. Ranajit Guha, "Not at Home in Empire," *Critical Inquiry* 23, no. 3 (1997): 487, 483–84.

4. George Orwell, "Shooting an Elephant" (ca. 1936), in *A Collection of Essays* (1946; repr., Orlando, FL: Harcourt, 1981), 148–56.

5. Søren Kierkegaard, *The Concept of Anxiety: A Simple Psychologically Orienting Deliberation on the Dogmatic Issue of Hereditary Sin*, trans. and ed. Reidar Thomte and Albert B. Anderson (Princeton, NJ: Princeton University Press, 1981). Guha cites Kierkegaard's distinction, as well as Heidegger's elaboration of it in *Being and Time*, on 486.

6. Gayatri Chakravorty Spivak, *Death of a Discipline* (New York: Columbia University Press, 2003), 26.

7. Here and throughout the book, I adhere to what I take to be a standard critical usage of "comparative" to mean "involving the use of comparison," and of "comparatist" to mean "promoting the use of comparison." The "-ist" in "comparatist," in other words, like the "-ist" in "transationalist" and "colonialist," conveys a stance of belonging, approval, or advocacy with regard to the word it modifies. This suffix has a different function in literary-critical uses of "modernist," as I discuss below.

8. Virginia Woolf, *A Room of One's Own*, ed. Susan Gubar (1929; repr., Orlando, FL: Harvest, 2005), 14.

9. In Woolf's usage, "modern" is not a prescriptive, or even a particularly descriptive, periodizing statement beyond its suggestion of the "modern" as current, both "now" and "new." Although the narrator of *A Room of One's Own* distinguishes between poetry before and after the war, she does not commit herself to the explanation that the war caused the shift she describes; she raises the possibility that it did but resists giving a definitive answer (Woolf 15). This characteristically open-ended mode of interpretation, which Woolf develops extensively in *Three Guineas* (a subject of chap. 4), encourages readers to imagine a more complex explanation for the shift, and with it a more indefinite period of what later came to be called modernist literary production.

10. While the uncanny difference of Woolf's cat with no tail is usually understood as a figure for women's sexual difference as read through Freud's theory of castration, it serves also as a figure for the cultural difference of what is anomalous and subordinate within British imperial culture, such as the Crown dependency of the Isle of Man, which Woolf makes a point of identifying as home to Manx cats. For an explanation of why Woolf would allude to Freud's sexist theory of castration in a text that attributes the dearth of women's writing to their historically unequal status and educational resources, see Patricia Klindienst Joplin's reading of "the lost tail as *tale*" in "The Voice of the Shuttle Is Ours" (1984), in *Rape and Representation*, ed. Lynn A. Higgins and Brenda R. Silver (New York: Columbia University Press, 1991), 38. Anne Fernald does not dispute that Woolf is critiquing Freud through the figure of the Manx cat, but she hints that there may be more to it when she notes that the "offhand manner" with which the cat is described conveys a sense of anxiety. See Anne Fernald, "*A Room of One's Own*, Personal Criticism, and the Essay," *Twentieth-Century Literature* 40, no. 2 (1994): 182.

11. I use "transatlantic modernism" when I am referring to multilingual literary currents on lands bordering the Atlantic since the early twentieth century. Before transnationalist and global modernist approaches proliferated over the past two decades, "modernism" in literary studies usually referred to European and Anglo-American aesthetic currents that emerged in the late nineteenth century and developed during approximately the first half of the next in reaction against literary and pictorial realism, and more broadly against cultural features of industrial modernity, such as scientism, individualism, and the mechanization of social and imaginative life. The "-ist" in this Eurocentric usage of "modernist" denotes a relationship of both belonging and resistance to modernity. "Transatlantic modernism" retains the sense of belonging and resistance to a culture of modernity, but its applicability to long-neglected South Atlantic cultures along with North Atlantic ones has expanded the periodization and the range of languages and attributes associated

with modernism. It has also accentuated the imperial dimensions of the modernity being absorbed and resisted.

12. Marjorie Perloff, *The Poetics of Indeterminacy: Rimbaud to Cage* (Evanston, IL: Northwestern University Press, 1981).

13. Dipesh Chakrabarty, *Habitations of Modernity: Essays in the Wake of Subaltern Studies* (Chicago: University of Chicago Press, 2002), 46–47.

14. Dipesh Chakrabarty, *Provincializing Europe: Postcolonial Thought and Historical Difference* (Princeton, NJ: Princeton University Press, 2000), 45–46. He refers to "fear and anxiety" in *Habitations* 46.

15. Dipesh Chakrabarty, "The Climate of History: Four Theses," *Critical Inquiry* 35, no. 2 (2009): 220, 221.

16. Édouard Glissant, *Philosophie de la relation: poésie en étendue* (Paris: Gallimard, 2009), 54. I consider these conceptions of wandering, trembling, and beauty in more detail in the book's conclusion.

17. The later Glissant's adaptation of Deleuze and Guattari's antiauthoritarian conceptions of rhizomatic identity and nomadism has been much discussed, but it is worth noting the emphatic language of deterritorialization through which these conceptions unfold. See, e.g., Gilles Deleuze and Félix Guattari, *A Thousand Plateaus: Capitalism and Schizophrenia*, trans. Brian Massumi (Minneapolis: University of Minnesota Press, 1987); originally published as *Mille plateaux*, vol. 2 of *Capitalisme et Schizophrénie* (Paris: Minuit, 1980): "If the nomad can be called the Deterritorialized par excellence, it is precisely because there is no reterritorialization *afterward* as with the migrant. . . . With the nomad, on the contrary, it is deterritorialization that constitutes the relation to the earth, to such a degree that the nomad reterritorializes on deterritorialization itself" (381).

18. Jacques Derrida, *The Other Heading: Reflections on Today's Europe*, trans. Pascale-Anne Brault and Michael B. Naas (Bloomington: Indiana University Press, 1992), 17–18; originally published as *L'autre cap* (Paris: Minuit, 1991).

19. Françoise Vergès writes that "l'avenir est ailleurs" in *Le ventre des femmes: Capitalisme, racialisation, féminisme* (Paris: Albin Michel, 2017), 121. Her phrase resonates with references to a similarly undetermined but still materially and dynamically constituted "elsewhere" by Glissant and Chamoiseau, to which I will return. Achille Mbembe has drawn out various, sometimes discrepant implications of the notion of "elsewhere" in black Africana thought. See, e.g., Achille Mbembe, *Critique of Black Reason*, trans. Laurent Dubois (Durham, NC: Duke University Press, 2017), 35, 53–54, 63, 112, 137–138; originally published as *Critique de la raison nègre* (Paris: Éditions La Découverte, 2013); and Achille Mbembe, "Afropolitanism," trans. Paulo Lemos Horta, in *Cosmopolitanisms*, ed. Bruce Robbins and Paulo Lemos Horta (New York: New York University Press, 2017), 105.

20. Brent Hayes Edwards, *The Practice of Diaspora: Literature, Translation, and*

the Rise of Black Internationalism (Cambridge, MA: Harvard University Press, 2003), 24. Edwards makes this point to challenge Glissant's critique of the "detour" to an elsewhere represented by Césaire's turn from Martinique to Africa and Fanon's even more decisive turn from Martinique to Algeria. Glissant's critique is not a nativist condemnation of detour, however, or an outright rejection of the detours that Césaire and Fanon conceived. Taking the "ruse" of detour in Caribbean letters as a precarious community's attempt to ground itself after having lost access to prior ancestral traditions (a predicament Glissant distinguishes from that of diasporic Jews, e.g., who as a group were able to maintain their inherited traditions and sense of communal continuity), Glissant distinguishes between two kinds of detour. There is the detour that "*leads nowhere*," i.e., creates no new possibilities for future development, and there is the detour that creates such possibilities and "*can therefore lead somewhere*." Glissant credits Césaire and Fanon with detours that "led us *somewhere*." See Édouard Glissant, *Le Discours antillais* (1981; repr., Paris: Gallimard, 1997), 40–57. Direct quotations above, with original emphasis, appear on 53, 51, and 56, and references to the Jewish diaspora pertain to 42 and 45. For an English translation, see Édouard Glissant, *Caribbean Discourse: Selected Essays*, trans. J. Michael Dash (Charlottesville: University of Virginia Press, 1989), 14–26, esp. 15, 17, 22, 23, and 25.

21. Variants of this distinction recur in Anglo-American literary formalism as well, as when I. A. Richards differentiates between "scientific" and "emotive" uses of language in *Science and Poetry* (New York: Norton, 1926) and when Cleanth Brooks and Robert Penn Warren contrast poetry's "*imaginative enactment*" of "*the multidimensional quality of experience*" to both "practical information" and scientific "statements of absolute precision," in *Understanding Poetry*, 4th ed. (1938; repr., New York: Holt, Rinehart and Winston, 1976), 9, 6.

22. In *Sovereignty*, the third volume of *The Accursed Share*, Bataille writes, "Now, language (discursive and not poetical language) carries within itself the 'signification' by which words constantly refer to one another: definition is the essence of [discursive] language." See Georges Bataille, *The Accursed Share*, vol. 3, *Sovereignty*, trans. Robert Hurley (New York: Zone Books, 1993), 382; originally published as *La Souveraineté* in *Œuvres complètes*, vol. 8 (Paris: Gallimard, 1976). Bataille often insists on the affinity of his own theoretical language to poetic and visual imagery in contrast to rational, especially scientific, discourse. For instance, he claims that his theory of political economy is unlike "the frigid research of the sciences" in the sense that "the object of my research cannot be distinguished *from the subject at its boiling point*." Georges Bataille, *The Accursed Share*, vol. 1, *Consumption*, trans.

Robert Hurley (New York: Zone Books, 1991), 10; originally published as *La part maudite* (1949; repr., Paris: Minuit, 1967).

23. This self-questioning poetics of anxious mastery is distinctly modernist in the sense elaborated above—modernist as simultaneously belonging to and resisting a culture of modernity. It articulates in varying degrees but also characteristically subverts positivist dichotomies used to justify modern imperial domination and its legacies of inequality.

24. Susan Stanford Friedman's "paratactic comparativism" is a method of reading evident in much of her work—most recently, *Planetary Modernisms: Provocations on Modernity across Time* (New York: Columbia University Press, 2015), where she develops the idea of a "comparative methodology of collage"; see esp. 77, 217–19, 278–80, 287. For her advancement of the idea with particular emphasis on parataxis, see Susan Stanford Friedman, "Cultural Parataxis and Transnational Landscapes of Reading: Toward a Locational Modernist Studies," in *Modernism*, ed. Astradur Eysteinsson and Vivian Liska (Amsterdam: Benjamins, 2007), 35–52. Laura Doyle frames her comparative readings of Anglo-Atlantic and African-Atlantic "liberty plots" over three centuries as examples of a "regional transnational approach" in *Freedom's Empire: Race and the Rise of the Novel in Atlantic Modernity, 1640–1940* (Durham, NC: Duke University Press, 2008), 452. Other important works that destabilize prevalent assumptions about transatlantic modernist politics through revisionist readings of literary form include Christopher GoGwilt's analysis of overlapping English, Creole, and Indonesian modernist modes of "decolonizing tradition" in *The Passage of Literature: Genealogies of Modernism in Conrad, Rhys, and Pramoedya* (Oxford: Oxford University Press, 2011); and Aarthi Vadde's analysis of "chimeric" literary forms that respond to "the growing unknowability of communities" in *Chimeras of Form: Modernist Internationalism beyond Europe, 1914–2016* (New York: Columbia University Press, 2017), 20.

25. One such intervention that pertains directly to the present discussion is Spivak's revisionist interpretation of the conclusion to *A Room of One's Own*. What interests Spivak in Woolf's conclusion is that it trades "verifiability" for a kind of "ghost dance" when Woolf "quite gives up" her earlier assertion that to be a writer a woman needs a room of her own and five hundred pounds a year, and instead invokes a future collectivity of women who, even without economic advantages, would in some unspecified way "work" for the ghost of Shakespeare's sister. Spivak argues that this illustrates fiction's capacity to teach us how "to let go" of verifiable certainties in the imagining of collectivity. See Spivak, *Death of a Discipline* 34–35.

26. See, e.g., Matthew Hart, "Threshold to the Kingdom: The Airport Is a Border and the Border Is a Volume," *Criticism* 57, no. 2 (2015): 173–89; Matthew Hart and Tania Lown-Hecht, "The Extraterritorial Poetics of W. G. Sebald," *MFS Modern Fiction Studies* 58, no. 2 (2012): 214–38; and Matthew Hart, *Extraterritorial:*

A Political Geography of Contemporary Fiction (New York: Columbia University Press, forthcoming).

27. Giorgio Agamben, *State of Exception*, trans. Kevin Attell (Chicago: University of Chicago Press, 2005), 1.

28. Françoise Vergès and Carpanin Marimoutou, *Amarres: Créolisations india-océanes* (Paris: L'Harmattan, 2005), 9.

29. Aimé Césaire, "Lettre à Maurice Thorez" (1956), in *Aimé Césaire: Poésie, théâtre, essais et discours, Édition critique*, ed. Albert James Arnold et al. (Paris: CNRS Éditions/Planète Libre, 2013), 1506.

30. Françoise Lionnet, *Écritures féminines et dialogues critiques: Subjectivité, genre et ironie/Writing Women and Critical Dialogues: Subjectivity, Gender and Irony* (Trou d'Eau Douce, Île Maurice: L'Atelier d'écriture, 2012), 13.

31. Françoise Lionnet, *Le su et l'incertain: Cosmopoliques créoles de l'océan Indien/The Known and the Uncertain: Creole Cosmopolitics of the Indian Ocean* (Trou d'Eau Douce, Île Maurice: L'Atelier d'écriture, 2012), 190–91.

32. Lionnet's characterization of the literary is one I see frequently articulated in interpretations of modernist writing, perhaps especially of Coetzee's fiction. Of course, all literature, indeed all writing, can be diversely interpreted, including "against the grain" or contrary to its apparent aims. But in defining transnational literary modernism as a multiform expression of anxious worldliness that throws imperial-era positivisms into doubt, I am differentiating its characteristic modes of questioning and qualifying orders of knowledge from the relative coherence and conclusiveness, however deconstructible, of *Medea* or *The Rape of the Lock*.

33. Shu-mei Shih and Françoise Lionnet, introduction to *The Creolization of Theory*, ed. Françoise Lionnet and Shu-mei Shih (Durham, NC: Duke University Press, 2011), 20.

34. Gary Wilder, *Freedom Time: Negritude, Decolonization, and the Future of the World* (Durham, NC: Duke University Press, 2015), 10.

35. Rita Barnard, "Post-apartheid Modernism and Consumer Culture," *Modernist Cultures* 6, no. 2 (2011): 215–16.

36. Watson and Wilder cite as examples of this trend Talal Asad, Walter Mignolo, Enrique Dussel, Aníbal Quijano, Frank Wilderson, and Dipesh Chakrabarty, among others. As my own engagement with Chakrabarty suggests, I interpret him as, on the whole, encouraging transnational and intercultural practices of comparison, an example being his reading of Tagore's heterogeneous poetics and their broader context of Bengali literary debates over the politics of realism versus modernism; see *Provincializing* 149–79. See Jini Kim Watson and Gary Wilder, "Introduction: Thinking the Postcolonial Contemporary," in *The Postcolonial Contemporary: Political Imaginaries for the Global Present*, ed. Jini Kim Watson and Gary Wilder (New York: Fordham University Press, 2018), 12. For Wilder's fuller critique of Chakrabarty, see *Freedom Time* 10–11.

37. Speaking generally of "the call for universalism" as "coming from all directions these days," Shih and Lionnet cite Gilroy's proposed "strategic universalism" as part of a "new *universalist turn*, the political implications of which are not yet clear" (14). Paul Gilroy advances the notion of strategic universalism, along with "planetary humanism," in *Against Race: Imagining Political Culture beyond the Color Line* (Cambridge, MA: Harvard University Press, 2000), 96, 220, 326, 327. Like Césaire, Gilroy opposes a "misanthropic humanism" with a utopian "heterocultural" humanism to come "conceived explicitly as a response to the sufferings that raciology has wrought" (334, 18). More recently, Mbembe has advanced planetary universalism in similarly utopian terms as a means of overcoming racial division, pointing out that "even when anticolonial struggles mobilized local actors, in a circumscribed country or territory, they were always at the origin of solidarities forged on a planetary and transnational scale." See *Critique of Black Reason* 172.

38. Paul Gilroy, *Postcolonial Melancholia* (New York: Columbia University Press, 2005), 64, 63. Gilroy polemically traces this notion back to what Freud, writing amid the rise of fascism, described as "a pathology of cultural communities," or what Gilroy paraphrases as "the psychological poverty and pathological character of groups that understand their collective life and fate in specifically cultural terms" to the neglect of other potential sources of solidarity (65). See also Sigmund Freud, *Civilization and Its Discontents*, trans. and ed. James Strachey (1930; repr., New York: Norton, 1961), 110.

39. See also *Critique of Black Reason* 32–34, where Mbembe attributes invocations of race by people historically oppressed by racialization to their paradoxical "desire for community" that a context of racism had denied them.

40. Shih draws on Glissant's theory of relation and his readings of William Faulkner's poetics to propose "relational comparison" as an alternative to comparison that presumes a hierarchical standard against which others are measured; see Shu-mei Shih, "Comparison as Relation," in *Comparison: Theories, Approaches, Uses*, ed. Rita Felski and Susan Stanford Friedman (Baltimore: Johns Hopkins University Press, 2013), 79–98. Also drawing on Glissant, Natalie Melas analyzes figures of "incommensurable relationality" in her theory of postcolonial comparatism in *All the Difference in the World: Postcoloniality and the Ends of Comparison* (Stanford, CA: Stanford University Press, 2007).

41. Anjali Prabhu and Adlai Murdoch, "Of Beauty, Cosmopolitanism, and History in Postcolonial Réunion," *International Journal of Francophone Studies* 11, no. 3 (2008): 403, 410.

42. Jean Bernabé, Patrick Chamoiseau, and Raphaël Confiant, *Éloge de la Créolité / In Praise of Creoleness*, bilingual ed., trans. M. B. Taleb-Khyar (Paris: Gallimard, 1993).

43. See Patrick Chamoiseau, *Césaire, Perse, Glissant: Les liaisons magnétiques* (Paris: Philippe Rey, 2013), 187–88; and Françoise Vergès, *Monsters and Revolution-*

aries: Colonial Family Romance and Métissage (Durham, NC: Duke University Press, 1999), 2–3. I discuss Chamoiseau's argument in relation to Glissant's critique of identitarianisms, including well-meaning multiculturalist ones, in chap. 3.

44. Édouard Glissant, *Faulkner, Mississippi*, trans. Barbara Lewis and Thomas C. Spear (Chicago: University of Chicago Press, 1999), 138; originally published as *Faulkner, Mississippi* (Paris: Éditions Stock, 1996).

45. Carrie Noland has criticized Chamoiseau's comparative method, as well as the conception of poetics by which he justifies it, as insufficiently historicist and thus politically suspect; I will return to such criticisms of Glissant and Chamoiseau in my conclusion. See Carrie Noland, "Césaire, Chamoiseau, and the Work of Legacy," *Small Axe* 19, no. 3 (2015): 102–20.

46. Gayatri Chakravorty Spivak, *An Aesthetic Education in the Era of Globalization* (Cambridge, MA: Harvard University Press, 2012), 452, 454; see also 450. It is worth noting that this use of *créolité* is not standard, and that in his recent work Chamoiseau, like Glissant, Vergès, Marimoutou, and others, is less concerned with delineating creolity or creoleness than with contextualizing, comparing, and extolling transnational processes of *créolisation*.

47. Ann Laura Stoler, *Along the Archival Grain: Epistemic Anxieties and Colonial Common Sense* (Princeton, NJ: Princeton University Press, 2010), 208–9.

Chapter 1. Troubling Classifications: Unspeakable Figures of *Métissage* in "Melanctha" and *Disgrace*

Epigraph: Françoise Vergès, *Monsters and Revolutionaries: Colonial Family Romance and Métissage* (Durham, NC: Duke University Press, 1999), 10.

1. Gertrude Stein, *Three Lives* (New York: Penguin, 1990), 56.

2. Chinua Achebe, *Things Fall Apart* (New York: Anchor, 1994), 208–9.

3. In 1965, Achebe wrote that in the previous year twenty thousand copies of *Things Fall Apart* were sold in Nigeria, in contrast to eight hundred in Britain and twenty-five hundred everywhere else. And, he continued, "most of my readers are young. They are either in school or college or have only recently left. And many of them look to me as a kind of teacher. . . . I would be quite satisfied if my novels (especially the ones I set in the past) did no more than teach my readers that their past—with all its imperfections—was not one long night of savagery from which the first Europeans acting on God's behalf delivered them." See Chinua Achebe, "The Novelist as Teacher," in *African Literature: An Anthology of Criticism and Theory*, ed. Tejumola Olaniyan and Ato Quayson (Malden, MA: Blackwell, 2007), 103, 105.

4. Although in the New Critical era after her death Stein was persistently described as an influential "personality" and arts patron rather than an accomplished literary innovator, this changed with the rise of cultural studies in the

1980s and 1990s. See Marianne DeKoven, "Introduction: Transformations of Gertrude Stein," *Modern Fiction Studies* 42, no. 3 (1996): 469–83.

5. Dipesh Chakrabarty, *Provincializing Europe: Postcolonial Thought and Historical Difference* (Princeton, NJ: Princeton University Press, 2000), 17.

6. Françoise Lionnet, *Écritures féminines et dialogues critiques: Subjectivité, genre et ironie / Writing Women and Critical Dialogues: Subjectivity, Gender and Irony* (Trou d'Eau Douce, Île Maurice: L'Atelier d'écriture, 2012), 10; my translation, second emphasis mine.

7. J. M. Coetzee, *Disgrace* (New York: Penguin, 1999).

8. Matthew Hart, *Nations of Nothing but Poetry: Modernism, Transnationalism, and Synthetic Vernacular Writing* (Oxford: Oxford University Press, 2010), 5.

9. In one of the more nuanced readings of how racial stereotypes function in Stein's poetics, Laura Doyle writes, "While Stein is arguably one of the most radical innovators in early twentieth century literature, her work at the same time contains some of the most openly racist descriptions of characters." For Doyle, these racist descriptions are Stein's attempts at parodying and critiquing common assumptions among white readers: "The narrators in *Three Lives* insult their characters with racial and ethnic slurs" whose "function is to echo the audience's racism in a way that makes readers squirm." She still faults Stein, though, for making "blacks serve a function" in what amounts to a dialogue between the author and her white audience, rather than imagining black characters and readers "as full human presences." See Laura Doyle, "The Flat, the Round, and Gertrude Stein: Race and the Shape of Modern(ist) History," *Modernism/Modernity* 7, no. 2 (2000): 256, 263.

10. Larsen's letter to Stein has been published as "From Nella Larsen" (1 February 1928), in *The Flowers of Friendship: Letters Written to Gertrude Stein*, ed. Donald Gallup (New York: Knopf, 1953), 215–16. Stein's response to Johnson (undated) is housed in the James Weldon Johnson and Grace Nail Johnson Papers, JWJ MSS 49, Series I. Correspondence, b. 20, f. 459, Beinecke Library, Yale University. For an early discussion of African American writers' responses to "Melanctha," in which Johnson is quoted, see John Malcolm Brinnin, *The Third Rose: Gertrude Stein and Her World* (London: Little, Brown, 1959), 121.

11. Richard Wright, "Gertrude Stein's Stay Is Drenched in Hitler's Horrors," *PM*, Sunday Magazine Section (11 March 1945), M15. Selections from Wright's review are reprinted in *Selected Writings of Gertrude Stein*, ed. Carl Van Vechten (1962; repr., New York: Vintage, 1990), 338.

12. Édouard Glissant, *Le Discours antillais* (1981; repr., Paris: Gallimard, 1997), 428–30. It is important to note that, in J. Michael Dash's frequently cited English translation of selections from this text, *métissage* usually appears as "creolization," even though *créolisation* is also a French word and one that figures significantly in Glissant's later writings. Moreover, Glissant's term *relation*, now routinely translated as "relation," usually appears in Dash's text as "cross-cultural" (though *métissage culturel* is rendered as "cross-cultural contact"). See Édouard Glissant, *Caribbean*

Discourse: Selected Essays, trans. J. Michael Dash (Charlottesville: University of Virginia Press, 1989), 140–42.

13. Françoise Lionnet, *Autobiographical Voices: Race, Gender, Self-Portraiture* (1989; repr., Ithaca, NY: Cornell University Press, 2018), 6.

14. Françoise Vergès, *Monsters and Revolutionaries: Colonial Family Romance and Métissage* (Durham, NC: Duke University Press, 1999), 9.

15. Arthur de Gobineau warned against the long-term corruptive influence of what he interchangeably called *mélanges ethniques* ("ethnic mixing") and *mélanges du sang* ("blood mixing"), whatever their "transitory benefits," in *Essai sur l'inégalité des races humaines*, 2nd ed. (1853; repr., Paris: Firmin-Didot, 1884), 219. Bénédict Augustin Morel influentially defined degeneration in *Traité des Dégénérescences Physiques, Intellectuelles et Morales de l'Espèce Humaine et des Causes qui produisent ces variétés maladives* (Paris: J. B. Baillère, 1857).

16. Glissant writes that "the poetics of *métissage* is the very same as that of Relation: non-linear and non-prophetic, woven with arduous patience out of irreducible derivations" (*Le Discours antillais* 430; my translation). Lionnet theorizes her own critical practice of *métissage* as "the weaving or plaiting of texts from diverse horizons that I put in transversal, intertextual and nonhierarchical relation in order to underline what these texts have in common despite their apparent distance" (*Écritures féminines* 16; my translation).

17. In their introduction to a special issue on "Migrations and *Métissages*," Pascale De Souza and H. Adlai Murdoch suggest that the rubric of "postcolonialism" is not adequate to "account for the somewhat anomalous geopolitical standing of the French Caribbean territories" relative to colonies that attained independence, and they propose the "'neither/nor' paradigm" of *métissage* as a means of addressing "the ongoing state of ambivalence" in France's overseas departments toward the metropole. See Pascale De Souza and H. Adlai Murdoch, "Caribbean Textuality and the Metaphors of *Métissage*," *Journal of Caribbean Literatures* 4, no. 2 (2006): vii–ix.

18. Susanna Pavloska offers an overview of contending responses to the depiction of race in "Melanctha" and urges that we read the story's "uses of blackness" with more attention to "Stein's grounding in nineteenth-century social science." By this, Pavloska means the influence of Stein's college professor and mentor, pragmatist philosopher and psychologist William James, on Stein's stated intention to give fictional form to "habits of attention" as conceived by James, or what Pavloska calls "the problem of consciousness divided against itself." See Susanna Pavloska, *Modern Primitives: Race and Language in Gertrude Stein, Ernest Hemingway, and Zora Neale Hurston* (2000; repr., London: Routledge, 2013), 34–36, 37, 40. Stein attests to James's influence on her attempts to represent "habits of attention" in "The Gradual Making of *The Making of Americans*," in *Selected Writings of Gertrude Stein*, ed. Carl Van Vechten (1962; repr., New York: Vintage, 1990), 243. For a discussion

of the influence that James had on the notion of (mind-)wandering in "Melanctha," see Lisa Ruddick, *Reading Gertrude Stein: Body, Text, Gnosis* (Ithaca, NY: Cornell University Press, 1990), 12–54.

19. Sir Francis Galton, *Memories of My Life* (London: Methuen, 1908), 310.

20. Francis Galton introduced the term and its definition in *Inquiries into Human Faculty and Its Development* (London: Macmillan, 1883), 30.

21. Francis Galton, *Hereditary Genius: An Inquiry into Its Laws and Consequences*, 2nd ed. (1869; repr., London: Macmillan, 1892), xx–xxvii, 130–40, 152; see also Francis Galton, "Hereditary Talent and Character," *Macmillan's Magazine* 12 (1865): 157–66. Galton's idea of "hereditary regression" served as a putatively scientific justification for opposition to interracial sex and marriage in the late nineteenth and early to mid-twentieth centuries.

22. Alfred J. Plötz coined the term *Rassenhygiene* in *Grundlinien einer Rassen-Hygiene* (Berlin: S. Fischer, 1895), a book Hitler claimed as an inspiration. Plötz cites Galton's theory repeatedly in support of his own; see 20, 22, 118, 215, 233.

23. Mieke Bal, *Narratology: Introduction to the Theory of Narrative*, 3rd ed. (Toronto: University of Toronto Press, 1997), 162. More generally, my uses of the term "focalization"—the perspective from which a narrative is told, often a fluid one—draw on Bal's extended definition of focalization's various types; see 145–64. Gérard Genette coined *focalisation* in *Discours sur récit*, in *Figures III* (Paris: Seuil, 1972), translated as *Narrative Discourse: An Essay in Method*, trans. Jane E. Lewin (Ithaca, NY: Cornell University Press, 1980), 189–94. For Bal, similar narratological concepts such as "point of view" and "narrative perspective" are less useful because "they do not make a distinction between, on the one hand, the vision through which the elements are presented and, on the other, the identity of the voice that is verbalizing that vision. To put it more simply: they do not make a distinction between those who see and those who speak. Nevertheless, it is possible, both in fiction and in reality, for one person to express the vision of another" (146).

24. Here I am drawing on Vergès's critique of postcolonial psychiatric discourse on "the Creole psyche," in which she discerns an enduring colonial bias. Many experts who contribute to this discourse assume that "the *métis* origin of the population" in Réunion "creates confusion about the individual's origins, a confusion leading to a lack of psychological foundations and a weakness of the sense of 'self.'" Vergès contends that "there is a relation between the notion of blood purity, which informed the idea of community defended by nineteenth-century writers and scientists, and a certain conception of selfhood that stresses wholeness" (197–98).

25. J. M. Coetzee, *White Writing: On the Culture of Letters in South Africa* (1988; repr., Johannesburg: Pentz, 2007), 142. Coetzee slightly amended the essay in 1988, but its argument is largely the same as what first appeared as "Blood, Flaw, Taint, Degeneration: The Case of Sarah Gertrude Millin," *English Studies in Africa* 23, no. 1 (1980): 41–58.

26. "To practice racism today even as it is rendered conceptually unthinkable, 'culture' and 'religion' have replaced 'biology.'" Achille Mbembe, *Critique of Black Reason*, trans. Laurent Dubois (Durham, NC: Duke University Press, 2017), 7.

27. Peter D. McDonald, "Disgrace Effects," *Interventions: International Journal of Postcolonial Studies* 4, no. 3 (2002): 322–23.

28. Quoted passages by Gerwal are McDonald's translations. The original texts from which McDonald quotes are SAHRC, *Inquiry into Racism in the Media: Hearings Transcripts* 14, no. 3/3 (2000): 123; and Jakes Gerwel, "Perspektief: Is *dít* die regte beeld van ons nasie?" (Is *this* the right image of our nation?), *Rapport*, 13 February 2000, 2.

29. Derek Attridge, *J. M. Coetzee and the Ethics of Reading* (Chicago: University of Chicago Press, 2004), 30.

30. Mark Sanders argues that Coetzee's use of the present tense in *Disgrace* signals a "resistance to the perfective," a play on the grammatical sense of "perfective" to denote an aspect of verbal inflection that indicates the completion of an action, event, or state. See Mark Sanders, "Disgrace," *Interventions: International Journal of Postcolonial Studies* 4, no. 3 (2002): 371.

31. In *The Translation Zone*, Apter explains that her concept of "zones" is intended to challenge both national and post-national delineations of language communities. For her definition and contextualization of the term, see Emily Apter, *The Translation Zone: A New Comparative Literature* (Princeton, NJ: Princeton University Press, 2006), 5–6. Well before that book's publication, however, she used "zones of untranslatability" in reference to Maryse Condé's first novel, *Heremakhonon*; see Emily Apter, "Crossover Texts / Creole Tongues: A Conversation with Maryse Condé," *Public Culture* 13, no. 1 (2001): 91. First published in 1976, *Heremakhonon* has proved prescient in a range of ways, including in its focus, long before *Disgrace*, on a promiscuous university teacher whose sense of sexual and political independence masks her entrenchment in colonial patterns of thinking about race and heritage. Like *Disgrace*, it is narrated in the present tense.

32. For the sake of brevity here and throughout the book, I use "human" and "animal" as shorthand designations for human and nonhuman animals, respectively, but by this I do not mean to deny the animality of the human.

33. DeKoven does not explicitly relate her recent work on Coetzee and feminist animality studies to her earlier, extensive work on Stein. See Marianne DeKoven, "Going to the Dogs in *Disgrace*," *ELH* 76, no. 4 (2009): 847.

34. "The dog is fascinated by the sound of the banjo. When he strums the strings, the dog sits up, cocks its head, listens. When he hums Teresa's line, and the humming begins to swell with feeling (it is as though his larynx thickens: he can feel the hammer of blood in his throat), the dog smacks its lips and seems on the point of singing too, or howling" (Coetzee, *Disgrace* 215).

35. Elizabeth S. Anker, "Human Rights, Social Justice, and J. M. Coetzee's *Disgrace*," *Modern Fiction Studies* 54, no. 2 (2008): 260.

36. See, e.g., DeKoven, "Going to the Dogs" 870; and Gayatri Chakravorty Spivak, *An Aesthetic Education in the Era of Globalization* (Cambridge, MA: Harvard University Press, 2012), 320, 324. Spivak argues that Lurie "learns to love dogs and finally learns to give up the dog that he loves to the stipulated death," although she complicates this claim when she undercuts its suggestion of Lurie's growth by reminding us that his "love [of] dogs as the other of being-human, as a source, even, of ethical lessons of a special sort" does not improve his "obvious race-gender illiteracy." Whatever ethical lessons he draws from learning to love dogs (which Spivak does not specify), they do not enable him "to touch either the racial or gendered other."

37. Rita Barnard, *Apartheid and Beyond: South African Writers and the Politics of Place* (Oxford: Oxford University Press, 2007), 39, 40.

38. Spivak makes Lurie's bathos an important marker of his interpretive deficiency in *Aesthetic Education* 324, 327.

39. Rushdie identifies "communalism" as a term Indians use to refer to sectarian religious politics, but his own uses of the word suggest his rejection of ethnic (including but not only religious) chauvinisms more generally, hence my use of the term. See Salman Rushdie, *Imaginary Homelands: Essays and Criticism 1981–1991* (New York: Penguin, 1992), esp. 380, 404; but see also 27, 31, 42, 43, 386.

40. J. M. Coetzee, *The Lives of Animals* (Princeton, NJ: Princeton University Press, 1999), 29–30. This text was incorporated into Coetzee's novel *Elizabeth Costello* (New York: Penguin, 2003), 74.

41. "To be a living bat is to be full of being; being fully a bat is like being fully human, which is also to be full of being." See Coetzee, *Lives* 33; *Elizabeth Costello* 77.

42. Rita Felski, *The Limits of Critique* (Chicago: University of Chicago Press, 2015).

43. In a letter to Louise Colet dated December 9, 1852, Flaubert compares the author to a distant creator-God after having just read *Uncle Tom's Cabin*, whose periodic authorial commentary violated his ideal of an impersonal narrative art. Flaubert reiterated the point in a letter to Marie-Sophie Leroyer de Chantepie on March 18, 1857. See Gustave Flaubert, *The Letters of Gustave Flaubert 1830–1857*, ed. and trans. Francis Steegmuller (Cambridge, MA: Harvard University Press, 1980), 173–74, 229–30.

44. Ulla Haselstein, "A New Kind of Realism: Flaubert's *Trois Contes* and Stein's *Three Lives*," *Comparative Literature* 61, no. 4 (2009): 389.

45. Spivak frames her point about counterfocalization within a larger critique of postcolonial claims to political exceptionalism: "In this essay I consider . . . not only fiction as event but also fiction as task. I locate in Rabindranath Tagore (1861–1941) and J. M. Coetzee (1940–) representations of what may be read as versions of the

'I' figured as object and weave the representations together as a warning text for postcolonial political ambitions" (*Aesthetic Education* 317–18). Her idea of the "I figured as object," exemplified by Coetzee's mode of undercutting Lurie's narrative authority by interspersing his account with the contradictions and silences of others (Lucy, Petrus, Bev, the attackers, the dog), is itself part of a nuanced debate in contemporary letters that should be credited as "postcolonial," notwithstanding Spivak's distrust of some articulations of academic postcolonialism that run the risk of overestimating their own moral and intellectual authority to change the world. It is also worth noting the confluence of her emphasis in this essay on intertextual "weaving" with that of Lionnet in her theorization of *métissage*.

46. Although Jennifer Fleissner's focus on "Melanctha" in the contexts of American naturalism and Freud's theory of the death drive is on the whole quite different from mine, she raises the pertinent point that "the problem of Stein's narration [is], at root, an issue of whether or not [Melanctha's] specific kind of desires can be *communicated*," and that "to suggest they might finally not be speakable at all would of course cut against every taxonomizing impulse of the book's narrative voice." See Jennifer L. Fleissner, *Women, Compulsion, Modernity: The Moment of American Naturalism* (Chicago: University of Chicago Press, 2004), 256.

47. Marianne DeKoven, *Rich and Strange: Gender, History, Modernism* (Princeton, NJ: Princeton University Press, 1991), 73.

48. Michael North, in *The Dialect of Modernism: Race, Language and Twentieth-Century Literature* (New York: Oxford University Press, 1994), has urged that we understand Stein's rendering of black vernacular in the context of her interpretation of Picasso's rendering of the African mask as "convention embodied, the sign of signs" that exposes "the conventional nature of all art" (63).

49. For a discussion of Stein's use of names in "Melanctha" and its relation to the theme of wandering, see John Carlos Rowe, "Naming What Is Inside: Gertrude Stein's Use of Names in *Three Lives*," *Novel: A Forum on Fiction* 36, no. 2 (2003): 219–43. Interpreting Stein as a poststructuralist *avant la lettre*, Rowe points to the incommensurable discursive roots and significations of Melanctha's name and argues that, rather than suggest the name's "'secret' or 'hidden' meaning," they imply "the 'natural' tendency of language to proliferate, refuse control and form, and exceed the intention of a discrete sender (author) or receiver (reader)" (220). Rowe does not consider the implications of the seemingly more straightforward name "Bridgepoint."

50. Frantz Fanon, *Black Skin, White Masks*, trans. Charles Lam Markmann (New York: Grove, 1967), 112; originally published as *Peau Noire, Masques Blancs* (Paris: Seuil, 1952).

51. Sianne Ngai, *Ugly Feelings* (Cambridge, MA: Harvard University Press, 2005), 255; Gertrude Stein, *The Making of Americans* (Normal, IL: Dalkey Archive Press, 1995). Stein wrote *Three Lives* (1905–6) just prior to *The Making of Americans*

(1906–11), although their publication dates are separated by sixteen years (1909 and 1925, respectively). Peter Nicholls has discussed Stein's use of the "continuous present" in these early works, in which "the sense of linear progression is broken by the 'layering' of one phrase against another"; see Peter Nicholls, *Modernisms: A Literary Guide* (Berkeley: University of California Press, 1995), 205.

52. Of course, the allusion here is to Gayatri Chakravorty Spivak, "Can the Subaltern Speak?," in *Marxism and the Interpretation of Culture*, ed. Cary Nelson and Lawrence Grossberg (Urbana: University of Illinois Press, 1988), 271–313, and to her subsequent reflections on its argument that the subaltern lacks the institutional means of being heard and in that sense cannot speak. See especially Gayatri Chakravorty Spivak, *A Critique of Postcolonial Reason: Toward a History of the Vanishing Present* (Cambridge, MA: Harvard University Press, 1999), 269–311; see also Spivak, *Aesthetic Education* 326.

53. Benita Parry, "Speech and Silence in the Fictions of J. M. Coetzee," in *Writing South Africa: Literature, Apartheid, and Democracy, 1970–1995*, ed. Derek Attridge and Rosemary Jolly (Cambridge: Cambridge University Press, 1998), 158.

54. Ato Quayson, *Aesthetic Nervousness: Disability and the Crisis of Representation* (New York: Columbia University Press, 2007), 149.

55. Neil Lazarus, *Nationalism and Cultural Practice in the Postcolonial World* (Cambridge: Cambridge University Press, 1999), 109.

56. For a revisionist defense of modernist primitivism, redefined with reference to anticolonial mobilizations of primitivist aesthetics by Césaire, Claude McKay, and Frantz Fanon, among others, see Ben Etherington, *Literary Primitivism* (Stanford, CA: Stanford University Press, 2017).

57. Fredric Jameson, *The Modernist Papers* (London: Verso, 2007), 345.

58. Even Stein's deliberately less radical and self-aggrandizing account of herself in *The Autobiography of Alice B. Toklas* (1933; repr., New York: Vintage, 1990) cleverly subverts its own narratorial authority by presenting as autobiography an explicit fiction whose ostensible author, speaker, and subject (Toklas) is actually a mask through which Stein projects her own voice and idealized image of herself. Toklas, lover, domestic, and secretary to the self-described genius Stein, haunts the narrative as one whose voice is everywhere performed but never, in fact, heard.

59. Though Barnard, focusing on Coetzee's aesthetic engagement with pastoralism, differentiates the pessimism of *Disgrace* from the intimations of utopianism she finds in his apartheid-era novels, we can align our reading of the politics of despair in *Disgrace* with her insight that "if Coetzee's fiction is in the main anti-pastoral and dystopian, then is it not our task as critics (following his own example) to read dialectically, to subvert the dominant, to discover in his work the utopian possibility, or pastoral impulse that cannot be expressed directly?" (32).

60. Timothy Bewes, *The Event of Postcolonial Shame* (Princeton, NJ: Princeton University Press, 2011), 140.

61. In *Diary of a Bad Year* (New York: Viking, 2007), J. M. Coetzee frames this problem in terms of the author's search for authority: "what if authority can be attained only by opening the poet-self to some higher force, by ceasing to be oneself and beginning to speak vatically?" (151).

62. Gertrude Stein, "What Are Master-pieces and Why Are There So Few of Them" (1936), in *The Gender of Modernism: A Critical Anthology*, ed. Bonnie Kime Scott (Bloomington: Indiana University Press, 1990), 495–96.

63. Achille Mbembe, *On the Postcolony*, trans. A. M. Berrett et al. (Berkeley: University of California Press, 2001), 190–91. Mbembe further elaborates this idea and its origins in "racial capitalism" in *Critique of Black Reason*, where he writes, "The world of the slave trade is the world of the hunt, of capturing and gathering, selling and buying" (136).

64. Mbembe analyzes Hegel's theory of the master-bondsman relation in terms of the role that recognition plays; see *On the Postcolony* 193.

Chapter 2. Troubling Sovereignties: Intimations of *Relation* in *The Waste Land* and *Cahier d'un retour au pays natal*

Epigraphs: Aimé Césaire, "Poetry and Knowledge," trans. Krzysztof Fijałkowski and Michael Richardson, in *Refusal of the Shadow: Surrealism and the Caribbean*, ed. Michael Richardson (London: Verso, 1996), 136; originally published as "Poésie et connaissance," *Tropiques* 12 (1945): 159; Aldous Huxley, "One and Many," in *Complete Essays*, vol. 2, *1926–1929*, ed. Robert S. Baker and James Sexton (Chicago: Ivan R. Dee, 2000), 306.

1. Derek Walcott, "A Letter to Chamoiseau" (1997), in *What the Twilight Says: Essays* (New York: Farrar, Straus & Giroux, 1998), 213–32.

2. I am drawing here on David Scott's influential interpretation of Hayden White's idea of "the mode of emplotment," which Scott defines as "the way the meaning or significance of a story is carried in the kind of story that is being told." See David Scott, *Conscripts of Modernity: The Tragedy of Colonial Enlightenment* (Durham, NC: Duke University Press, 2004), 46. Scott discusses modes of emplotment with reference to numerous works by White; see esp. Hayden White, *Metahistory: The Historical Imagination in Nineteenth Century Europe* (Baltimore: Johns Hopkins University Press, 1973); and Hayden White, *The Content of the Form: Narrative Discourse and Historical Representation* (Baltimore: Johns Hopkins University Press, 1987).

3. Michael Levenson, *Modernism* (New Haven, CT: Yale University Press, 2011), 240–41.

4. Peter Nicholls, *Modernisms: A Literary Guide* (Berkeley: University of California Press, 1995), 256.

5. Franco Moretti, *Signs Taken for Wonders: Essays in the Sociology of Literary Forms* (London: Verso, 1983), 222.

6. By "untimely," I do not mean "premature" or "inopportune" as the word's colloquial usage implies, but rather as "out of joint" with modern historical conventions of demarcating time and identities in time. For an explanation of how philosophers such as Nietzsche, Deleuze and Guattari, and Derrida have used the concept of the untimely (and, in Derrida's case, the phrase "time out of joint") to challenge these conventions, see Jonathan Gil Harris, *Untimely Matter in the Time of Shakespeare* (Philadelphia: University of Pennsylvania Press, 2009), 11–12. Harris makes the important distinction that Nietzsche's "*unzeitgemässe* does not simply connote the persistence of the past in the present; it also has a critical dimension. By resisting absorption into a homogeneous present, it brings with it the difference that produces the possibility of a new future even as it evokes the past" (11). Gary Wilder similarly argues for the emancipatory critical potential of "untimely vision" as conceived by Aimé Césaire and Léopold Sédar Senghor; I will return to his sense of the untimely as a dialectical interpenetration of past, present, and future in chap. 4. See Gary Wilder, *Freedom Time: Negritude, Decolonization, and the Future of the World* (Durham, NC: Duke University Press, 2015), esp. 224, 233, 280.

7. Eliot writes this in the 1930 preface to his first published translation of Perse's poem. In a prefatory note to the revised 1949 edition, Eliot explains that he has modified his earlier translation in collaboration with Perse. See St.-John Perse, *Anabasis*, trans. T. S. Eliot (1949; repr., New York: Harvest, 1977), 10; originally published as "Anabase," *La Nouvelle Revue Française* 124 (January 1924): 46–62.

8. Michel Crépu and J. M. G. Le Clézio, "Une Lettre de J. M. G. Le Clézio," *Revue des Deux Mondes* (2006): 75–76; my translation. The communal narration of Stein's "Melanctha," a subject of the previous chapter, well preceded that of Joyce but proved harder to recognize than the more overtly multiperspectival variations that followed, especially those that drew directly from classical mythology, such as *Ulysses* and *The Waste Land*.

9. For Eliot's laudatory 1923 review of *Ulysses* in which he credits Joyce with replacing an outdated "narrative method" with the "mythical method" of "manipulating a continuous parallel between contemporaneity and antiquity," see T. S. Eliot, "*Ulysses*, Order, and Myth," in *Selected Prose of T. S. Eliot*, ed. Frank Kermode (San Diego, CA: Harcourt, 1975), 175–78.

10. It must be said that Walcott dismisses the *Éloge* on grounds the *créolistes* anticipated in their prologue, where they defend themselves against the charge of writing from within a theoretical framework: "These words we are communicating to you here do not stem from theory, nor do they stem from any learned principles. They are, rather, akin to testimony. They proceed from a sterile experience which we have known before committing ourselves to reactivate our creative potential,

and to set in motion the expression of what we are." Jean Bernabé, Patrick Chamoiseau, and Raphaël Confiant, *Éloge de la Créolité / In Praise of Creoleness*, bilingual ed., trans. M. B. Taleb-Khyar (Paris: Gallimard, 1993), 75. Like Walcott, they follow Glissant in using "theory" as a shorthand designation for any abstract, systematizing language, though the quintessential example and catalyst of all these critiques is the speciously rationalist discourse of colonialist domination and racial science.

11. See also Walcott's brief critique of the *Éloge* in his earlier essay "The Muse of History" (1974), reprinted in *What the Twilight Says* 51. Maryse Condé has also criticized the *Éloge de la Créolité* for its prescriptiveness about the future of Caribbean literature and its dismissiveness toward Caribbean literary production that preceded it. See Maryse Condé, "Order, Disorder, Freedom, and the West Indian Writer," *Yale French Studies* 97 (2000): 151, 158–60, 164–65.

12. Césaire's neologism contributed to efforts already underway in the 1920s among black diasporic intellectuals, notably Lamine Senghor, to claim and revalue the word *nègre*, as Brent Hayes Edwards explains in *The Practice of Diaspora: Literature, Translation, and the Rise of Black Internationalism* (Cambridge, MA: Harvard University Press, 2003), 28.

13. The first phrase is taken from Timothy J. Reiss, *Against Autonomy: Global Dialectics of Cultural Exchange* (Stanford, CA: Stanford University Press, 2002), 47. Reiss gives a valuable overview of earlier critiques of negritude by an array of African and Caribbean thinkers with whom he agrees, including Es'kia Mphahlele, Wole Soyinka, Okot p'Bitek, Chinua Achebe, Fanon, Glissant, Chamoiseau, and Raphaël Confiant; see esp. 46–54. The second phrase is from Susan Stanford Friedman's interpretation of the *Cahier* in *Planetary Modernisms: Provocations on Modernity across Time* (New York: Columbia University Press, 2015), 300, 306.

14. Nick Nesbitt, *Voicing Memory: History and Subjectivity in French Caribbean Literature* (Charlottesville: University of Virginia Press, 2003), 83–84. I agree with Donna Jones that "it short-circuits the argument" to assert, as Nesbitt does, that because "blood" and pre-rationality were idealized in fascist discourse, contemporaneous idealizations of them, such as Césaire's in the 1930s, were necessarily fascist as well. See Donna V. Jones, *The Racial Discourses of Life Philosophy: Négritude, Vitalism, and Modernity* (New York: Columbia University Press, 2010), 174.

15. I will return in chap. 3 to Milan Kundera's use of this phrase in French, "rencontre multiple," to describe Martinican culture in his essay "Beau comme une rencontre multiple," in *Une Rencontre* (Paris: Gallimard, 2009), 117, 121; translated as "Beautiful Like a Multiple Encounter," in *Encounter: Essays*, trans. Linda Asher (New York: Harper Perennial, 2010), 81, 84. Kundera appears to be adapting Césaire's line "RENCONTRE BIEN TOTALE" ("TRULY TOTAL ENCOUNTER") from the title poem of *Corps perdu* (1950), in *The Complete Poetry of Aimé Césaire: Bilingual Edition*, ed. A. James Arnold, trans. A. James Arnold and Clayton Eshleman (Wesleyan, CT: Wesleyan University Press, 2017), 497.

16. C. L. R. James, "Appendix: From Toussaint L'Ouverture to Fidel Castro," in *The Black Jacobins: Toussaint L'Ouverture and the San Domingo Revolution*, 2nd ed. (New York: Vintage, 1963), 391–418.

17. Césaire published four versions of the *Cahier* between 1939 and 1956. The first version appeared in the avant-garde journal *Volontés* in 1939. Two distinct revised editions, both prefaced by André Breton, were published in 1947, one by Brentano's, New York, and the other by Bordas, Paris. Finally, the best-known, most politically explicit version, and the one to which I refer throughout this chapter, was published in 1956 by Présence Africaine. A genetic edition of these four versions was published in A. James Arnold et al., eds., *Aimé Césaire: Poésie, théâtre, essais et discours, Édition critique* (Paris: CNRS Éditions/Planète Libre, 2013), 63–219. Arnold also offers a detailed history and analysis of the successive versions in his English-language introduction to *The Original 1939 Notebook of a Return to the Native Land: Bilingual Edition*, ed. and trans. A. James Arnold and Clayton Eshleman (Middletown, CT: Wesleyan University Press, 2013), xi–xxii; see also "A Césaire Chronology" in the same volume, 71–72. For an earlier textual history of the *Cahier*, see Lilian Pestre de Almeida, "Les Versions successive du *Cahier d'un retour au pays natal*," in *Césaire 70*, ed. M. a M. Ngal and Martin Steins (Paris: Silex, 1984), 35–90.

18. Frantz Fanon, *The Wretched of the Earth*, trans. Richard Philcox (New York: Grove, 2004), 151; originally published as *Les damnés de la terre* (Paris: François Maspero éditeur, 1961).

19. Though this appears not to be a direct quotation of Karl Marx, James is referring to a core idea running through Marx's works, namely, that the real history of humanity, no longer impeded by illusory ideals, will begin after the emancipation of the proletariat through revolutionary struggle.

20. Aimé Césaire, *Cahier d'un retour au pays natal*, ed. Abiola Irele (1956; repr., Columbus: Ohio State University Press, 2000), 33. Although page references hereafter are to this edition, Irele's introduction, notes, and commentary have been reprinted in N. Gregson Davis's translation and bilingual edition of the *Cahier*, *Journal of a Homecoming/Cahier d'un retour au pays natal* (Durham, NC: Duke University Press, 2017).

21. Edward W. Said, *Culture and Imperialism* (New York: Vintage, 1993), 279–81. For a response to Said's discussion of James, see John Marx, "Postcolonial Literature and the Western Literary Canon," in *Postcolonial Literary Studies*, ed. Neil Lazarus (Cambridge: Cambridge University Press, 2004), 90–91.

22. For examples of postcolonial criticism that treats Eliot as representative of an unambiguously conservative modernism, see Robert J. C. Young, *Colonial Desire: Hybridity in Theory, Culture and Race* (London: Routledge, 1995), 51–52; and Neil Lazarus, *Nationalism and Cultural Practice in the Postcolonial World* (Cambridge: Cambridge University Press, 1999), 152. Contemporaneous with these books was future barrister Anthony Julius's influential scholarly prosecution of Eliot's work for

anti-Semitism, *T. S. Eliot, Anti-Semitism, and Literary Form* (Cambridge: Cambridge University Press, 1995).

23. For analysis and theoretical framing of Césaire's "poetic knowledge" as "a dialectical form of knowing" that overcomes what Césaire calls "the law of identity" and "the law of noncontradiction" and through poetic images transcends modern antinomies of "one and the other," "Self and World," see Wilder, *Freedom Time* 39. For analysis of Eliot's "dialectical imagination" and the implications of his philosophical relativism for the interpretation of his poetry, see Jewel Spears Brooker, *T. S. Eliot's Dialectical Imagination* (Baltimore: Johns Hopkins University Press, 2018), esp. 1–11; and Jewel Spears Brooker, *Mastery and Escape: T. S. Eliot and the Dialectic of Modernism* (Amherst: University of Massachusetts Press, 1994), 3, 16–20, and 172–90. In critical readings that encompass Eliot's doctoral critiques of philosophical dualism and the dialectical patterns of his poems and essays, Brooker has traced a "resistance to binary thinking resulting in a simultaneous embrace of such opposites as tradition and originality"; Jewel Spears Brooker, "Yes and No: Eliot and Western Philosophy," *A Companion to T. S. Eliot*, ed. David E. Chinitz (Malden, MA: Wiley-Blackwell, 2009), 53. In the same volume, Michael Levenson also reads Eliot's poetry and criticism from the 1920s with reference back to Eliot's early philosophical work, especially his "'theory of points of view,' which held that we can construct reliable—though never indubitable—judgments through the accumulation of many immediate perspectives." See Michael Levenson, "Eliot's Politics," in *Companion to T. S. Eliot* 377.

24. T. S. Eliot, "The Dry Salvages," in *Four Quartets*, in *The Complete Poems and Plays 1909–1950* (1941; repr., New York: Harcourt, 1980), 136.

25. David Damrosch, *What Is World Literature?* (Princeton, NJ: Princeton University Press, 2003), 50.

26. At the Modern Language Association in 2015, Joseph Slaughter delivered an address titled "Another Modernism?" in which he criticized "the global expansionism of the New Modernist Studies." Slaughter subsequently developed this argument in the published version of his 2017 presidential lecture to the American Comparative Literature Association, "Locations of Comparison," and in his formal response to a cluster of "opinion papers" on the lecture. See Joseph R. Slaughter, "Locations of Comparison," *Cambridge Journal of Postcolonial Literary Inquiry* 5, no. 2 (2018): esp. 216n25, 224n65, 224–25; and Joseph R. Slaughter, "More Locations of Comparison: On Forum Shopping and Global South Envy in a Globalizing Discipline," *Cambridge Journal of Postcolonial Literary Inquiry* 5, no. 3 (2018): esp. 287–88, 293.

27. Jahan Ramazani, *A Transnational Poetics* (Chicago: University of Chicago Press, 2009), 115. In this influential book, Ramazani builds on the theory of postcolonial poetics he introduced in *The Hybrid Muse: Postcolonial Poetry in English* (Chicago: University of Chicago Press, 2001) to offer a more expansive theory of transnational poetics spanning diverse translocal and cross-regional contexts, including transatlantic and expatriate modernisms.

28. C. L. R. James, *Mariners, Renegades and Castaways: The Story of Herman Melville and the World We Live In* (1953; repr., Lebanon, NH: Dartmouth College Press, 2001).

29. Édouard Glissant, *Le Discours antillais* (1981; repr., Paris: Gallimard, 1997), 56–57; Édouard Glissant, *Caribbean Discourse: Selected Essays*, trans. J. Michael Dash (Charlottesville: University of Virginia Press, 1989), 26; trans. mod.

30. Prescott S. Nichols, "Césaire's Native Land and the Third World," *Twentieth-Century Literature* 18, no. 3 (1972): 157–66. Unmentioned in Nichols's essay but relevant to any reading of the *Cahier* and *The Waste Land* as expressions of the West's decline is Oswald Spengler's *The Decline of the West*, trans. Charles Francis Atkinson (New York: Knopf, 1957), the influential first volume of which was initially published in German in 1918.

31. Abiola Irele, introduction to *Cahier d'un retour au pays natal*, by Aimé Césaire, ed. Abiola Irele (Columbus: Ohio State University Press, 2000), lix.

32. Natalie Melas, *All the Difference in the World: Postcoloniality and the Ends of Comparison* (Stanford, CA: Stanford University Press, 2007), 180.

33. See Michael North, *The Dialect of Modernism: Race, Language and Twentieth-Century Literature* (New York: Oxford University Press, 1994), 77–99. North interprets Eliot's experiments with black speech as attempts to "deterritorialize" English by giving voice to "nonstandard speakers" (87–89), but where Césaire unsettles racial stereotypes, Eliot is prone to reiterate them.

34. Stéphane Mallarmé, "Crisis of Verse," in *Divagations*, trans. Barbara Johnson (Cambridge, MA: Belknap, 2007), 203–4; originally published as "Crise de Vers," in *Divagations*, *Œuvres* (1897; repr., Paris: Garnier, 1992), 271–72.

35. For Césaire's tribute to Mallarmé, see his "Vues sur Mallarmé," in Arnold et al., *Aimé Césaire* 1329–35. For other discussions of Mallarmé's poetics in relation to that of Césaire, see Carrie Noland, *Voices of Negritude in Modernist Print: Aesthetic Subjectivity, Diaspora, and the Lyric Regime* (New York: Columbia University Press, 2015), esp. 44–57; Wilder, *Freedom Time* 43; and A. James Arnold, *Modernism and Negritude: The Poetry and Poetics of Aimé Césaire* (Cambridge, MA: Harvard University Press, 1981), 65–67, 276–77. For a study of symbolism's importance to twentieth-century modernism, with particular attention to Mallarmé's significance as a theorist of modernist poetics, see Levenson, *Modernism* 12–38, 106–68. For Levenson's discussion of Eliot and symbolism, see *Modernism* 163–68. For a study of the network of influences connecting the symbolists, Eliot, the negritude poets, Perse, and other New World writers, see Anita Patterson, *Race, American Literature and Transnational Modernisms* (Cambridge: Cambridge University Press, 2008).

36. Jean-Paul Sartre, "Orphée Noir," in *Anthologie de la Nouvelle Poésie Nègre et Malgache de Langue Française*, ed. Léopold Sédar Senghor (1948; repr., Paris: Presses Universitaires de France, 1969), xix; my translation.

37. In addition to Ramazani's work, other important transnationalist accounts of Eliot's considerable influence on Anglophone Caribbean and world poetry, and of

how to read Eliot's work differently in light of postcolonial engagements with it, include Matthew Hart, *Nations of Nothing but Poetry: Modernism, Transnationalism, and Synthetic Vernacular Writing* (Oxford: Oxford University Press, 2010), 106–41; and Charles W. Pollard, *New World Modernisms: T. S. Eliot, Derek Walcott, and Kamau Brathwaite* (Charlottesville: University of Virginia Press, 2004). For transnationalist interventions in the intellectual history and political import of negritude, see Wilder, *Freedom Time*; and Gary Wilder, *The French Imperial Nation-State: Negritude and Colonial Humanism between the Two World Wars* (Chicago: University of Chicago Press, 2005). As I have already suggested, Wilder interprets Césaire's and Senghor's writings, including their poems, with a commitment to understanding how they might inform our current vision of progressive political engagement.

38. Lawrence Rainey, *Revisiting "The Waste Land"* (New Haven, CT: Yale University Press, 2005), x.

39. Christopher L. Miller, *The French Atlantic Triangle: Literature and Culture of the Slave Trade* (Durham, NC: Duke University Press, 2008), 328. Other close readings of the *Cahier* that demonstrate the poem's resistance to being reduced to a fixed theory of negritude include Wilder, *French Imperial Nation-State* 278–94; and Doris L. Garraway, "'What Is Mine': Césairean Negritude between the Particular and the Universal," *Research in African Literatures* 41, no. 1 (2010): 71–86. Mireille Rosello takes a similar position regarding Césaire's work generally in "The 'Césaire Effect,' or How to Cultivate One's Nation," *Research in African Literatures* 32, no. 4 (2001): 77.

40. Chinweizu, Onwuchekwa Jemie, and Ihechukwu Madubuike, *Toward the Decolonization of African Literature* (Washington, DC: Howard University Press, 1983), 163–238. See esp. their opposition between negritude and the "euromodernism" of Eliot (172–73, 177) and their suggestion that Césaire, one of their book's dedicatees, exemplifies an alternative African poetic tradition (v, 195). For condemnations of negritude that define it with reference to an isolated strand of Senghorian thought, see Wole Soyinka, "Cross-Currents," in *Art, Dialogue and Outrage: Essays on Literature and Culture* (Ibadan, Nigeria: New Horn, 1988), 180; and Henry Louis Gates Jr., "Writing 'Race' and the Difference It Makes," in *"Race," Writing, and Difference*, ed. Henry Louis Gates Jr. (Chicago: University of Chicago Press, 1985), 13. See also the critique of Césaire's negritude in Bernabé, Chamoiseau, and Confiant, *Éloge de la Créolité* 79–83. For a defense of negritude and Senghor's thought specifically, see Robert J. C. Young, *Postcolonialism: An Historical Introduction* (Oxford: Blackwell, 2001), 265–73.

41. Souleymane Bachir Diagne, *African Art as Philosophy: Senghor, Bergson and the Idea of Negritude*, trans. Chike Jeffers (London: Seagull, 2011), 27.

42. See Pound's editorial comments in *The Waste Land: A Facsimile and Transcript of the Original Drafts Including the Annotations of Ezra Pound*, ed. Valerie Eliot (San Diego, CA: Harcourt, 1971).

43. T. S. Eliot, *The Waste Land*, in *The Complete Poems and Plays 1909–1950* (New York: Harcourt, 1980), 5.427–34.

44. T. S. Eliot, "The Art of Poetry No. 1," *Paris Review* 21 (1959): n.p., http://www.theparisreview.org/interviews/4738/the-art-of-poetry-no-1-t-s-eliot.

45. "Entretien avec Aimé Césaire," with Jacqueline Leiner, in *Tropiques* 1 (Paris: Éditions Jean-Michel Place, 1978), xxii. For Chinweizu, Jemie, and Madubuike's directly contrary view of literature's communicative function, notwithstanding their sense of solidarity with Césaire, see *Toward the Decolonization* 187–88, 217.

46. T. S. Eliot, "Dante," in *Selected Prose* 206.

47. T. S. Eliot, "From *The Music of Poetry*" (1942), in *Selected Prose* 111.

48. For a discussion of how the hermeneutics of suspicion is aligned with "symptomatic reading" practices now being variously critiqued, supplemented, and superseded by "surface reading," see Stephen Best and Sharon Marcus, "Surface Reading: An Introduction," *Representations* 108, no. 1 (2009): 1–21, esp. 2, 5, 8–9, 16, 19. Definitions of symptomatic and surface reading that sharply distinguish these practices from each other do not quite accommodate the mode of reading I advance here, one that neither seeks to excavate latent meaning presumed to be a text's master code nor attends to what is directly denoted or easily perceptible in a text without also casting a suspicious eye on less immediately apparent textual attributes.

49. Édouard Glissant, *Poetics of Relation*, trans. Betsy Wing (Ann Arbor: University of Michigan Press, 1997), 25; originally published as Édouard Glissant, *Poétique de la relation* (Paris: Gallimard, 1990), 37.

50. Rebecca L. Walkowitz, *Cosmopolitan Style: Modernism beyond the Nation* (New York: Columbia University Press, 2006), 7.

51. When Anna Tsing writes that the concept of "assemblage" has been useful for ecologists seeking to avoid "the sometimes fixed and bounded connotations of ecological 'community,'" she makes clear what a transnationalist project of imagining "history without progress" has to gain from reorienting itself toward the "never settled" encounters of assemblage, which she likens to polyphony's "separate, simultaneous melodies": "Assemblages are open-ended gatherings. They allow us to ask about communal effects without assuming them. They show us potential histories in the making." See Anna Lowenhaupt Tsing, *The Mushroom at the End of the World: On the Possibility of Life in Capitalist Ruins* (Princeton, NJ: Princeton University Press, 2015), 22–23.

52. Ranjana Khanna, *Algeria Cuts: Women and Representation, 1830 to the Present* (Stanford, CA: Stanford University Press, 2008), 237–38.

53. Donald E. Pease, introduction to James, *Mariners* xviii, xv.

54. Aimé Césaire, *Notebook of a Return to the Native Land*, trans. Clayton Eshleman and Annette Smith (Middletown, CT: Wesleyan University Press, 2001), 49. I have made a number of modifications to the translation. See also the recently

published translation and critical edition of the 1939 *Cahier*, which does not contain the lines quoted and discussed above, or those quoted further on regarding the prince and the queen: Aimé Césaire, *The Original 1939 Notebook of a Return to the Native Land: Bilingual Edition*, ed. and trans. A. James Arnold and Clayton Eshleman (Middletown, CT: Wesleyan University Press, 2013), reprinted in Aimé Césaire, *The Complete Poetry*, bilingual ed., trans. A. James Arnold and Clayton Eshleman, ed. A. James Arnold (Middletown, CT: Wesleyan University Press, 2017).

55. Sophocles, *Elektra: A Play*, trans. Ezra Pound and Rudd Fleming (1949; repr., Princeton, NJ: Princeton University Press, 1989).

56. Natalie Melas, "Untimeliness, or Négritude and the Poetics of Contramodernity," *South Atlantic Quarterly* 108, no. 3 (2009): 563–80.

57. Abiola Irele, "Commentary and Notes," in Césaire, *Cahier*, ed. Irele, 145–46.

58. On lost authority figures in *The Waste Land*, see Levenson, "Eliot's Politics" 378. On Eliot's appeal to an outside source of authority despite the poem's formal radicality, see Marjorie Perloff, *21st-Century Modernism: The "New" Poetics* (Malden, MA: Blackwell, 2002), 38.

59. Césaire again associates "la Reine" with the state in his later poem, "La Justice écoute aux portes de la beauté" (1982), trans. as "Justice Listens at the Gates of Beauty," in *Lyric and Dramatic Poetry, 1946–82*, bilingual ed., trans. Clayton Eshleman and Annette Smith (Charlottesville: University Press of Virginia, 1990), 160–61. In this poem, the Queen serves as the figurehead of a beautiful and obfuscatory regime, who "puts down her crown" (*dépose sa couronne*) but persists in obscuring the nature of justice.

60. For a feminist critique of how colonial notions of virility came to influence ideals of decolonized masculinity in the thought of Césaire, Fanon, Albert Memmi, and Ashis Nandy, see Françoise Vergès, *Monsters and Revolutionaries: Colonial Family Romance and Métissage* (Durham, NC: Duke University Press, 1999), 221–22.

61. J. Michael Dash, introduction to Glissant, *Caribbean Discourse* xiii, xxi.

62. Ranjana Khanna, *Dark Continents: Psychoanalysis and Colonialism* (Durham, NC: Duke University Press, 2003), 126, 128.

63. It is tempting to allow the autobiographical dimension of the *Cahier* to determine one's reading of the speaker and his language. Carrie Noland has argued that Sartre's identification of Césaire with surrealism too often leads to his poetry being read as if it were a kind of automatic writing and therefore "the revelation of some personal, or even collective unconscious" rather than "a dialogue between a situated subject and equally situated means." She warns against equating "an aspect of subjectivity—the writer's inscription in a particular field of cultural production" with "the writer's identity—understood either as his ethnic affiliation (his politics) or his unique psychological being." See Noland, *Voices of Negritude* 50.

64. I will return to this scene in chap. 3. In the *Éloge*, the *créolistes* write that they wish to "free" Césaire from the accusation that he was hostile to Creole. They

somewhat sympathetically contextualize the poetics of negritude but in the process compare it unfavorably to their own poetics of *créolité*. See Bernabé, Chamoiseau, and Confiant, *Éloge de la Créolité* 17–18 and 79–80.

65. My reference to the plot of heroic romance is indebted to Scott's discussion of heroic romance and tragedy as modes of emplotment through which James narrates the story of Toussaint Louverture in *The Black Jacobins*; see Scott, *Conscripts of Modernity* 46–47 passim.

66. The notes did not appear with the poem when it was first published, either in the October 1922 issue of the *Criterion* or in the New York periodical *The Dial* the following month. Eliot added the notes when *The Waste Land* was first published in book form in December 1922.

67. For the idea that the *Cahier* "undogmatically explores the 'fit' of various racial selves (masks of Negritude, so to speak) from contingent vantage points," see Gregson Davis, *Aimé Césaire* (Cambridge: Cambridge University Press, 2008), 27.

68. Jewel Spears Brooker and Joseph Bentley, *Reading "The Waste Land": Modernism and the Limits of Interpretation* (Amherst: University of Massachusetts Press, 1990), 54.

69. For Levenson's earlier and more extensive reading of points of view in *The Waste Land* and their relation to Eliot's early philosophical theory of points of view, see Michael H. Levenson, *A Genealogy of Modernism: A Study of English Literary Doctrine 1908–1922* (Cambridge: Cambridge University Press, 1984), 169–93.

70. My own reading of "Sweeney Erect" centers on the poem's nostalgic juxtaposition of a lost, ethically infused imaginative order to a chaotic present devoid of shared values. See Mara de Gennaro, "Man Is Man Because . . . : Humanism Wars, 'Sweeney Erect,' and the Makings of Modernist Imagination," *Paideuma: Modern and Contemporary Poetry and Poetics* 41 (2014): 159–93, esp. 177–86.

71. Brent Hayes Edwards, "Aimé Césaire and the Syntax of Influence," *Research in African Literatures* 36, no. 2 (2005): 9.

72. T. S. Eliot, "Tradition and the Individual Talent" (1919), in *Selected Prose* 38.

73. See Ovid, vol. 3, *Metamorphoses*, vol. 1, book 6, trans. Frank Justus Miller, 3rd ed., rev. G. P. Goold (Cambridge, MA: Harvard University Press, 1984), 329–35.

74. Again, see Patterson, esp. 9–92, 115–19. Also see Césaire's ambivalent poetic tribute to Perse, "Cérémonie vaudou pour Saint John Perse . . . ," in *Noria* (1976), in Césaire, *Complete Poetry* 811–13; as well as his earlier, respectful citation of Perse in a lecture published as "Discours prononcé par Aimé Césaire à Dakar le 6 avril 1966 dans le cadre du Colloque sur l'art dans la vie du peuple qui marqua l'ouverture du Premier Festival mondial des arts nègres (30 mars–21 avril 1966)," *Gradhiva* 10 (2009): 209.

75. Achille Mbembe, *Critique of Black Reason*, trans. Laurent Dubois (Durham, NC: Duke University Press, 2017), 173.

Chapter 3. Traversing Bounds of Historical Memory: Dethroning the Narrator and Creolizing Testimony in *A Passage to India* and *Texaco*

Epigraphs: Michel-Rolph Trouillot, *Silencing the Past: Power and the Production of History* (Boston: Beacon, 1995), 15; Édouard Glissant, *Poetics of Relation*, trans. Betsy Wing (Ann Arbor: University of Michigan Press, 1997), 138–39; originally published as *Poétique de la relation* (Paris: Gallimard, 1990), 153.

1. E. M. Forster, *The Hill of Devi* (San Diego, CA: Harvest, 1953), 7.

2. Edward W. Said, *Culture and Imperialism* (New York: Vintage, 1993), 201. See also Joseph Conrad, *Heart of Darkness*, ed. Paul B. Armstrong (1899; repr., New York: Norton, 2006).

3. R. Radhakrishnan, "Why Compare?," in *Comparison: Theories, Approaches, Uses*, ed. Rita Felski and Susan Stanford Friedman (Baltimore: Johns Hopkins University Press, 2013), 20.

4. Benita Parry, *Postcolonial Studies: A Materialist Critique* (London: Routledge, 2004), 174–75.

5. In light of postcolonial critiques of *A Passage to India* that have proliferated since the late 1980s, it is tempting to underestimate the novel's salutary deviation from more conventional interwar representations of British imperialism, as Parry has noted (174–75). Edward Thompson's *Suttee* was a "perfect specimen of the justification of imperialism as a civilizing mission," writes Gayatri Chakravorty Spivak in *A Critique of Postcolonial Reason: Toward a History of the Vanishing Present* (Cambridge, MA: Harvard University Press, 1999), 303. Whereas Forster sends Mrs. Moore from Chandrapore with a realization of India's prodigious diversity—she wishes she could "disentangle the hundred Indias" she sees in Bombay alone (E. M. Forster, *A Passage to India* [1924; repr., San Diego, CA: Harcourt, 1984], 233)—Thompson in no way qualifies his "construction of a continuous and homogeneous 'India'" that warrants British control, nor does he qualify his own narratorial persona as "'a man of good sense' who would be the transparent voice of reasonable humanity" in so representing India (Spivak 303–4). Spivak's critique of transparency here is closely aligned with that of Glissant: a text produces transparency through translational distortion and, in the process, legitimizes domination conceived as humane beneficence.

6. Michel-Rolph Trouillot, *Silencing the Past: Power and the Production of History* (Boston: Beacon, 1995), 141.

7. We learn of Adela Quested's intent—"I want to see the *real* India"—before we even learn her name. This intent is restated repeatedly in similar terms.

8. Trouillot writes, "Historical representations—be they books, commercial exhibits or public commemorations—cannot be conceived only as vehicles for the transmission of knowledge. They must establish some relation to that knowledge.

Further, not any relation will do. Authenticity is required, lest the representation becomes a fake, a morally repugnant spectacle" (149).

9. Jenny Sharpe, *Allegories of Empire: The Figure of Woman in the Colonial Text* (Minneapolis: University of Minnesota Press, 1993), 122.

10. Ian Baucom, *Out of Place: Englishness, Empire, and the Locations of Identity* (Princeton, NJ: Princeton University Press, 1999), 134.

11. Édouard Glissant, *Poetics of Relation*, trans. Betsy Wing (Ann Arbor: University of Michigan Press, 1997), 191–92; trans. mod. "Il y a dans ce verbe comprendre le mouvement des mains qui prennent l'entour et le ramènent à soi." See Édouard Glissant, *Poétique de la relation* (Paris: Gallimard, 1990), 206.

12. Paul Gilroy, *Against Race: Imagining Political Culture beyond the Color Line* (Cambridge, MA: Harvard University Press, 2000), 55–56. For Hegel's disparagement of Africans in comparative, world-historical terms, see G. W. F. Hegel, *The Philosophy of History*, trans. J. Sibree (Mineola, NY: Dover, 1956), 93–99.

13. Urmila Seshagiri, *Race and the Modernist Imagination* (Ithaca, NY: Cornell University Press, 2010), 58.

14. In her influential reading of homoeroticism in *A Passage to India*, Sara Suleri argues that Forster replaces "the Orientalist paradigm in which the colonizing presence is as irredeemably male as the colonized territory is female" with "an alternative colonial model" in which "the most urgent cross-cultural invitations occur between male and male, with racial difference serving as a substitute for gender." In Forster's depiction of the punkah wallah, an "ostensibly casual invocation of caste further complicates the muddied gender boundaries of the text" by extending the meaning of "untouchable" from the punkah wallah's caste alone to his "embodiment of homosexual desire." See Sara Suleri, *The Rhetoric of English India* (Chicago: University of Chicago Press, 1992), 133, 135.

15. See chap. 1, note 43.

16. For Forster's descriptions of "the herd" and of Fielding's detachment from it, see *Passage* 65, 183.

17. E. M. Forster, "What I Believe" (1938), in *Two Cheers for Democracy* (1951; repr., London: Edward Arnold, 1972), 66.

18. Leela Gandhi, *Affective Communities: Anticolonial Thought, Fin-de-Siècle Radicalism, and the Politics of Friendship* (Durham, NC: Duke University Press, 2006), 29; see also 10.

19. Aamir R. Mufti, *Enlightenment in the Colony: The Jewish Question and the Crisis of Postcolonial Culture* (Princeton, NJ: Princeton University Press, 2007), 123.

20. Milan Kundera, *The Curtain: An Essay in Seven Parts*, trans. Linda Asher (New York: Harper Perennial, 2006), 166; originally published as *Le Rideau: Essai en sept parties* (Paris: Gallimard, 2005), 202. Further references are to Asher's translation.

21. In *Colonial Desire: Hybridity in Theory, Culture and Race* (London: Routledge,

1995), Robert J. C. Young concedes that colonialisms differ but also insists on their shared basis: "Clearly the ideology and procedures of French colonialism, based on an egalitarian Enlightenment assumption of the fundamental sameness of all human beings and the unity of the human race, and therefore designed to assimilate colonial peoples to French civilization, differed very substantially from the indirect-rule policies of the British, which were based on an assumption of difference and of inequality"; however, "most forms of colonialism are after all, in the final analysis, colonialism, the rule by force of a people by an external power." Young reminds us that it was "Third World theorists, such as Fanon, Nkrumah or Said, who needed to invent such categories precisely as general categories in order to constitute an object both for analysis and for resistance" (164–65).

22. Said cautions against overstating the distinction between the British "'departmental view'" and the French "assimilationist enterprise" from the late nineteenth century on, because after 1880 the French "ideological theory of colonial assimilation begun under the Revolution collapsed, as theories of racial types . . . guided French imperial strategies. Natives and their lands were not to be treated as entities that could be made French, but as possessions the immutable characteristics of which required separation and subservience, even though this did not rule out the *mission civilisatrice*" (169, 170).

23. As I note in this book's introduction, *créolité* continues to be defined mostly in terms laid out in the *Éloge de la Créolité*, as well as in a subsequent interview about the *Éloge* with its authors; for the latter, see Patrick Chamoiseau et al., "Créolité Bites," *Transition* 74 (1997): 124–61. Chamoiseau is still cited in Anglophone world literature debates most often for his coauthorship of this manifesto. In these forums, the proponents of *créolité* call for more recognition of Creole as a potential literary language whose hybrid character evokes Caribbean cultural diversity as colonial European languages, and French in particular, cannot. Their argument, written in French, was criticized by numerous Caribbean and Francophone writers as unfair and simplistic; as I discuss in the previous chapter, some of these writers, such as Derek Walcott, have contrasted the prescriptive definitions of *créolité* in the *Éloge* with the highly inventive, Creole-inspired, freewheeling French of Chamoiseau's fiction. See Derek Walcott, "A Letter to Chamoiseau" (1997), in *What the Twilight Says* (New York: Farrar, Straus & Giroux, 1998), 222–31; and Maryse Condé, "Order, Disorder, Freedom, and the West Indian Writer," *Yale French Studies* 97 (2000): 158–60, 164–65.

24. Pierre Choderlos de Laclos, *Les Liaisons dangereuses* (1782; repr., Paris: Gallimard, 1998); William Faulkner, *As I Lay Dying* (1930; repr., New York: Vintage, 1987).

25. Jacques Stephen Alexis, *L'Espace d'un cillement* (Paris: Gallimard, 1959); translated by Carrol F. Coates as *In the Flicker of an Eyelid* (Charlottesville: University of Virginia Press, 2002). Kundera could also have mentioned this novel's correlation of

political conditions in Haiti with conditions in Batista's Cuba. The US military's occupation of Haiti, together with Trujillo's racist dictatorship in the Dominican Republic, also inspires Alexis's relativizing juxtapositions in his earlier novel *Compère Général Soleil* (Paris: Gallimard, 1955); translated by Carrol F. Coates as *General Sun, My Brother* (Charlottesville: University of Virginia Press, 1999).

26. Kundera cites the French version of Alejo Carpentier's *El siglo de las luces* (1958), namely *Le siècle des lumières*, trans. René L.-F. Durand (Paris: Gallimard, 1962). The English version is translated from the French by John Sturrock as *Explosion in a Cathedral* (Minneapolis: University of Minnesota Press, 2001).

27. C. L. R. James, *The Black Jacobins: Toussaint L'Ouverture and the San Domingo Revolution*, 2nd ed. (New York: Vintage, 1963); Eric Williams, *Capitalism and Slavery* (1944; repr., Chapel Hill: University of North Carolina Press, 1994).

28. Milan Kundera, "Beautiful Like a Multiple Encounter," in *Encounter: Essays*, trans. Linda Asher (New York: Harper Perennial, 2010), 92–93; originally published as "Beau comme une rencontre multiple," in *Une Rencontre* (Paris: Gallimard, 2009), 132. The original French-language essay was first published in 1991, a year before the publication of Chamoiseau's acclaimed *Texaco*.

29. Patrick Chamoiseau, *Solibo Magnifique* (Paris: Gallimard, 1988); Patrick Chamoiseau, *Texaco* (Paris: Gallimard, 1992); translated by Rose-Myriam Réjouis and Val Vinokurov as *Texaco* (New York: Vintage, 1998).

30. The inscription reads, "*Pour Édouard Glissant, Pour Véra Kundera . . . ô estimés . . . P. C.*" (For Édouard Glissant, For Véra Kundera . . . O esteemed ones . . . P. C.). The English translation of *Texaco* erroneously identifies Milan Kundera instead of his wife as Glissant's fellow dedicatee.

31. Patrick Chamoiseau, *Césaire, Perse, Glissant: Les liaisons magnétiques* (Paris: Philippe Rey, 2013), 204–5; my translation.

32. This positively inflected use of "poor" is consistent with the uses of "poor theory," "poor college," and "poor analogies" discussed in detail in the next chapter.

33. "Une phrase soudain m'habita. Je lui demandai de me la répéter. Puis, je lui pris le livre que je lus seule, sans y comprendre hak, me laissant juste porter par l'énergie invocatoire qui me négrait le sang" (401). Réjouis and Vinokurov translate "sans y comprendre hak" as "without understanding a word." It is notoriously difficult, and often impossible, to prevent Chamoiseau's shifts from French to Creole from being lost in translation. The Martinican Creole word "hak" means "nothing," which I have here translated as "squat" in accord with Réjouis and Vinokurov's translations of "hak" elsewhere in *Texaco*. This gives a better sense of the colloquial character of Marie-Sophie's sudden shift into Creole. "Squat" (or any similarly colloquial English term for "nothing," such as "zilch") is not an ideal translation either, because "squat" is an English word, while "hak" is not a French word.

34. Forster's distinction between an imperialist European order and a teeming indigenous disorder that escapes it is echoed in Chamoiseau's distinction, a fre-

quent reference point in the urban planner's notes to the Word Scratcher, between "an occidental urban logic, all lined up, ordered, strong like the French language" and "the open profusion of the Creole language in the logic of Texaco," "a mosaic culture" that is "multilingual, multiracial, multihistorical, open, sensible to the world's diversity" (Chamoiseau, *Texaco* 220; trans. mod.).

35. Elleke Boehmer, *Colonial and Postcolonial Literature: Migrant Metaphors* (Oxford: Oxford University Press, 1995), 152, 101.

36. *The Journals and Diaries of E. M. Forster*, ed. Philip Gardner (London: Pickering & Chatto, 2011), 174. Forster wrote this on August 30, 1909, after receiving an unfinished letter addressed to him by C. C. Gaunt, who had died before completing it. Forster wonders if it was Gaunt's final letter and regrets he cannot feel the loss of his acquaintance more acutely, writing that while "we cannot expect to know" where the dead have gone, "the fact of their departure might strike us more."

37. The English translation of this passage does not convey Marie-Sophie's vernacular: "Jourd'hui-encore, peu de nègres soupçonnent leur existence. Or bondieu seul sait en quel état tombé sans eux nous fûmes toujours" (63).

38. The narrator's ironic detachment from an untroubled rationalist sensibility is pronounced in numerous passages involving not only Ronny, an easy target ("Ronny's religion was of the sterilized Public School brand, which never goes bad, even in the tropics. Wherever he entered, mosque, cave, or temple, he retained the spiritual outlook of the Fifth Form, and condemned as 'weakening' any attempt to understand them"; Forster, *Passage* 286), but also the more nuanced Fielding and newly humanized Adela as well: "There was a moment's silence, such as often follows the triumph of rationalism" (268). On the other hand, reason is treated as a trustworthy alternative to prejudice, an attribute that raises Fielding well above his English colleagues, as here: "He was still after facts, though the herd had decided on emotion. Nothing enraged Anglo-India more than the lantern of reason if it is exhibited for one moment after its extinction is decreed" (183).

Chapter 4. Traversing Bounds of Solidarity: Poor Analogies and Painful Negotiations in *Three Guineas* and *The Farming of Bones*

Epigraphs: Aimé Césaire, *Discourse on Colonialism*, trans. Joan Pinkham (1972; repr., New York: Monthly Review Press, 2000), 75; originally published as *Discours sur le colonialisme* (Paris: Présence Africaine, 1955); Ngũgĩ wa Thiong'o, *Globalectics: Theory and the Politics of Knowing* (New York: Columbia University Press, 2012), 20.

1. Edwidge Danticat, "Our Guernica," in *Create Dangerously: The Immigrant Artist at Work* (Princeton, NJ: Princeton University Press, 2010), 165.

2. Bruce Robbins, "Too Much Information," *Novel: A Forum on Fiction* 43, no. 1 (2010): 80–81.

3. "Unbearable present" is Robbins's phrase; see 81.

4. Albert Camus, "Create Dangerously," in *Resistance, Rebellion, and Death* (1957; repr., New York: Vintage, 1995), qtd. in Edwidge Danticat, "Create Dangerously: The Immigrant Artist at Work," in *Create Dangerously* 13.

5. Césaire's *Discours sur le colonialisme* appears to have taken shape over the course of at least seven years. Daniel Delas identifies three stages of its composition, each culminating in a distinct published version. A little-known and very brief early version was published as "L'impossible contact" in the journal *Chemins du Monde* in 1948. Subsequently, the *Discours sur le colonialisme* was published by Éditions Réclame in 1950 and then in its final form by Présence Africaine in 1955. For all three versions, see Delas's genetic edition of the *Discours*, in A. James Arnold et al., eds., *Aimé Césaire: Poésie, théâtre, essais et discours, Édition critique* (Paris: CNRS Éditions/Planète Libre, 2013), 1443–76.

6. Aimé Césaire, *Discourse on Colonialism*, trans. Joan Pinkham (1972; repr., New York: Monthly Review Press, 2000), 74, 32.

7. More directly, Danticat does not let us rest in the assumption that the Haitian earthquake's ravages came of altogether natural causes: "This is a natural disaster, I explained, but one that had been in the making for a long time, partly owing to the complete centralization of goods and services and to the import-favoring agricultural policies that have driven so many Haitians off their ancestral lands into a capital city built for two hundred thousand that was forced to house nearly three million" ("Our Guernica" 158).

8. I will return to Ngũgĩ wa Thiong'o's use of "poor theater," which he takes from Jerzy Grotowski's *Towards a Poor Theatre*, to mean theater that makes do with minimal resources.

9. Gary Wilder, *Freedom Time: Negritude, Decolonization, and the Future of the World* (Durham, NC: Duke University Press, 2015), 130, 131.

10. Robert J. C. Young, "The Postcolonial Comparative," *PMLA* 128, no. 3 (2013): 686, 688.

11. Rey Chow puts it well: "But that alibi—of not having enough time or not being available to know everything—is precisely the heart of the matter here because it is, shall we say, a one-way privilege. Such an alibi is simply not acceptable or thinkable for those specializing in non-Western cultures. . . . On these scholars, the pressure is that of an imperative to acquire global breadth—to be cosmopolitan in their knowledge—even if they choose to specialize in esoteric languages and subject matters." See Rey Chow, *The Age of the World Target: Self-Referentiality in War, Theory, and Comparative Work* (Durham, NC: Duke University Press, 2006), 13.

12. Woolf is surprisingly often read as rejecting the concept of feminism when the speaker of *Three Guineas*, equated with an earnest Woolf herself, calls for the word "feminist" to be burned; see Virginia Woolf, *Three Guineas*, ed. Jane Marcus (1938; repr., Orlando, FL: Harcourt, 2006), 120–21. Woolf's argument is consider-

ably more complex than this and not at all a rejection of feminism, a point that should be clear from the discussion that follows. The short response is that the word "feminism" is to be burned only after the word "tyrant" has also been burned; the idea is that when we no longer have tyrants, we will no longer need a word to designate them (121–22). When that happens, the word "feminism," which designates the movement that opposes tyranny, will also be obsolete and happily consigned to oblivion.

13. To date, *Three Guineas* has entered little, to my knowledge, into postcolonial and global South debates, but its advocacy of a cosmopolitan ethos against a backdrop of rising international conflict has made Woolf's text a more frequent focal point in the field of global modernist studies. For comparative treatments of *Three Guineas* that engage with its themes of social justice, see Jessica Berman, *Modernist Commitments: Ethics, Politics, and Transnational Modernism* (New York: Columbia University Press, 2011), 184–236; and Susan Stanford Friedman, "Wartime Cosmopolitanism: Cosmofeminism in Virginia Woolf's *Three Guineas* and Marjane Satrapi's *Persepolis*," *Tulsa Studies in Women's Literature* 32, no. 1 (2013): 23–52. For other transnationalist comparative interpretations of *Three Guineas*, see Rebecca L. Walkowitz, "For Translation: Virginia Woolf, J. M. Coetzee and Transnational Comparison," in *The Legacies of Modernism: Historicising Postwar and Contemporary Fiction*, ed. David James (Cambridge: Cambridge University Press, 2011), 243–63; and Gayle Rogers, *Modernism and the New Spain: Britain, Cosmopolitan Europe, and Literary History* (Oxford: Oxford University Press, 2012), 125–62.

14. These would include the *Discourse*'s conflation of Jews and other diverse victims of Nazi violence as fitting neatly into a larger collectivity of "the white man," a conflation that Michael Rothberg criticizes in *Multidirectional Memory: Remembering the Holocaust in the Age of Decolonization* (Stanford, CA: Stanford University Press, 2009), 71. They might also include Césaire's lack of differentiation between men and women in his delineation of the human, and they would certainly include Woolf's omission of black African slaves in *Three Guineas*'s analogies involving slavery, to which I will return.

15. Winkiel makes this argument in a comparative chapter on *Three Guineas*, C. L. R. James's play *Toussaint Louverture*, Césaire's *Cahier d'un retour au pays natal*, and two short essays by Césaire and Suzanne Césaire, respectively, from their surrealist journal *Tropiques*. See Laura Winkiel, *Modernism, Race and Manifestos* (New York: Cambridge University Press, 2008), 191–231, esp. 191–93.

16. Françoise Vergès, *Monsters and Revolutionaries: Colonial Family Romance and Métissage* (Durham, NC: Duke University Press, 1999), 16.

17. Gary Wilder, *The French Imperial Nation-State: Negritude and Colonial Humanism between the Two World Wars* (Chicago: University of Chicago Press, 2005), 257.

18. Gary Wilder, "Here/Hear Now Aimé Césaire!," *South Atlantic Quarterly* 115, no. 3 (2016): 593–94.

19. Laura Doyle, *Freedom's Empire: Race and the Rise of the Novel in Atlantic Modernity, 1640–1940* (Durham, NC: Duke University Press, 2008), 448.

20. *The Years* and *Three Guineas* were initially conceived as parts of one experimental, genre-crossing book called *The Pargiters*. Woolf considered the experiment a failure and eventually divided the novel from the essay to form two distinct texts, but they remain closely related through their shared preoccupations with freedom, complicity, and the interpenetration of political and domestic spheres.

21. Anna Snaith, "The Hogarth Press and Networks of Anti-Colonialism," in *Leonard and Virginia Woolf: The Hogarth Press and the Networks of Modernism*, ed. Helen Southworth (Edinburgh: Edinburgh University Press, 2010), 121.

22. In an extensive unnumbered endnote on Woolf's uses of the word "guineas," Jane Marcus writes, "In all cases the reference is to black Africa" (*Three Guineas* 224). While Marcus's discussion is compelling and valuable, the certainty with which she writes this obscures how very indirectly Woolf is alluding to black African slaves, if indeed she is alluding to them. We need to raise the question of why Woolf, a descendant of abolitionists, is indirect about it, and not about female slaves in ancient Egypt. Her one explicit reference to black slavery pertains to a point of difference, not affinity; see 55.

23. In a chapter on the implications of Woolf's reference to "a very fine negress" in *A Room of One's Own* ("It is one of the great advantages of being a woman that one can pass even a very fine negress without wishing to make an Englishwoman of her"), Jane Marcus argues that Woolf was less egalitarian than her abolitionist forebears: "A century of ideological racism had taken its toll on the English radical tradition," so that Woolf "was not so quick to claim equality or recognize a common humanity with her negress, and she seems nervous, too, about sisterhood under the skin." See Virginia Woolf, *A Room of One's Own*, ed. Susan Gubar (Orlando, FL: Harcourt, 2005), 50; and Jane Marcus, *Hearts of Darkness: White Women Write Race* (New Brunswick, NJ: Rutgers University Press, 2004), 29. Woolf's ironic aside about the "negress" conveys what she no doubt considered a humane skepticism of the English colonialist "civilizing" project, with its presumptuous aims of acculturating immigrants and colonials of African descent, especially those whose appearance was consistent with English standards of beauty at the time. On the other hand, Woolf's phrasing has been criticized for its presumption of a divide between black women and Englishwomen, as if a black woman could not be authentically English without such acculturation. My view is that the phrasing leaves indeterminate whether the presumption is in fact hers or only that of the Englishmen she is focalizing.

24. Qtd. in Eric Williams, *Capitalism and Slavery* (1944; repr., Chapel Hill: University of North Carolina Press, 1994), 180. For a more detailed account of Stephen's specific accomplishments in the fight against slavery, see Paul Knaplund, "Sir James Stephen: The Friend of the Negroes," *Journal of Negro History* 35, no. 4 (1950): 368–

407. See also Marcus, *Hearts of Darkness* 27–29, esp. where she writes, "Stephen stands out among the antislavery agitators as deeply outraged at the racial basis of slavery" (28).

25. Susan Sontag, *Regarding the Pain of Others* (New York: Picador, 2003), 13.

26. For a critique of Sontag's reading that interprets Woolf's withholding of the photographs as a form of resistance to the use of photographic evidence as propaganda, see Berman, esp. 64–76.

27. In *Cruel Optimism* (Durham, NC: Duke University Press, 2011), Lauren Berlant disputes the "fundamentally ahistoricizing logic" of trauma discourse "from Caruth to Agamben," specifically this discourse's definition of trauma as "an exception that has just shattered some ongoing, uneventful ordinary life" (9–10). She suggests that we replace the "logic of exception" with a "post-traumatic" logic of "crisis ordinariness," a sense of crisis as embedded in everyday life and navigated continually and variably (10, 54). Sibylle Fischer has also called for more historical contextualization of traumas too often conflated in generalizing psychoanalytic frameworks; see Sibylle Fischer, *Modernity Disavowed: Haiti and the Cultures of Slavery in the Age of Revolution* (Durham, NC: Duke University Press, 2004), 144.

28. Ngũgĩ wa Thiong'o, *Globalectics: Theory and the Politics of Knowing* (New York: Columbia University Press, 2012), 2. Ngũgĩ's wordplay here alludes back to E. P. Thompson's critique of Louis Althusser, *The Poverty of Theory*, which had alluded back to *Poverty of Philosophy*, Marx's playfully titled critique of Proudhon's *System of Economic Contradictions, or Philosophy of Poverty*. Ngũgĩ explains, though, that given his background in "poor theater" he associates poor theory more with Jerzy Grotowski's *Towards a Poor Theatre* than with these other works; see *Globalectics* 5.

29. Ngũgĩ wa Thiong'o, *Decolonising the Mind: The Politics of Language in African Literature* (Oxford: James Currey, 1986), 94.

30. M. Jacqui Alexander, *Pedagogies of Crossing: Meditations on Feminism, Sexual Politics, Memory, and the Sacred* (Durham, NC: Duke University Press, 2005), 109.

31. In the detailed endnote that follows, Woolf criticizes a trend of upper-class writers giving accounts of working-class experiences they know little about and concludes, "Meanwhile it would be interesting to know what the true-born working man or woman thinks of the playboys and playgirls of the educated class who adopt the working-class cause without sacrificing middle-class capital, or sharing working-class experience" (*Three Guineas* 209n13). Standing in contrast to this trend and supplementing what Woolf's speaker feels able to imagine are two books Woolf recommends: one by members of a working-class women's cooperative and another about working-class life as seen "at first hand and not through pro-proletarian spectacles" (210n13).

32. Alexander delivered an early version of "Whose New World Order?

Teaching for Justice" as a keynote address at the 1994 meeting of the Great Lakes Colleges Women's Studies Association in Indianapolis; see *Pedagogies of Crossing* 91. Three of the four chapters in *Decolonising the Mind* also originated as lectures at a variety of venues in Africa and Europe, which Ngũgĩ enumerates in his acknowledgements (iii).

33. Edwidge Danticat, *The Farming of Bones* (New York: Soho, 1998).

34. While Danticat's focus is principally on Haitian domestics and plantation workers who have few rights and freedoms even before the massacre, she also portrays more affluent victims well established in the region; see *Farming* 186. Similarly, Lauren Derby and Richard Turits have challenged the now-common assumption, which they trace back to Dominican nationalist discourse, that ethnic Haitians living on the borderlands were mostly migrants, economically marginal and little integrated into Dominican social life. They argue that many victims of the massacre had been born in the Dominican Republic, were Dominican citizens, and were well integrated into the frontier community before the massacre. See Lauren Derby and Richard Turits, "Temwayaj Kout Kouto, 1937: Eyewitnesses to the Genocide," in *Revolutionary Freedoms: A History of Survival, Strength and Imagination in Haiti*, ed. Cécile Accilien, Jessica Adams, and Elmide Méléance (Coconut Creek, FL: Caribbean Studies Press, 2006), 137–38.

35. Virginia Woolf, "Speech before the London/National Society for Women's Service, January 21 1931," in *The Pargiters: The Novel-Essay Portion of "The Years,"* ed. Mitchell A. Leaska (New York: Harvest, 1978), xlii.

36. Though Judith Butler does not include *Three Guineas* in her discussion of Western philosophical interpretations of Antigone, her critique of the tendency to make Antigone a representative of the pre-political, an outsider to a state she opposes, is useful in considering Woolf's different implications when the speaker of *Three Guineas* analogizes Antigone defying Creon to women like herself defying a patriarchal order. Butler argues that even as Antigone speaks out she is absorbing the language of the state she opposes, assimilating the very terms of sovereignty that she refuses. See Judith Butler, *Antigone's Claim: Kinship between Life and Death* (New York: Columbia University Press, 2000), 11, 23. While Woolf's speaker makes no such point about Antigone, it is worth noticing that her reference to Antigone's confrontation with Creon follows from her suggestion that women who seek to "enter the professions and yet remain civilized human beings, human beings who discourage war," do so not simply by retaining the virtues Woolf's speaker ascribes to daughters of educated men, such as poverty and "freedom from unreal loyalties," but by judiciously qualifying them in practice when necessary (*Three Guineas* 96–97).

37. Martin Munro, "Writing Disaster: Trauma, Memory, and History in Edwidge Danticat's *The Farming of Bones*," *Ethnologies* 28, no. 1 (2006): 81–98.

Conclusion. The Beauty of a Trembling World

Epigraph: Virginia Woolf, *Orlando: A Biography*, ed. Maria DiBattista (1928; repr., Orlando, FL: Harvest, 2006), 236–37.

1. Virginia Woolf, *To the Lighthouse* (1927; repr., San Diego, CA: Harvest, 1981), 142.

2. Walter D. Mignolo, *Local Histories/Global Designs: Coloniality, Subaltern Knowledges, and Border Thinking* (Princeton, NJ: Princeton University Press, 2000), 240.

3. Patrick Chamoiseau, *Migrant Brothers: A Poet's Declaration of Human Dignity*, trans. Matthew Amos and Fredrik Rönnbäck (New Haven, CT: Yale University Press, 2018), 76; originally published as *Frères migrants* (Paris: Éditions du Seuil, 2017), 91.

4. Chris Bongie, *Friends and Enemies: The Scribal Politics of Post/Colonial Literature* (Liverpool: Liverpool University Press, 2008), 330–31.

5. See Chris Bongie, "(Not) Razing the Walls: Glissant, Trouillot and the Post-Politics of World 'Literature,'" in *Transnational French Studies: Postcolonialism and Littérature-monde*, ed. Alec G. Hargreaves, Charles Forsdick, and David Murphy (Liverpool: Liverpool University Press, 2010), 125–45. An influential critique of Glissant's late work on which Bongie builds is Peter Hallward's *Absolutely Postcolonial: Writing between the Singular and the Specific* (Manchester: Manchester University Press, 2002). For persuasive challenges to these critiques, all of which question the narrow definition of "politics" propounded by Hallward, Bongie, and their allies, see Sam Coombes, *Édouard Glissant: A Poetics of Resistance* (London: Bloomsbury, 2018), esp. 88–109; Jaime Hanneken, *Imagining the Postcolonial: Discipline, Poetics, Practice in Latin American and Francophone Discourse* (Albany, NY: SUNY Press, 2015), 70–94; and John E. Drabinski, *Glissant and the Middle Passage: Philosophy, Beginning, Abyss* (Minneapolis: University of Minnesota Press, 2019), 220n13, 230–31n26.

6. Édouard Glissant, *Poetics of Relation*, trans. Betsy Wing (Ann Arbor: University of Michigan Press, 1997), 20; trans. mod.; originally published as Édouard Glissant, *Poétique de la relation* (Paris: Gallimard, 1990), 33.

7. Édouard Glissant and Patrick Chamoiseau, *L'Intraitable beauté du monde: Adresse à Barack Obama* (Paris: Éditions Galaade/Institut du tout-monde, 2009), 28–29.

8. Édouard Glissant and Patrick Chamoiseau, *Quand les murs tombent: L'identité nationale hors la loi?* (Paris: Éditions Galaade/Institut du tout-monde, 2007), 26.

9. Glissant and Chamoiseau quote this passage from *Quand les murs tombent* in their conclusion to *L'Intraitable beauté du monde*, 56. They leave all such quotations unattributed, labeled only as "Répétitions."

10. Édouard Glissant, *Philosophie de la relation: poésie en étendue* (Paris: Gallimard, 2009), 54.

11. Virginia Woolf, *A Room of One's Own*, ed. Susan Gubar (1929; repr., Orlando, FL: Harvest, 2005), 16–17.

12. Virginia Woolf, *Orlando: A Biography*, ed. Maria DiBattista (1928; repr., Orlando, FL: Harvest, 2006), 236–37.

13. Patrick Chamoiseau, *Césaire, Perse, Glissant: Les liaisons magnétiques* (Paris: Philippe Rey, 2013), 135, 205.

Index